THE
BLUE
PLATEAU

AN AUSTRALIAN PASTORAL

ALSO BY
MARK TREDINNICK

The Land's Wild Music (editor)
The Little Green Grammar Book
The Little Red Writing Book
A Place on Earth (editor)
The Road South (poems)
Writing Well

THE
BLUE
PLATEAU

AN AUSTRALIAN PASTORAL

MARK TREDINNICK

milkweed
editions

Published 2009 by Milkweed Editions
Printed in Canada
Cover design by Betsy Donovan
Cover photo courtesy of Max Hill
Author photo by Tony Sernack
Interior design by Steve Foley
The text of this book is set in Chaparral Pro.
09 10 11 12 13 5 4 3 2 1
First Edition

Please turn to the back of this book for a list of the sustaining funders of
Milkweed Editions.

Library of Congress Cataloging-in-Publication Data

Tredinnick, Mark.
  The Blue Plateau : an Australian pastoral / Mark Tredinnick. — 1st ed.
    p. cm.
  ISBN 978-1-57131-320-1 (pbk. : alk. paper)
1. Blue Mountains Region (N.S.W.)—Poetry. 2. Blue Mountains Region
(N.S.W.)—Description and travel. 3. Wilderness areas—Blue Mountains
Region (N.S.W.) 4. Human ecology—Blue Mountains Region (N.S.W.) I. Title.
  PR9619.4.T74B68 2009
  821'.914—dc22
                    2009021234
                    CIP

This book is printed on acid-free, recycled (100% postconsumer waste) paper.

For Maree and for Roland

THE BLUE PLATEAU

I am what is around me . . .
These are merely instances.
—Wallace Stevens, "Theory"

Nobody likes erosion anymore . . . now that all the scenery
is made.
—James Galvin, *Fencing the Sky*

THE
BLUE
PLATEAU

AN AUSTRALIAN PASTORAL

PROLOGUE

SOME OF THE PARTS

I am made of pieces and of the spaces between them where
other pieces used to be. I am a landscape of loss. Most of me is
the memory of where else, and who else, and with whom, I have
been and no longer am.

And so it is with the plateau; she, too, is a landscape of loss.

We are not—none of us, not I and not this place—ever whole;
we are never of a piece. Who we are is how what's left of us falls
back toward some kind of coherence much older than we are.

The real book is the one you do not write, the one that orders
the pieces that remain; and the real plateau is the work to which
all the pieces almost amount, the order they all imply—the
heath and the ironstone, the escarpment and the late afternoon
light, the valley wind and the early summer fire, the way the
plateau came in and the way it's going out again, the first
peoples and the second, the time before men and the time of
men and the time of no men to come, the falling water and the
deepening drought, the sandstone and the black cockatoo and
the gray kangaroo and the horse and the rider and the fifteen
hundred kinds of plants and the birds that know the difference,
and the valley's turns of phrase in the mouths of the women and
the men, most of them now gone.

All we can ever know is some of the parts, and here some of them are, each an allusion to the same kind of truth, most of it eroded long ago and borne away east by slim and persistent streams.

CAST

KANIMBLA VALLEY

Jim Commens

Judith, his wife

George William, his father

Helen, his mother

George William, his grandfather

Julia, his grandmother

Grady boys, Julia's brothers

Ron Flynn, stockman and friend of Jim's father, mentor to
    young Jim

Dave, Jim's friend

Guy Teseirero, neighbor and captain of the Kanimbla Valley
    Rural Fire Service

John Underhill, neighbor and member of the Kanimbla Valley
    Rural Fire Service

KATOOMBA

Mark Tredinnick

M., his wife

KEDUMBA VALLEY

Les Maxwell

May, his wife

Norm, her son; Les's stepson

Ross, Norm's son

William Maxwell, Les's grandfather

Mary-Anne, Les's grandmother

George William (known as Billy), Les's father

Olive Beatrice, Billy's wife, Les's mother

Jim (known as Jimmy), Les's brother

Dan Cleary, Les's boss and landlord, founder of the Kedumba
    Pastoral Company

Bill, his son and Les's boss and landlord, after Dan

Ken, Dan's other son

Terry, a National Parks and Wildlife Ranger

David C., a boy who gets lost in the valley

David I., a second boy who gets lost in the valley

COX'S RIVER

Oonagh Kennedy, leader of a party of riders in the Cox's River,
    August 1967

Clem, Mark, Lynne, and Margaret, the other members of
    the party

Bert Carlon, whose guesthouse and riding school in Megalong
    they left from

DARGAN

Henryk Topolnicki

Philippa, his partner

I

VALLEY

WHAT IS ESSENTIAL IS INVISIBLE TO THE EYES

Les wakes before dawn and walks outside.

It's hard to say just when day comes to the Kedumba, for the valley is deep and it grows light long before the sun makes it up over the eastern rim. But if morning dawns slowly on the valley, it dawns all at once on Les, and he rises without question into the blue tailings of the night and the crying of the kookaburras and leaves the house as though he knows that morning will not come unless he gets up and goes out and walks the morning down.

Though the house has an inside toilet, Les never could kick the habit of going outside to pee. It isn't just for that, though, that he leaves the house and walks across the paddock to the creek or down the two-wheel track toward the woolshed or east to his grandfather's grave through the frost or the rising fog or the tepid blue-gray silence.

Les goes outside to remember who he is. He leaves the house to become the place again—no longer just the lean old wreck of a man who's slept all night on the kitchen floor, or sometimes in the narrow bed, where he fell after midnight saturated with

5

sherry. Every morning, as another man might dress, Les puts on the valley again.

So this particular morning Norm is not surprised to see Les in overalls and gumboots walking in the predawn like some condemned man across the paddock, making for the sheoaks on Waterfall Creek. A dozen roos and some Bennett's wallabies closer to the crossing have their heads down grazing, and when Les walks through, none of them raises its head, none of them shifts or shoots him a glance. Les passes among them like a ghost, like an understanding they share, an aspect of the morning's ritual. Norm watches from the window of the front room as Les walks to the river to check its height and to splash his face and wet his hair and to drink in that sweet water, and then Norm watches the old man come back the way he went out, straight through the animals, as though he were no one at all. At the top of the stairs Les kicks off his boots and comes into the house in his socks and clears his throat.

"You'se'd better rouse yourselves before the day's half gone," Les calls out from the hall. "Thought you said you wanted to catch some fish." This is for Norm's son Ross and the woman he's brought here this time, and for Ross's goodfornothing mate who's snoring down the back. Then Norm walks into the kitchen in his shorts and a jumper and Les sees him and winks. "Morning boy," he says.

While his stepfather fixes tea and cuts slabs of bacon and drops them in the pan on the stove, Norm decides to test a notion. He goes out to the hall where Les hangs his overalls and he pulls some on and rolls up their gray legs and arms and buttons them; he pulls on Les's boots and he shuffles down two steps from the porch to the drive; he hitches up the overalls and straddles the top rail and follows Les's trail across the paddock.

6

Ten feet along, a dozen roos and nine or ten wallabies raise their heads and freeze. Norm slows and tries to shuffle in Les's way, but he's fooling no one. Three more strides and twenty-one animals turn and bound away. Not panicked; more disappointed than anything. Norm's been coming to the valley since Les cut the road in, but Norm isn't what the valley is and he knows he never will be. He's a part-time predator in some ill-fitting pieces of the morning's clothing.

The roos disappear into the timber, and Norm turns for home. "They can see you, boy. They can smell the big smoke on you," says Les, when Norm tells him what's happened. "You gotta come from here like they do, before they stop actually seein' you."

WHY I CAME AND WHEN

I came to the plateau in the winter of '98. A place a thousand meters in the air, a hundred ks west of the city. Not far west, but far enough. A world of sandstone and eucalypt and unregenerate weather, a place just fallen from the sky. The pitch of the night and the closeness of the stars within it and the sky asleep in the valleys at dawn: I came for that, and for the faces of the vermilion stone that no one would ever own. And I stayed because there was real estate here, nonetheless, in all this inalienable wilderness, that even I could afford.

I came to leave the city behind, a place that never wanted as much of me as I had wanted of it; I came to live with a woman I loved in a landscape that never ended, and I thought I'd like to be here yet if it did.

The house we found in May and moved into in August was a plain timber cottage, caught somewhere between Federation and California Bungalow on the south side of Katoomba. Since 1911, when the allotment was cut from woodland near the cliff's edge, it had sat without pretension through all the years in all the wind above the valley of the Kedumba. A stand of trees, peppermints and silvertop ash, geebungs and banksias, kept the house from the valley and the valley from the house, and most days I took the path through those assembled and restless trees to the edge of the scarp and looked down to where the plateau had once been, where now only the valley remained.

To live in the plateau is not to live high, but deep; it is to cleave to a landscape, most of which is gone and most of which is space and most of which is down below you. To live in the plateau is to live inside something, not upon it. Katoomba sits on a narrow ridge, and canyons gape all about. They surround you; they are where your eye wanders and your mind falls. The valleys are the larger part of what the plateau is now, and they are what it will all one day become. And down in the deepest, the one below my place, Les Maxwell got up and went to work most of the days of his life.

But Les had been dead two years by the time I learned that the clearing I looked down upon each morning, from the end of the track through the trees, had been almost his entire life.

THE SOUND OF HOME

Before the place we went to live was made over into a suburb trying to resemble a resort town where those from Sydney's better suburbs might come to take the waters and breathe the bracing air, and before that, when it was a mining town knocked up in timber and set down several stories above the coal seam its inhabitants descended to by funicular each shift—before all that, no one used to stay here through the winter. On top of the plateau the first peoples danced and traded and courted and left, for it wasn't where they lived. The Gundungurra wintered in the valleys.

8

For Katoomba blows hard through the middle of the year, and under the weight of an August wind, the cottage quaking about us at night, it seemed certain more than once this was the night the house would end up in the valley where the plateau's first people had gone. The place doesn't mean you to stay. Not forever; not for a year; maybe not at all. Any kind of title to the top of the plateau feels more tenuous in life than it looks on the deed. That's what I learned again each winter.

The people who were too smart to winter here named the place how it sounded. *Katoomba* is what they called it, and that is how they carried the place on their tongues for so many thousands of years we may as well call it forever. It sounded tough and lugubrious, as if it were making its way downstream, as if it were plummeting slowly away. As if it didn't mean to stay. *The place of falling water* is what we think those people thought *Katoomba* meant. And *Kedumba*—the name of the creek that all the waters that begin up here become—Kedumba is the way the same idea ran in the valley. It's where it went in the winter; it's where the place of falling water falls.

And in this falling place, above the valley where it's headed, I lived for seven years at the edge of a cliff. They were seven years of drought—just the beginning, it turns out now—in which the place of falling water fell on, but the water itself fell less and less often.

THE TALKING CURE

"You won't get much out of him," his neighbors told me, the first time I went to see Jim Commens—a man who'd never known another place than the plateau, a man I hoped in my early years might unpack some of it for me.

But I set out anyway along the gravel road and I walked through the antique light of morning and its winter shadows past the horses in the fields and the paperbarks and grey gums at the foot of the escarpment beside me to Jim's gate, and I unlatched the gate and walked through it and I closed the gate behind me again and went on down the drive and through the open door of Jim's great green shed, and I found Jim there in the cavernous twilight saddling six horses to lead a party of riders out, and I told him my name and I mentioned the book that mentions his granddad and he said, "Yeah I got a copy of that, read it maybe fifty times," and then he said, "Can you ride?" I said I could and he said, "I'll get you a horse, we can talk as we ride." He got me a horse and we started to talk and for seven years we never stopped.

NO MATTER WHAT YOU CALL IT

People started calling the plateau the Blue Mountains when they started selling it to Sydney. But these are not mountains; nor are they especially blue.

Griffith Taylor, an eccentric but perspicacious geologist, named the place the Blue Plateau in the 1930s. Though the name never stuck, it gets the place right. For this is a dissected sandstone plateau. And it's blue enough sometimes.

The plateau is a slab of sandstone laid down by rivers, solidified, dead, buried, and risen again, and crazed by time and subsequent streams so that within the plateau many smaller plateaux stand, islands of stone marooned in steep valleys— buttes and mesas and buttresses and all manner of remnants. And some of them look a lot like mountains, but orogeny had no part in it; they're just what's left of the original basin. And together, they compose the Blue Plateau.

The plateau only looks blue till you're in it. It's about as blue as any high ground seen from far off. Blueness is a trick that distance plays upon light, and here the trick is performed in air scented and oiled by the breathing of gum trees; their exhalations are the specific density of the blueness of the plateau.

The plateau is very much like the sky, which is always blue somewhere, but never merely blue. The plateau's escarpments, for instance, are ocher, purple, white, and black, and there are legends written upon them that the shadows in the late light bring out. And in some of the valleys the plateau is made of grasses, which shift from summer green to the bleached bone of winter, and along the river that cuts through those pastures and runs through this plateau the black, spare riveroaks sing the plateau away to the sea.

TELLING IT

I'm going to tell some stories here, and most of them are Les's, and some of them are Jim's, and some of them are Henryk's, and then there are some others still, and one or two of those are mine, and some of them aren't even stories at all, and what connects them is my living for a time among them on a piece of ground where they all meet. And if I tell them, these broken pieces of a broken plateau, you might hear the place as I heard it now and then, telling me who it really was for as long as I stayed. Which wasn't long enough.

LIKE IT WAS

Another day, a year after I'd first met him, I was riding with Jim again, and I asked him if he knew anything about the clearing I could see from up near my house, and he said, turning on his horse and talking out of his blond beard, that for five years in the eighties, when he was working midweek up at the Clarence Colliery, he'd run his steers into the Kedumba. "By then," he said, "the whole Kedumba belonged to the

Clearys, and the Waterboard wanted it and Cleary was makin' 'em wait.

"The piece you're talkin' about used ta belong t' the Maxwells before the Clearys got hold of it. Not sure how all that 'appened. Can't even say how I got onta the Clearys now, mighta been through Chris Grady, that's the son a Kevin Grady, who spent about twenty years walkin' in front a Les Maxwell blazing trees so Les could knock 'em over with 'is 'dozer. Les used ta say 'It took me twenty years ta catch that bastard Grady,' but I had no idea of any a that then. Les was just the funny old bugger livin' down there that everyone knew about.

"Anyway, there was a lot of cattle run wild down there over the years, an' Bill Cleary said I could leave me steers there, run 'em up inta Cedar Creek where the best grass was, for as long as it took me ta get 'is stragglers out. All the boys from the mountains'd been goin' down on their horses trying ta chase 'em in, but ya don't get cattle in this area with horses. The horses are just for keepin' up with the dogs, and for sittin' on while you're bein' the brains behind the operation. But it's the dogs that get the cattle in. Always is in this country.

"Well, I had a coupla good dogs, and Ronnie Flynn had a couple more, and we knew how to keep our 'alf-decent horses outa the dogs' way, let 'em get a good work on the cattle. We just shitted it in really. Those cattle, they'd seen plenty a horses and the bloody idiots who rode 'em, an' they knew how ta get away from horses, but they 'ad no answer to workin' dogs. The dogs'd sniff 'em out one by one, bite 'em on the nose or heel 'em or whatever, and as soon as they got bit once or twice the game was all up for those cattle. Soon the dogs 'ad fifty or more an' they'd just all bunch together an' we'd crack a bit of a whip an' bring 'em 'ome like we'd chased 'em outta the scrub ourselves. But as I say, it was the dogs did all the work.

"Cleary'd been tryin' for years with these cowboys, he'd call 'em, who 'ad no idea at all. 'E just said, 'Run the cattle inta the yards an' truck 'em ta Camden for me.' Well, we got all that done in a few months. But I got talkin' ta Les some nights, and that's 'ow we got started goin' over there ta Kedumba with our families, Dave an' I over the years, after Ronnie died, right up till when Les got shunted off an' the Water Board locked the gate.

"Our best memories, mine and Judith's, come from those times. All those school holidays camped on Waterfall Creek, talkin' ta Les at night till both of us were shitfaced, an' next day ridin' round where we were never s'posed t' ride, somehow not fallin' off.

"One afternoon Dave an' I got a bit of a fire goin' in the scrub by Reedy Creek, an' the wind got up an' all of a sudden the thing got away from us an' was runnin' up the slope toward the house an' sheds an' that. We only just got on top of it. Girls an' kids an' everyone just about, even the bloody dogs, 'ad ta pitch in an' stamp the thing out. When we drove back past Les's later in the dark 'e was on the front step lookin' a bit worried. 'Just a bit of a bonfire, Les,' we called out.

"An' there was the time we dropped one a the kids, Mel I think it musta been, out the back a the ute drivin' along the airstrip paddock there. Looked around and saw a bundle in the track behind us. Bundle started bawlin' an' tryin' t' get up. Realized it was one a the kids."

THE VALLEY

That's what Les Maxwell called the whole catchment of the Cox's, that republic of grasses, that federation of rivers. Everyone used to call it that. The Valley—capital V. The heart of it, where the soils were best and the valley stretched widest, they called the Burragorang. And it was the Burragorang that drowned in 1960 when the Warragamba filled with the Cox's. They dammed the river and they flooded the Valley, so that a city on the coast might take the water that falls on the plateau. Under all that water, where the Cox's now backs up, lie the paddocks of the Pippens and Maxwells, the Galvins and the McMahons, the Lakemans and the Pearces; under it lies the country of the Gundungurra and half their dreaming.

Les called Lake Burragorang, when it flooded the Valley, the Gambie. He called it the Big Water. And big it is. There's a whole way of life lost in it. Two ways, if you count the first people, whose way had been lost long before the big water came.

But the whole Valley didn't drown. For the Valley reaches all the way up the Kedumba Creek, between the Kings Tableland and Mount Solitary, to the Kedumba's headwaters at Katoomba. And the Valley's jurisdiction runs west past Narrowneck into the Megalong and the Kanimbla, and the big water never got that far. So these valleys upstream of the ruined Burragorang are all that's left of the Valley now until the city drinks the plateau dry.

KEDUMBA

The Kedumba River, having fallen off the escarpment, tries to shake the township by making a bunch of sudden moves among weathered hills that look like mullock heaps down there in the valley, all of them teeming with gums. She cuts down into tough old Devonian stone, the folded bedrock of the plateau. She starts looking for a way around Mount Solitary. And when she finds it, the little river turns south, still making out she's lost, and just before she picks up Waterfall Creek, she broadens and slows and runs her finger between two breasts.

These hills have no names on the maps. Les, who lived here longer than anyone, used to call the more easterly of them Sunset Hill because its tip caught the last of the sun, when shadow had inundated the rest of the valley. The other was Sunrise Hill, because it caught the morning before anything else on the valley floor.

Those are good names. But these are breasts, and their form is lovely, and Les, for one, never weaned himself off them. And you'd like to rest your head where Les spent his childhood—here among these hills, which are unlike anyplace else in the valley. They belong to another gender altogether than the angular and unforgiving scarps between which they lie. They are flesh scantily clad in timber, and a river runs between them.

And just beneath the valley's breasts, until the next big fire carries it off, stand the remains of the hut where Les Maxwell was once a child. North of them, the head of the valley lolls to the west, asleep at the bend of the river, hair hiding her face.

The Kedumba is a fallen woman. She has her feet in the Big Water, and she has a lapsed pastoral property in her belly.

THE MEETING OF THE WATERS

On high ground just above the place two creeks meet—Waterfall Creek and the Kedumba River—there's a slab hut from which the soul has departed. It's been empty longer than it was ever full; it's ninety years since it held the voices of the children it was built to house, and sixty since the hands that raised it ceased, and now it's falling back fast into the forest it was cut from.

Looking at the hut, you'd think you'd found the first house ever made in the Kedumba. It's built of slabs, timbers hewn from felled trees, Bentham's Gums or white mahogany, all of them adzed square and stood vertically; each slab is cut just as long but only roughly as thick and wide as the next and fit as tightly together as a man could manage, the cracks filled with clay to baffle the wind. The whole thing, six rooms in all and verandas on three sides, has ironbark stumps for footings, a timber that doesn't know how to rot. The house is well made and inside some of the blue plaster still clings to the boards, and some of the things the children wrote there remain.

The Burragorang was settled with houses like this, houses roofed with stringybark held down with battens and rocks. But this one's roofed in corrugated iron. The tin, you'd think, was a later improvement, for surely this must be a pioneer's shack; this, you'd imagine, as I did standing beside it one hot January day in 2002, must be the house that Les Maxwell's grandfather William built when he settled the Kedumba.

But you'd be wrong; the story of the hut is fifty years—a whole generation—younger than that. The hut was built the only way Billy, the son of William and the father of Les, knew how, the way houses had always been done in the Valley. This hut might have been built in 1824; in fact it was put up a century later. My house had already stood a dozen years, it already belonged to a newer and a faster time, when this hut, a late expression of the pre-modern world, got built. Here were two houses, then, in neighboring parishes, not twenty miles apart; here were two eras abutting as though the plateau cared nothing for such distinctions, as though all manner of time zones ran here at once.

In this cottage, when Les was a boy of five or six, his father got a note from a neighbor. Mr. A. L. Bennett owned land downstream on Reedy Creek. He was a city man, and he came and went, but he'd made himself a student, over the years, of the language of the Gundungurra, whose country this had always been, and that's what this note was about.

All his life Les kept Bennett's note in a wooden box along with other important things—his grandfather's will, his own marriage papers, photographs of his wife and the valley—and he left the box to his stepson, Norm. The note's still folded there, the way Bennett folded it to send to his neighbor:

nadgyung	water
wolway	waterfall
bambaroo	falling
nadgyung bambaroo	water falling
kurra dulla	meeting of the waters (a junction)
dulan	a river
walluk walluk dulan	a crooked river
murung	a creek
gargure	a gully
murrung	a valley
boombi	spring

The above are a few names I have obtained from W. Russell.
And you may choose which you prefer. They are the names of the
Gundong-gorra tribe, which belonged to the Burragorang and Cox's
River Tribe.
Yours truly
A. L. Bennett

There's no date on the note, so it's hard to be sure. But I'd guess it's about as old as the slab hut, and it's an answer to a question, but what was the question?

I'm guessing Maxwell was asking what names the valley knew for water, so he might christen the six-room hut he'd just put up where two waters meet. No one can say now which Gundungurra words he chose for what; but we know that he asked, which speaks well of him. And we know what he learned—this small poem of the sound of water falling in a valley.

THE FATE OF A VALLEY

After Billy Maxwell died, when in time the hut and the paddock at the joining of the rivers fell, with the whole valley, into the hands of another family and they named it all the Kedumba Pastoral Company, and after a few more years passed and the 1960s arrived, the elder son of the man who'd built this hut so well and named it so gently returned to his family's end of the valley, which was theirs no longer. In the summer, to be precise, of 1965, Les Maxwell returned to take care of the whole Kedumba for the family who owned it now.

And by the time, nearly thirty years later, that the KPC got the price they wanted for their seven thousand acres of valley, Les had half-filled with sherry flagons the hut where he'd spent his first fifteen years. When he returned as a man to the valley he'd left as a boy, Les didn't move back to the hut. Until 1990 he lived in a weatherboard demountable brought in on the bed of a truck and set down on the other side of Waterfall Creek: the caretaker's house, part of the KPC compound.

For many years before that, Herb Bowen had taken care of the valley for the Clearys; he'd lived with his wife in the caretaker's house till he died one day in January 1965. That month, fires burned the Kedumba Valley right up to the house, and Les was down there fighting them, and one day the cross on his grandfather's grave burned to the ground, and another day Herb Bowen dropped down dead. In mid-February, Mrs. Bowen left, and Dan Cleary asked Les and May to move in and take over. But there was work to do first. The weather was hot and dry all February and well into March, and Les and May were down in the Kedumba every other day, driving in from Camden, keeping water up to the garden and the corn, and running repairs on the house. And then Les was tending fires up at Newnes. So it wasn't until the fourteenth of March, a Sunday, the fires stanched and the house as ready as it was ever going to get, that Les and May came to the Kedumba and stayed, and their first night was as cold as buggery.

All up, Les lived in that house twenty-seven years, alone for more than half of them, and from the front veranda Les looked out every evening as the light swelled in the Kedumba Walls and then the scarp fell back to dreaming. He sat there alone, Mount Solitary behind him swallowing the sun. He drank a lot; he stared at the light; he remembered.

A SHORT HISTORY OF BELONGING I

Once there was a people who belonged to a Valley. They kept the Valley tame; they spoke the words it gave them.

The people had a name for the grasslands that they kept the trees from taking back; they called them burrangorang. Pretty much the name the white men took for the Valley when they took the Valley from the people who spoke its name and nature when they opened their mouths. For when white men discovered the Burragorang, it was already a place sweet with grasses, made long ago into pasture by the fire farming of the people they took it from.

And when white men found the Valley, they found the cattle who'd found it first. The cattle had escaped the white men's colony almost as soon as they walked off the boats, and they'd found their way to the burrangorang, where they fattened and prospered and increased. When the pioneers came twenty years

later, finally discovering the paths along the rivers that the
cattle had followed a generation before them and the old people
had known since the beginning, they saw cattle grazing
inside the plateau, horns as wide as your extended arms,
grasses up to their backs. And by then—not that the men
with guns gave a damn—there were already cattle in the first
people's dreamings; there were bulls on the walls of the caves
where the old people lived.

But they fell, most of the Valley's people, to violence and
disease. They succumbed to the new people who came to the
Valley and thought it should belong to them. They were shot;
they fell ill; they went away. If a place is your life, if it is the
very words in your mouth, and it is taken, what do you say,
and who are you then, and where? You grieve; you fall silent;
you pass. Or you weather, and you scatter like so many of the
plateau's former lives among the townships of the plateau's
current incarnation, and you carry on. And some did that.
Like Werriberri, a *kooradjie*, a leader of his people, whose
name was a river, and who learned cricket and horsecraft
and gave some words for water to Billy Maxwell's neighbor.
Or you get sent away and one day, a hundred years on, you
come back, as your descendants, from a city or a station or a
convent school, from someone else's country somewhere, and
you make a home again inside the plateau, though not in the
Valley, for it's got too wet, and some of the old words and the
stories they came from get shared again, up in the gully where
the Valley begins. And you begin to speak the plateau slowly
together again.

But that's later. This is the settlement story of the Burragorang,
and it's the same old settlement story—just add water.

First there was the river and the trees. Then there were men
and fire; there were grasses and kangaroos—the *burru* whom

the grasses brought forth. For many hundreds of generations, the first men and women had the Valley for themselves and the river; they danced it and fought for it and passed it to their children in song; they came and went along it, and in time the Valley thought of those people as its own. Then there came cattle. And soon after them, white men came with horses and fences, with more cattle, with sheep, with corn and pigs and rabbits. Oh, yes, the rabbits, who stole the grasses and laid the ground bare. At last they went, poisoned to hell, but the men and their houses and their fences and pigs and orchards and rampant garden plants and, near the finish, their roads stayed on. And after all that came the water. Now the water sinks, but the grasses are gone. And the people, too, are gone. From the Valley anyway.

Wherever he moved earth up in the Kedumba, making dams, pushing roads, leveling the block south of Waterfall Creek where the Clearys built their compound, Les turned up axe-heads; he bent and picked up chipping stones, sharp-edged fragments of rock that did not belong to the stones of the Valley floor. And he knew these were the tools and leavings of the people who first belonged to the Valley. He knew that those people had come and stayed by the meeting of these two waters, and gone again according to the season. It was their steep and difficult road up the escarpment his father and mother had taken to Wentworth Falls weekly in his youth, the bridle track he still took until he blasted the road across the Kedumba Walls.

Les knew his people were not the first to inhabit his end of the Valley; he knew because of the stones and because of the stories his grandfather told his father, who told Les, who told Norm. Because of the painted places he had seen in the scarps. So Les knew there might have been pasture here by the river for twenty thousand years before his grandfather rode into it in the middle of 1858.

A SHORT HISTORY OF BELONGING II

Twin boys were born in Sydney Town in April 1832. The first was christened John; the second William. This is where Les's story begins.

Thomas Maxwell, their father, had come out from County Roscommon in 1823, a counterfeiter of money; Elizabeth Osborne, their mother, a stealer of yarn, arrived from County Monaghan in July 1831. When she landed, Thomas Maxwell stood waiting at the quay for a wife, and he found her. By then he had his ticket of leave and was working in the Burragorang for the Valley's constable, and he had ideas in his head about buying a piece of land and making something of himself, and a wife and children would come in handy for that.

Thomas Maxwell was a Catholic, as you might expect, but Elizabeth Osborne was a Belfast protestant who'd gone south to find work and found trouble instead, and she was a good two inches taller than Thomas. But these were not the times and this was not the place for being particular. The twins were conceived, apparently, before Elizabeth had even found her land legs, for along they came nine months after her ship docked. And Thomas and Elizabeth took the boys back down to the burragorang, and they got themselves a plot of land and had themselves five more children before they got around to marrying in August 1839.

Four years later Thomas drowned in the Wollondilly River, where the Maxwells farmed, and four years after that Elizabeth married again and settled on the Nattai and set about making another family. And soon after, her firstborn boys, John and William, left her home and wandered all over the Valley, running cattle and mending fences for other men and finding caves high in the escarpment decorated with the red hands of black women and following songlines sung for tens of thousands of years upriver, and John walked right out of the story.

William, though, married Mary Anne Thompson in the Catholic Church at Campbelltown in July of 1855, and Les had their marriage certificate in his box of things when he died. His grandparents had marked their names on the certificate, each of them, with an X.

William found them a good small piece of ground in the loop the river used to take at Black Gooler, and the very next year their first child arrived, a boy they named James Thomas for their fathers, and three years later a second child came, a girl they named Margaret Elizabeth for their mothers. The next two decades are a litany of children, and one or two of them died, until in the end there were ten. But all these years, William Maxwell can't have been home much more often or for too much longer than it took to make these children, for he ran other men's cattle up and down the Burragorang—McMahon's and Lakeman's and others'—and he chased them out of the river flats and sedge swamps where the Valley men let their cattle run wild and fatten, way up along the Nattai and the Wollondilly and the Kedumba, and he got them to market and made other men rich, and in between he rode and climbed in the gorges and escarpments of the plateau, where one or two high places are named for him still. And one summer day in 1858 or '59 he rode right up the Kedumba and came out into the clearing where a small creek he later called Waterfall joined it and heavy sheoaks bunched, and he sat on his stockhorse, stunned.

Roos were grazing, though he could barely see them in the grass. Late afternoon was lighting up the Kedumba Walls. When he rode out into the tall grasses it was like riding into his past and into his future all at once; it was like coming into country he had dreamed of, though he couldn't have told you when. He hobbled his mare and walked in the grasses and down to the creek beds, and he made camp in the clearing that night. And when he had eaten and when he had rolled out his bedding in the elbow of the streams and put his fire out, he felt the cold air come down off the cliffs and he looked up at sharper stars in blacker sky than he had ever known, and it was like looking from the bottom of a well.

In the morning, he caught a blackfish in the Kedumba, and he ate it and drank tea. He waded out into the grasses again and found a place a little raised up from the bottomlands, which he told himself he would come back to and put up a hut, but now he must find these cattle and push them back home. He took the hobbles off his mare and saddled her and rode out of the clearing, his billy setting up a clangor against his pan on the flanks of the horse and butcherbirds singing their sweet and menacing phrases as he went, and an hour later he rode up a low-running creek that cut across the river, and he found a little way along its course some cattle with Lakeman's brand on their rumps where he had put it the year before, and with them five or six long-horned cleanskins. He drove them out and followed them all that day and half the night to the Burragorang to join the others yarded there.

But he never really left the clearing, not that day, not in the months between then and when he came in the winter and put up a bark hut, and not in all the thirty years that followed, when sometimes he never saw it for four years or five at a stretch.

When the land surveyor rode into the clearing by Waterfall Creek late in 1859 and put it on the map, part now of the Parish of Kedumba in the County of Cook, he found Maxwell's hut, but no one was in it and the circle of stones where a fire had been was cold. He saw no fences nor any evidence that the ground had been improved. He declared the valley untenanted and rode away.

SOLITUDE, 1980

It's a spring morning, and Les sits down on the back step in his boots. He's been up and after it for hours, and now he's cut a sandwich in the kitchen and brought it out here into the sun. It's made from week-old bread and some kind of cold meat so old it would be of interest to archaeologists. He's chewing on it, tasting nothing and looking up at the mountain.

The plate with the other half of the sandwich is sitting on the bottom step. Two female blue wrens are a foot away from him, feeding on the crumbs. Another is on the china plate, one of his mother's, picking at the sandwich. And on Les's left boot, the male in his blue cap is fanning out his lairy cobalt tail, hopping from side to side, opening his mouth and talking up a high-pitched storm at Les, like some overexcited toddler. It's not that Les doesn't know the birds are there. He knows who's here on this land before they know it themselves. It's just that this is how it goes. A bird on his foot is no stranger than a shadow beside him in the afternoon.

He picks up the enamel cup with his free hand. He takes a sip of sweet black tea and tips the dregs on the ground. He tosses the rest of the sandwich over the hedge for the goanna—the eight-foot lizard that patrols the yard—to find later. Les feeds it like a pet. Nothing odd about that, either. Where you have a goanna, you don't have snakes. Or not so many. Saves on bullets.

SOLITUDE, 1888

Who can say how many kinds of loneliness are known to a boy of twelve left by himself at the far end of a valley?

Who can say how many ways he might learn to pull eel from the river; how many times, hungry as a horse, he might skin and cook the thing before he learned the one way to make it palatable; how many calls of birds he might commit to memory while felling trees and making fence; how many times he might look up to the cliff-tops at Katoomba and wonder what town life might feel like; how many times he might look south along the vestigial road he'd come in on and hope to see the rising dust that would tell him his father was coming to fetch him.

Being left like this, alone in a bark hut, with only two horses and the back of Mount Solitary for company, could be the best way to make a man of you. It could be the best way to learn how to check your cot for brown snakes before falling into it; the best way to get good at hitting what you aimed at or go hungry; the best way to master the knife and the axe, the adze and the saw; the best way to find out what timber burns, and what timber lets itself be made into fence or yard or shed; the best way to get yourself lost and let your horse lead you home in the dark from the back country; the best way to learn to bind your swollen ankle and bathe your wounds and keep working; the best way to cry out in anger and yearning and fear under the cold stars, to hear your voice, barely broken and broken again now with anguish, come back to you from the godforsaken walls, and yet not go mad.

Who knows? Maybe this is what his father had in mind when he brought young Billy up into the valley and left him with a few supplies and told him he'd be back for him in a month or two.

And maybe it worked. Billy Maxwell grew into a big man, strong, deft with his hands, sparing with his words, a stayer. This boy, abandoned for a time in the valley, lost his childhood there and found the man he would become. He foresaw the place the whole valley would become a hundred years later, a grassland among the timbered sandstone keeps, watched over—though he probably didn't see this bit coming—by his son Les.

Who can say how deep that kind of solitude lodges you in a place? It might break you like a horse, or like a heart. It might make you want to run, to lose yourself in the timber and die. It might defeat you and send you home in shame, never to be a man. Or it might make you never want to leave. Such an arid baptism, such an initiation in a place, might make you hers forever. So it was with Billy Maxwell.

His father sent him there with a real-estate purpose in mind, if nothing more: so that Portion 46 in the Parish of Kedumba would be occupied if the surveyor happened through again. As he did, and found there a thirteen-year-old boy, who said he was clearing the land and making fences for his father.

The first time Billy Maxwell came to the valley, he came as a down payment. He came as an advance party of one. He stayed until his father came to fetch him, and shortly after he came back with his parents for keeps. He came and learned what his son would have to learn a century later—how to stay in this fallen piece of heaven, and how to do it alone.

A SHORT HISTORY OF BELONGING III

By October 1889 all of William Maxwell's children were dead or married, all but the youngest, Billy, who at thirteen was already taller than his father. And so at the age of fifty-seven, William and his aging wife and his youngest son rode upriver to pioneer the land he'd first fallen in love with three decades before, the place he'd sent his son Billy to stake a claim in the winter.

The men built a slab hut, like the one they'd lived in at Black Gooler, and around it they planted fruit trees, and Mary dug a vegetable bed. In a year, William and Billy cleared the two acres about the house and ring-barked a further ten acres beyond and put up two thousand feet of three- and four-rail fence, enough in the surveyor's eyes to make the land theirs.

In 1891, William Maxwell claimed in his son's name the parcel of forty acres adjoining this first lot (Lot 2) to the south, and Maxwell and his son ran a three-rail fence along the boundary between the two plots, and on Lot 2 they put up a six-room house to replace the hut they'd made in haste two years before, and on the new lot (Lot 46) they built a shed, stockyards, and a larger enclosure, so that by 1892 near the head of the Kedumba, ninety-three acres had been alienated from the Crown, severed from their long, slow past and estranged from the forest about them. On these acres the grass was spreading; the timber was falling. There were cattle and sheep. There were plum trees and apples. There were garden vegetables. There were two men and a woman. And Dawson just over the ridge.

THE PLACE OF FALLING WATER

Rain falls on the Blue Plateau. M. falls asleep beneath these hands of mine, which run along ridges and hold for small moments the high ground of a shoulder, then drop and settle into the low places of her body. On the metal roof above us, on the corrugated iron and its peeling green paint, baffled by a carpet of needles, rain falls in a slow, irregular beat.

A cypress stands by the house and reaches its arms over the roof. The tree was planted here, along with the timber cottage, back when the first war had just ended in Europe, and this April night in a new century it still catches and orchestrates the rain and lets it fall, in round heavy notes, on the roof; the water runs down to gutters flush with moult, and it spills over them hard to the ground.

And this is how the place speaks tonight. We fall asleep in the sound of falling water.

CATCHMENT I

The plateau, this sandstone platform worn down by water, drains into one river with two names.

The river is the Hawkesbury-Nepean, and it rises, as the Nepean, in rough sandstone country south of Camden; it picks up the waters of the Cox's and flows down into the fertile shale flats of Bents Basin. It enters once into the escarpment below Lapstone and comes quickly out again into the plain. Then, for a while, it travels north on a wide alluvial bed at the escarpment's foot. Where the Grose joins it, at Grose Wold, the river changes its name to the Hawkesbury, and it bends east above Richmond to receive the Colo and the MacDonald, and it keeps on bending until at Wiseman's Ferry it's running southeast, after which it passes in deep meanders through the sandstone country north of the Cumberland Plain—the country of my childhood—and empties at last all the waters of the plateau into Broken Bay.

The plateau leans east, and its streams cut their deep and narrow, spare and convoluted ways toward this twice-named river at its feet. The whole plateau is a catchment, and it's making for the sea.

A SHORT HISTORY OF BELONGING IV

In 1893 the Maxwells crossed Waterfall Creek, and by 1898 Billy owned forty-two acres in a rough triangle formed by the two creeks and the base of the Kedumba Walls. On the knoll above the junction of the creeks Billy put up his own two-roomed slab hut and beside it a cooking shed, and he roofed them both in stringybark. In 1898, Billy was twenty-two and his father was sixty-six, and between them they held title to 135 acres at the far end of the Valley: marginal, heartbreaking ground, set down in some of the finest scenery the gods ever dreamed of.

The native grasses fed roos well enough, but they didn't fatten cattle. This pretty land could carry only one beast per ten acres. If you worked at it you could conjure enough vegetables from the ground and enough eggs from the fowls to keep from starving, but it must have been clear to the Maxwells by the turn of the century that they were destined to remain paupers in a parsimonious paradise.

The Maxwells had cleared and fenced as much land as they had strength for, and they had done it pretty fast. But they could only stay and pay for what they'd won so hard by sending Billy downriver. Billy became a stockman and farm hand like his father, and he was away from the sharp end of the Kedumba, where his parents aged fast, for months at a time. Then, in the winter of 1907, his mother, Mary-Anne, died, and they took her in a bullock dray to lie in the Catholic cemetery in Burragorang.

This was land you'd live for, but not land you could live from. It wouldn't keep you; it would suffer you; it would go that far. And for William Maxwell that was far enough. To live with these cliffs and the light they harbored, the weather and the cries of curlew at night and the bellowing of cattle; to spend his old age in a place promised to him, as he saw it, by the plateau in his youth—this felt like a miracle to him, renewed each day at dawn.

But it had to end one day, and on July 28, 1914, it did. When news of William's death came downriver, old John Maxwell sent a dray and ten oxen to bring his twin out of the Kedumba and back to the Cox's River, to lay him beside his wife. Billy set off south behind the bullocks, his father's body bouncing along

in a coffin Billy had banged together, and they'd just crossed
Reedy Creek when they met the priest coming the other way.
The weather was warm for winter, and soon the old man's body
would start to go off, and here was the Church come to them, so
Billy turned the bullocks round and took his father back to his
land and buried him there under the Kedumba Walls.

THE SYNTAX OF STREAMS

Les used to draw his water from Waterfall Creek, just above its
junction with the Kedumba. Not that he bothered much with
water. The water of Waterfall Creek was sweet because it rose in
a spring on Kedumba Mountain. He knew that because he and
May had lived up there in a caravan for most of 1963, when he
was building a road somewhere. He knew where the Waterfall
rose before it falls into the valley; and he knew that it ran clean
all the way to the house—no one but the old Gundungurra had
ever lived in its headwaters, and all the ground it cuts through
coming along the valley floor had been Maxwell land since it was
taken from the forest. All the old words still ran in the *Wolway*.
But other words, less easy to stomach, tainted the Kedumba.
Words like *runoff* and *effluent*. This was already true when Les
first left the valley in the thirties, and even truer when he left it
for the last time in the eighties. The Kedumba's diction has long
been corrupted.

For the Kedumba rises in a swamp in an upland valley,
and the whole town, including my place, is in its catchment.
It carries the stain of settlement, of careless humanity
packed closely together. It's not only water and words for
water's falling that drop from the escarpment's tongue into
the valley. .

The day I first came to the valley, I didn't drink the water.
At the ford over the Waterfall, the creek had been reduced by

drought, abstracted to a string of stagnant pools; if it was pure, it didn't look it. And though I thought the Kedumba, when I came to it, the loveliest river I'd seen, cutting as it does just below the slab hut through a small sandstone gorge, attended along its length by the worshipful riveroaks and tenanted by eagles, I would not have drunk its water either. For I, too, know where this river starts, the place from which it falls and the suburban curses it carries.

THE GULLY

But nothing, of course, is pure, and it turns out the Kedumba rises on holy ground.

The river rises in a sedge swamp in a hanging valley that has always been the center of Indigenous life on the plateau. It was where the people of the Burragorang and of the valleys to the plateau's north met and relaxed, traded songs and women, I guess, and lies and liturgies—or kept them secret together. The usual deal: a place both sacred and profane.

And when that net of suburban streets was dropped across the slender ridge, the swamp poked a hole in it and stayed; some of it was cleared and drained and turned to paddock; some of it, right in back of the falls, was fashioned into picnic grounds; and the rest of it became a shantytown encircled by Katoomba, and here some of the plateau's original people fabricated houses from kerosene tins and clay and hessian, and drew water from wells sunk in the old swamp, and they made a community and sang in the local churches and drank in the local pubs and played in the local cricket competition and fought and sometimes died fighting bushfires and went down into the valleys to pull out white bushwalkers who, inevitably, lost their way.

The headwaters of the Kedumba—this swamp and the humpies and sheds and wells about it—were known as the

Gully. And families, some of them large, grew and married and sat on their balconies and drank tea and fought and forgave and finally died, some of them, in the Gully. Until in the 1950s the town bulldozed the Gully back into the swamp and built a raceway there. The racetrack lasted thirty years until the locals, especially the owners of the guesthouses, got sick of the noise. And then the swamp started coming back, and people started to walk in the Gully again and to wonder what it had once been.

A SHORT HISTORY OF BELONGING V

One day in 1910, Billy went up the goat track to Katoomba and came back down with a wife.

I've seen photographs of her, this petite, intelligent, and determined-looking woman who married Billy Maxwell. When Billy found her, she was working for a minister in Katoomba; that's all Norm remembered of all Les remembered about how his parents met. She reminds me of my own grandmother. Both of them dairy farmer's daughters from up on the north coast of New South Wales, both of them tiny, gentle, indomitable, dignified to the point of solemnity.

I imagine that Billy courted Olive awhile in Katoomba, a town made—with all its romantic lookouts, its bridal-veil falls, its honeymoon points—for wooing and winning. (It was where, as it happens, my nana came to honeymoon, but that was twenty years later.) I see them courting up in Katoomba, along the escarpment's edge, along the Cox's River, in the middle burragorang, and I imagine Billy walking her down to Echo Point and showing her the land he farmed, the paddocks he and his father had cleared from the timber. To see your future so far down in front of you and so far back in time and surrounded by so much exquisite difficulty—this must have seemed a sublime temptation, an offer easier to refuse than forget.

I think Olive knew something else, which a poet later put like this: You can look as long as you like, but you're going to have to leap. Leap, or stay there on the precipice of the rest of your life for the rest of your life. Olive knew this, for she had left home in Kempsey and come to the city to work and live and then to Katoomba, where, look, she had this landscape about her, where Billy had found her and offered her a valley. So she jumped.

It took six years but in 1916 a child came along—Les—and a year and a bit later another boy, Jim, and then no more. Billy built them a bigger hut and named it for the waters, and Olive painted the walls eggshell blue inside and planted roses and flowering cherries in the garden and watched her boys grow and made them do their lessons and supervised her small dominion. She is registered in 1923 as the proprietor of the OM brand for cattle and horses, and she is named as *Olive Beatrice Maxwell of Olivedale, via Wentworth Falls.*

THE FIRST PHOTOGRAPH

It's the tenth day of January 1927, and the Maxwells are standing out in the front of their home. Les would be nearly eleven. A young cattle dog is licking his left hand, and the boy is trying hard to ignore the dog's affection and look straight into the newspaper man's camera, but he's not quite pulling it off. His face is caught midway between devilry and obedience. He has his white shirt buttoned to the neck and tucked into dark long shorts, and he has no shoes on his feet. His face is thin; his nose is long. His father's face, except for the mouth, which is his mother's—a sarcastic, dogged, embarrassed line.

Billy Maxwell stands like a tree. A man going nowhere fast.

Behind him in the doorway is Olive, still shorter than her husband by half a head though she stands on the step and he on the ground. She looks at him, not at the camera, and her mouth is clenched in a grimace meant to be a smile. She seems impatient and proud, perhaps a little ashamed that this old white dress is the best she has and that how she's dressed the boys is the best they will ever look.

To Les's right stands Jimmy, and he looks like a boxer waiting for the bell. He's got his eyes on someone off camera, and he's ready.

Behind them, the house looks as unfinished, as unvarnished, as the Maxwells.

But the family looks well. They seem to be prospering in the same way cattle might, or kangaroos, on good ground, but no more than that. As though the place is enough, but barely. You'd call them poor, and whether you'd call them happy depends on what you think happiness entails, and whether you think they want anything much more than they have; and it doesn't look like they know there's anything more than this place to want. So let's say they're happy.

They look like they're living a century earlier than they are.

THE ONES THAT GOT AWAY

Once a year Billy took some men from downriver—and when they were old enough, which was pretty soon, the boys too—and they shook as many heifers and steers as they could find out of the profound and serpentine cover of the forests up around Cedar Creek where the grasses were uncommonly good. They brought them in and drove the fat ones down the Kedumba and down the Cox's and up out of the Valley to market in Camden; the breeders they kept. Fifty years later, Jim Commens was still fetching from the timber the ones that got away.

But it was never much of a cattle empire; it never could have been. The soil in the valleys was too poor, and the country around was too steep. But Olive knew that Billy wasn't really running a business; he was living the only life he could imagine in the only place he could imagine living it.

THE SECOND PHOTOGRAPH

Here's Les, a boy of seventeen now. Already long and sure enough to make a good fist of seeming a man. Old enough for war and work; almost old enough for love or grief.

Here are Les and Jim on horses in the valley. And here, in front of them, feet on the ground, is their father. He holds in his hand a knife, the kind you'd use to work a saddle or mend a boot or carve a name. The way he holds it, in his fist, blade pointing back and up, out of harm's way, tells you he's a bushman. This knife is a tool in deft hands. Maybe sometimes a weapon.

He looks kind. He is a bullock, with a bullock's perseverance and sadness and the potential for rage.

Among these men there is no softness anywhere; there is no sentiment. There may be love, but there is no affection; there is no sympathy. They have been hard with each other, you can tell, and they have been hard with this place. There's confidence, though, in the boys' faces; there's something like delight at where they are and what they know how to do.

And look at these fine-boned, handsome horses they sit upon. They stand resigned beneath the boys, thin-nosed and stoic. Both horses are grays, and they look like stockhorses, bred for chasing cattle in up-and-down, in-and-out country like this.

The Kedumba Walls rise behind them. This is Australian Pastoral, no water anywhere. The boys are sitting far apart from each other and from their dad. Jim sits his horse like it's an armchair, leaning back, his off leg out of its stirrup and draped over the pommel. It looks like he's holding a cigarette in his left hand, his wrist cocked below his chin. Les is behind, half obscured by his father's bulk. He's pushing his feet down hard in the stirrups and forward and he's looking out with a wry and awkward smile.

These are boys who'd like you to think they have no softness anywhere in their hearts for these elegant beasts or this country. Just off to muster cattle; just doin' our dreary jobs. They're dressed like stockmen in sturdy pants and khaki shirts, sleeves rolled, hats made for keeping sun off and scooping water and shooing cattle and swatting flies, not for anything fancier. Narrow-brimmed town hats, not your showy cowboy models. The valley hadn't heard of cowboys then.

This is a picture of a life you wish you'd led in a place you wish you'd led it in. You know that you're discounting all the hurt and hunger and sunburn and downright cruelty—and not only for these men—that it took for two young men and their father to have come to belong so well in this grassy, stone-walled valley. But without doubt, there is a kind of sly joy here, and there is accomplishment that does not think of itself as anything so fancy as that, as though this is just the way things are. There is also the taciturn pride of men—in each other, in son, in father, in valley, in horse, in the day's work ahead they know they will perform with ease in timber and water and the wild fresh air. They long for nothing else but this moment, which is theirs. Here is a world, and here its citizens.

REAL ESTATE DREAMING

Billy Maxwell's father dreamed a valley; Billy worked his whole life squaring the valley to the dream.

Sixty-six years he spent trying to make it come true. Some men wander and imagine and begin; other men settle and consolidate and die—some of them—exhausted. Billy was the second kind of man. He kept the family poor buying up the other pieces of the valley floor around the meeting of the creeks. And, with the help of his own boys, until they left—long before the work was done—he fired and felled and grubbed and sowed and fenced and stocked the acres he won: he did what he had to do on these portions to fulfil the terms of his conditional purchases. All the acquiring he did he'd done by 1921, when Les was four and Jimmy three, and Billy himself was forty-four. But the work had barely begun.

For twenty-two years after that, he worked to keep the land in the family. He never stopped mustering and yarding and branding those pieces of that valley. He gathered up these acres almost by himself. He corralled these four hundred acres for his father, and for his own wife and sons. No man could have worked harder at a task. And when he died on the sixth day of the sixth month of 1943, a man exhausted by sixty-six years of claiming a valley, 437 acres of it had his name on them—seven portions of land, all of them contiguous except the 54 acres up on Dawson's Wold.

From up there, in his last days, hardly strong enough to let his horse carry him up the ridge, he looked down on his holdings, and he saw how small they were in the valley's larger scheme of things, and yet how beautiful—his few cattle upon the grasses, his horses, the house he'd made, the fences he'd built—and in his mind he could still see his small sons carrying water in pails strung from rods across their small backs up from the river to their mother's kitchen garden. In late October 1942, hearing his death approaching perhaps in the breath that failed him as he worked and walked, he sent word asking friends Enoch Donoghoe and Stephen Jarvis to come down from Katoomba to witness his will. Like the hut it was written in, the will could have been made a century earlier. It belongs in style to a time now passed. It is an imitation of the one his father had made fifty years before. It's made in a painstaking calligraphy upon a sheet of foolscap. And it tries to continue what his father began.

Billy bequeathed all his land to his wife and his two sons indivisibly. All but one acre. He wanted to keep the valley whole. Though his sons had been gone the better part of ten years, working in Camden, coming down rarely, he wanted to keep his family whole, too, and to give them back to the valley.

And that single acre? That he asked to be set aside for the Roman Catholic Church as a burial ground. It was the land around his father's grave. That's where he hoped to be laid to rest, beside his father in the valley. And that's where he thought his family would come to join him later. When he died eight months after signing his will, he thought he was passing the valley and his aspirations for it and its memories of him and his father into the hands of his family.

THY WILL BE UNDONE

And if none of this happened, Billy Maxwell is not really to blame. He misjudged his family, and he made a mistake: He named no executor in his copperplate will. A friend like Enoch, who ran the riding school in Katoomba, might have worked to keep the lands together. He might have seen the family cemetery consecrated and old Billy interred there. He might have talked Les and Jimmy into taking on the property and tending the graves of their father and grandfather and, in time, their mother.

But Enoch had no say in it. And Jimmy, who, upon his father's death, hastened to have himself named administrator of the estate, had another idea, though it took him seven years to work out exactly how to carry it out.

Jimmy's idea was to sell the place: cash it in and be

done. And no one—not Les and not Olive—was giving him an argument. Les had left the valley late in the 1930s, and by the time his father died Les was married and settled in Camden, driving trucks for the Clearys. Jimmy was working for them, too, and when their father died the boys leased a fibro house in Camden from the Clearys and moved their mother into it.

Les paid the funeral expenses. They buried the old man in the cemetery in Camden. Probably no one would have let them stick the old man in the ground beside his father, even if they'd thought of asking. It was already the modern and secular world.

All of Billy's acres were worth just £625 when he died. He still had £7 to pay the Crown for Dawson's Wold and another £26 for Portion 106, the largest and the farthest south. Once these debts were paid, the whole lot, Billy Maxwell's entire life's work, came out at under £600. He had £43 in his account at the Commonwealth Bank at Katoomba and sixteen head of mixed cattle. Jimmy sold off the cattle for £56 and I suppose he gave that and the £43 in the bank to his mother. But for seven years he did nothing more to execute his father's will; he neither worked the land nor sold it. There was a war on, I suppose, and the acres were worth so little. I guess he thought he'd wait and see.

For seven years the valley lay fallow. Everyone abandoned it but old William Maxwell lying in his grave. For seven years the trees encroached upon the ground that Billy had taken from them. His dream lay down in the silent paddocks and died.

And for seven years Jimmy haunted the place. You'd find him there some weekends when he had nowhere else to go and nothing else to do, passed out on the ground or in the back of a borrowed ute, walking the paddocks at night, like a boy looking

for something—a stone or a rubber ball or a coin—he'd dropped
and now needed more than he'd ever needed anything.

SELLING IT ALL

Then in October 1950 Jimmy Maxwell knew what to do. The
war was over, and a dam was coming. The Burragorang was
going under, and up in the Kedumba the landholders thought
their days were numbered, too. The dam would make an island
of the valley, swallowing the only decent road in and out—the
switchbacks up to Camden. Nearly everyone was selling up,
getting what they could for their desolate parcels. But Jimmy
saw it differently, and so did his employers.

For some years, Dan Cleary and his brother had owned a large
piece of ground across the Kedumba River from the Maxwells—
this was how the boys had met them in the first place—and like
Jimmy they'd been waiting for the time to be right, and now it
was. Now they could see the future. No one would ever make
a small holding pay, but think of the economies of scale if you
owned it all. Seven thousand acres might make a going concern.
So that was their plan: buy up the valley cheap; run some cattle
and cut some trees and grow some corn, whatever you could
turn a dollar or make a useful loss from; and—the crucial part—
punch a road up the Kedumba Walls and get to market that way.

Jimmy saw the way their thinking was headed. Seven full
years after administration was granted to him, Jimmy got
registered as the proprietor of his father's lands, and his single
act as owner was to sell those lands to the Clearys. He drove the
bargain hard; he screwed them for the four hundred Maxwell
acres, without which there could be no road out of the valley
and no monopoly over it. The sale went through on January 22,
1951, the eve of his brother's birthday, and the lands that Billy
Maxwell had won so hard were lost.

I suppose some of the money from the sale found its way back to his mother and his brother. If most of it stayed in Jimmy's pocket, that may explain the animosity that grew between the brothers and blew up later, the year their mother died, when Les was back in the Kedumba and Jimmy had lost a leg out west and made a fortune and couldn't believe how much he still coveted the childhood he'd traded away.

THE THIRD PHOTOGRAPH

The old world has eroded now. It has retreated into the figure of this ruined man, who has spent too long slouching in a valley, who has spent a lifetime bowing to other men, bent over hard work, indentured to a place on earth. It is 1990. And it is Les. He still looks poor. His clothes seem soiled, and his hair is thinning. He wears a parka, baggy jeans, and old lace-up boots. You know that if he has other clothes, they would all look like this, steeped in the air he's breathed and the dirt he's worked most of his life. He looks dirt poor, and more or less ruined. He looks like he's waiting for someone to tell him what to do next, no more at home, but also no less, than he was at ten. And his expression, though it's taken on more of his father's animal resignation, still falls between meekness and pride, humor and despair.

He has eroded, too. If you're going to stay your ground, you're going to have to weather. He's bent like a tree in the prevailing wind. And his form tells the history of the valley over eighty years and of all his labor in it. He seems to know that this is how you end up when you let a place have its way with you; he looks as though he'd like to look as though he didn't care.

If he looks sad, it's because the world has just been taken from him. The valley, these last ten years, has ebbed and ebbed, and now it is dry. It's over. And he looks about over, too.

He's been gone from the Kedumba some years now. These

men have brought him back, to show them where he used to live. If you didn't know better, you'd take him for a homeless man. He looks like he's left his life someplace else and crashed here in someone else's valley. He's been sleeping rough and drinking hard, you'd think he knew nothing of this place, when, in fact, there is nothing about it he doesn't know as well as his own name.

Sometime before this photograph was taken, Les stood at his grandfather's grave below the Kedumba Walls in the gray afternoon and declaimed—in a voice that's his geriatric version of the voice he was taught as a boy to use for poetry—the entire poem A. L. Bennett wrote when Les's grandfather died. To this vagrant, the valley has committed its memory. There's not a line of it he doesn't know by heart, and many of them he lived himself. In the dam paddock Les stands and speaks a poem. His voice is thick with years and smoke and drink and probably sorrow. He slurs, and he looks off toward the flanks of Solitary where the words seem to live. And he recalls them all, and in them he recalls the first white man the valley fell for, whose dream—the man's dream, the valley's for the man—this old exile has spent his life seeing through to its close.

At the end of the poem, it seems to Les suddenly that the place is finished, too; it's all been sung and it's empty now. He's woken here in his grandfather's dream to find it was only really a valley after all.

THE HOMELESS MAN

When May had died and there was only Les and the valley, a hobo came and stayed a month or so. He camped in Smith's hut for a bit, and then in Les's abandoned caravan over Reedy Creek. But by the time Les found his fires and the mess he'd made of those places, the bugger had moved on.

Les would hear the dogs barking or the hens going off, or the horses stirring, and know it was the hobo. Now and then he went out with his gun and poked about. "Bugger off and don't come back," he yelled into the violate dark. In the morning there'd be eggs gone, once a whole chook. And twice by day, as Les came back from town in the Holden, he glimpsed the hobo slipping off the road, but by the time he'd stopped the car, the bloke had disappeared, and Les had left his rifle at the house. But Les had seen enough: the filthy beard and the old army disposal jacket. It was hard to tell how old the bloke was, but he must have been younger than he looked, because Les had seen him move pretty quickly. And it angered Les that this bastard thought he could walk in here and treat the valley as his own.

When Norm came down, Les went on about it. "There he goes, now," Les said one Saturday afternoon, looking up toward the two hills where the road disappears into timber, looking at nothing that Norm could make out.

"Where?"

"Didn't ya see the dust in the air? He's got his bloody dog with him."

"His dog?"

"I can tell, boy. You learn to notice when there's something here that shouldn't be. He stinks so bad, I can smell him from here. But he's there all right, goin' up the road as though 'e owns the place. Got a mind to drive up and help him on his way."

Norm is thinking—on the subject of how bad the guy smells—*look who's talking*. "Have another beer, Les. You're seeing things."

Next morning, over tea, Les sits suddenly upright. He stares south along the road to where it disappears. "He's coming this way," he says.

"Shit, Les. You're makin' this up."

"Look at the dust risin' óff the road again. It's 'im and 'is dog."

Les gets up. "I'm gonna send him a little message." And he walks into the house and takes his rifle from the rack and comes back with it to the veranda.

Les raises the rifle and sights something and he fires one shot and then another and after a moment a third.

"Watch it, Les, you might've killed the mother," says Norm.

"If I'd meant to kill 'im, 'e'd be lyin' dead now," says Les. "I shot a good foot over 'is 'ead. Jumped like a rabbit and ran."

"The sherry must be improving your eyes, Les," says Norm.

"Nothin' to do with the sherry, boy." He puts the rifle down. He hasn't looked this happy in all the years since May passed on. "Might 'ave the place to meself for a bit now."

THE ART OF LOSING

The Kedumba came to Les three times. It came with birth; it came with his father's death, when Les thought he didn't want it; it came later with a job, when Les knew that he did. And three times he lost the valley—four, if you count his dying. All up, he spent fifty years in the valley and never owned it once. He left it for a long stretch in the middle of his years and wandered, but it never did leave him.

The first time Les lost the valley, he left to find a bigger world. It was 1936; he was twenty; it was about time. He got as far as Central Burragorang. There, he ran the mail from the Cox's River Post Office to Nattai and back, three times a week. For three years he made that run on horseback, leading a packhorse carrying the mail; sometimes, when there were passengers prepared to pay, he drove horse and sulky. In 1940, he bought a 1927 Studebaker and made the run by car; the next year, his Studebaker failed and he bought Jack Pippen's 1928 Buick and drove the mail in and out six days a week until he was tired of it.

That happened in 1941, when Les gave up the run and lost the valley a second time and went to work for the Clearys, who were busy with military contracts around Camden. Camden in wartime was about as big as Les needed the world to get, so he stayed, and for a couple of years after the war Les drove passengers from Camden railway station to the guesthouses in the Lower Burragorang. He did this until his brother, Jim, sold off Kedumba to the Clearys. Then, with the Big Water coming and no home left to him by Waterfall Creek, he went off west to help Jimmy move earth and dig tanks in the flat red country. The third time he lost the valley.

But something had happened in Camden during the war. Someone, actually.

MAY

She was Susannah May, though she thought "Susannah" too fancy and went by "May," and she was never what you'd call beautiful; she was no one's idea of thin. Or tall, for that matter. But her breast, in its day, was ample, and her day was during the war years when Les first met her.

In 1943 she worked as a cook at the Camden Hospital. She was separated from her two boys and adrift from her husband, who was living with another woman down in the army camp at Liverpool. He drove the buses there, name of Maurice. Les had met Maurice, had met him and not liked him much, even before Les met May and had some more reasons not to like him. The boys were still young, and Maurice had no money to send. So May had sent Mervyn, who was eight, into an orphanage, and Norman, who was six, she'd sent to Maurice's parents, in Camden.

May lived in Camden too—a flat above the jewelers on the main street. She saw Norman most days, and some evenings she sold hot dogs and hamburgers to the American airmen. She was twenty-six, pretty enough to catch a lonely man's eye, but not, in most cases, to hold it long. She was neither free nor unfree. A mother but not a parent; married but no one's wife. She was short, and she could be sweet. She cooked; she flirted; she saved money to pay for her boys' care. And she tried to keep herself from expecting anything too much.

It was like this, piecing herself together, that she met Les one night. She was serving hamburgers, and he was hungry.

Les was twenty-seven. He was ready, after his wandering, which had not gone all that far, but had already been quite long, for a wife. And like most men about that stage and about that age, he was ready again for a mother, though he wouldn't have seen it that way. May had curves in some of the right places; that's more what Les was looking for. She was good with her hands; he'd have seen that. She could cook, and there she was. It's sometimes enough.

So Les fell for Susannah May Peck, who liked to call herself May, over a hamburger stand in Camden in the middle of 1943. Les and May waited out the war and they waited out Maurice. When he did nothing, May filed in early 1945 on the demonstrable grounds of desertion, and the divorce came through in December. Maurice took two weeks to marry his new woman. And Les married May on the second day of February in 1946 at Ingleside, where her parents lived. The Catholics wouldn't have them; May was a married woman as far as they could see and manifestly a mother. The Anglicans were more accommodating.

THE YEARS GO BY

At the war's end the boys went to live with their father and stepmother in a new house in Prospect, and it was ten years

before May saw much of them. She lived in a caravan on the
road with Les, who loved her though he forgot to mention it
for months at a time. She caught fish, and she shot the snakes
that got in under the van, and once she shot a goanna that got
right inside. From the caravan's windows she shot the crows that
plucked the eyes from the newborn lambs. In a pressure cooker
on the campstove she cooked strings of fish, and she cooked eels
and cockatoos and rabbits and wallabies and even wombats now
and then, and all of it was pretty good. She had a gift for food.
She had a good eye and a steady hand with a gun. She could run
repairs. She could drive a tractor. She could cut timber, and she
could split logs. She could paint a caravan, and she could trap and
skin a rabbit, but she could never quite get the hang of happiness.

By the mid-1950s, her boys had grown up and entered the
world. They learned to drive; they came to visit their mother.
Norm and, less often, his brother drove out to camp with May
and Les where they were, down on the Murrumbidgee, or up
along the Hunter, or out at Cullen Bullen. Norm never let more
than two weeks pass without going to stay with his mother and
Les. Les and May were closing in on the plateau again by then,
working the roads into that nursery of fires, drawing back closer
to the Kedumba.

And then at last came all her Kedumba days, eleven years of
weekend visits from the boys, and in between, the valley and the
weather and a plenitude of time.

May spent the rest of her life with Les, and if she'd known
how to be happy she would have been, and she went where Les
went until he ended up back where he began, where she stayed
until the end. Until she drowned in landscape.

THE FATHER OF THE MAN
In Camden during the war, young Norman had lived with his

father's parents, and one day an old woman moved in next door, and Norm soon learned that her name was Mrs. Maxwell and her husband Mr. Billy Maxwell had just died in the Kedumba.

The old girl swung an axe like a man, a woman thin as a stick and tough as a snake and just as likely to bite you. Sometimes Norm's grandparents spoke of her by her full name, Mrs. Olive Beatrice Maxwell, and one day, when he was seven and trying to sound grown up, not trying to be funny, he called out to her over the fence, "Morning, Olive Beetroot." She glared at the boy and called him over and hit him with a stick. "That'll teach you some manners," she said. And she might have been right.

A bit later Norm met this old woman's son Les, when Les started walking out with Norm's mother, and then Norm started learning some more things. Before too long Les was taking the boy out shooting rabbits along the river flats in the jeep. At first Les just let the boy run and fetch the animals Les brought down. Bullets, those days, were hard to come by, and Les would never have more than two or three. "There's nothing so good for improvin' your aim," he said once to Norm, "as not eatin' meat for a week if you miss." Les didn't miss too often. Later, when Les could beg a bit more ordnance from the army boys, he let Norm shoot a bullet or two. And Norm soon got his eye in and most Fridays he got a rabbit or two, and that was the only meat the boy ever ate in the three years he stayed with his father's parents.

LANDSCAPE PHOTOGRAPHY

It's early September, the driest month of the year, and the valley is rolling over into summer. The sun has been out all day, and now what's left of it has fallen into the valley and is lying there on the yellow grasses like whiskey in a glass. This is light that should not be here at all. For Solitary's side is black with shadow and the sun itself has fallen behind it. This is light that bends and picks up the tint of the escarpments it bends over; it carries traces of the bark of eucalypts and suggestions of their parsimonious way with water. The light is sclerophyll—austere, dry as the soil it affects to bless. The light comes to the valley out of the west, over the outflung arm and the ribs of the plateau, through the sharp blue breath of eucalypts, bearing within it fragments and undertones of the western plains. And someone has daubed the cured grasses with it.

Norm is coming home, driving along the Valley Road north from a day's fishing lower down the Kedumba. His esky is full of trout. And an eel. He's got himself a black duck, fished it out of a dam with his fishing rod, for that is where it fell when he shot it out of the sky, and he had no dog to fetch it. He is content. He, too, is steeped in the light of the end of winter. He's a practical man who thinks himself unmoved by pretty things, least of all sunsets. But he comes over the rise into Dawson's paddock, and he is pulled up short by the look of the grass and the rock beyond it in this light.

Three eastern greys are black stumps on the ground. They've heard the Rover's approach and have stilled themselves in case that saves them the trouble of flight. They too are blessed by the afternoon, by the light that silhouettes them, because when Norm stops the car and shoots, it's a camera he aims at them, at the yellow ground and the dark bulk of Solitary, the sidelit face of Mount Kedumba, the dusky nipple of Sunset Hill, and the bleached blue of distance with which the plateau at this end of the valley is colored. Just the kind of blue of which nostalgia is made; just the tone that gave the mountains, which are not mountains but which look like them from here, their name.

The wheel tracks ahead of him are mauve with shadow, and the eucalypts stand like Japanese calligraphy in the paddocks.

Night has already fallen on the house ahead, where his stepfather Les Maxwell waits. Norm knows as he closes the shutter that this is a picture of everything he loves, caught in one of the moods in which he loves it best.

THE PIECES OF A MAN

He'd been talking for three hours, and I'd run out of tape. "Lunchtime, anyway," said Norm. He stood and I stood too, and then he said, "There are some things of Mum's and Les's you might as well take a look at." He walked out to the garage and came back with a cardboard box. He put it down on the laminex top of the table we'd been sitting at, out on his deck in Blacktown.

"This is all Les had when he died," said Norm, "apart from the pyjamas he died in. And a few shirts and pairs of pants, which weren't much use to anybody. I tossed those out. But I kept this box. Don't really know what to do with it. But I can't chuck it out."

Norm reached in and pulled out a blue diary, and then another, brown. The brown one still had the little pencil it came with lodged between the spine and the plastic binding. "Mum kept these diaries. Every year, I think, right till the end. Les kept 'em close by when she went. I've never looked at 'em myself, but you might find something in 'em. You never know."

I took the diaries from him and set them back on the table. In the box lay all that remained of all that mattered to Les. There were the diaries, twenty of them it looked like, arranged on the bottom like library books on a shelf, spine out. There were three watches, and I took one out of the box.

"Les was a man who had to have the time on him," said Norm. "You'd never catch him without a watch."

I found small black-and-white photographs, a compass, a

student's writing block, a Christmas card some woman sent him in 1979 as though he were some kind of prophet, some bills, a pair of spectacles, clippings from aged newspapers, typescript pages Norm said were joke letters Les used to write but never send to the authorities, and a wooden box inlaid with mother-of-pearl. I opened that and found more photographs of people who turned out to be May and Les and friends of theirs from a time and in a light that looked like they belonged to a foreign country but were just the valley in a former life. And there was Les leaning on his elbow by a creek. His white shirtsleeves rolled to his biceps. His other hand, resting on the ground, holds up a bottle of beer, and someone's child is sitting beside him. Les is looking into the camera, smug and embarrassed and sunburned and pissed.

I found May's divorce papers from her first marriage, then Les and May's marriage certificate, some letters from solicitors, a very old letter written by hand to Les's father, Billy, a gun license, Les's motorcycle license from 1938, clippings of the fires of 1958 and a man sitting on a bulldozer above the caption *Mr. Lesley Maxwell clearing the new firetrails.*

Here in a box were the fragments of a man. Some of the parts of which Les was the whole. Here was a life eroded into the very few pieces that held it together. And twenty of those pieces were May.

TAKING NOTE

Down in the valley, through the sixties and the seventies, there was a woman keeping note of the days. Few of them went anywhere without her noticing. They entered May's diaries, year after year, compressed notations of weather and work and family and health. She complained, but not at length. Mostly she just observed—*very hot again; Les moved gravel all day alone;*

Les drilling at Nellies Glen; crane collapsed; flies v bad; storm in afternoon; twelve points. Like that she transposed each day into a few lines in a book, a week to an opening, making a blue biro a kind of calligraphy of witness. The lines became volumes, and the volumes became years, and the years became a poem, in which the valley was spoken.

FOR INSTANCE

Wednesday, August 1. Windy & fine. / Les clearing stumps. / Very
   cold night.
Thursday, August 2. Big frost. / Les grading & carting / sand on
   Mtn. / Went shopping / after work.
Friday, August 3. King size frost. / Les on Mtn again.
Saturday, August 4. Frost & / fog, overcast. / Les went to work
   with Kevin. His / saw broke down, home / at 11 am, he had / it
   fixed & returned. / I went fishing / alone as usual. / Nice day.
Sunday, August 5. Nice day. We went fishing / had no luck. /
   Mild night.
Monday, August 6. Les grading Mtn / again. / Warm day & / night. /
   Yarded stears / late.
Tuesday, August 7. Fog early / then sunny. / Men drafting & /
   drenching stears / fixing fences. / Les got into strife / with
   stears at Kedumba Crk / while Brian cut a / load of wood for
   him- / self.
Wednesday, August 8. Cloudy & / cool. Les in strife / with stears
   again. / Started plowing. / Stears broke / fence / he fixed / that
   & got them in. / Started on back / paddock again. Very /
   cold night.
—1973

THE FIRST TIME

I'd thought at first that Les was born in the valley.

But the first time Les came into the valley, he was already six weeks old. He was conceived down there and for eight months the valley carried him. A month from term, straight after Christmas 1915, Billy took his wife out of the valley by cart to Narromine, where he had a sister.

Narromine's a fair way west of the plateau, and it was a long way to go to give birth, but in 1916 there was a war on and there was only the goat track into the Kedumba and you wouldn't expect a doctor to get down there, not in a single piece, in time to help you drop a child. So Billy took Olive to stay with the Tolimans—his sister, Caroline, and her prosperous husband and their comfortable house—for the last month of her confinement.

They had to take the cart out through Burragorang and up the jump-back to Camden. Then they traveled north against the eastern flank of the plateau to find the Western Highway. And they took that through the plateau again, bouncing in that sulky behind the horses, taking a narrow and bending track across the main ridge, dreading fire and enduring instead rain, and then they dropped down the pass from Mount Victoria into the Kanimbla, out of the sandstone country and all the way west through Lithgow and Bathurst to Dubbo—and finally to Narromine. There, on January 23, 1916, in Nurse Chamberlain's Hospital on Booth Street, Leslie William John Maxwell was born.

Billy went home on horseback to see about the cattle and do a job of droving for someone in the Burragorang. Five weeks later he collected his wife and firstborn son and took them back to the Kedumba.

So it was early March when Les first knew the valley. Some of his first days there were hot and all of them were humid and some of them were wet. But the nights were growing cool.

In the paddocks close to the creeks, the finches flocked and the friarbirds—"leatherheads," Billy called them—fledged their Christmas offspring and began to think of leaving for the winter. Some nights, the pure and disconsolate chorus of stone-curlews washed over the house and the sleeping child from out of another world. Olive would shiver if she heard it, for it sounded like death to her. She'd rise and listen for her baby's breathing, in case the birds had carried it off. And in the dusk and dawn of the last days of March, from the gully where the creeks met, the baby would have caught the sweet and myriad shrill callings of the lyrebird.

In Les's first weeks in the valley, there would have been currawongs and grass parrots and gang-gangs with their ratchet voices up in the riveroaks; he would have heard the elegiac calls of black cockatoos, leaving in their twos and threes for the coast; there would have been bulbuls in the fruit trees with their sweet queep-quillyas and spinebills with their limpid, shapely rondos and flame robins flitting the fences; and, in the tall gums along the Kedumba, he'd have heard tree martins in their lithe congregations. Not that he'd have known what he was hearing; but what he heard in the beginning is what he would still be hearing at his end.

Up on the breasted hills the red bloodwoods were putting out creamy flowers. The blue gums and the white gums were shedding their skins in long careless ribbons, and deep in the gullies the whistling tree frogs were starting to bell and chorus. And the snakes were beginning to think of winter, the first time Les came into the valley.

Les came into the valley by the light of the lamp his grandfather had first brought there in 1889, the same oil lamp that William Maxwell had got from his mother, who'd bought it on a street in Sydney in the 1830s, the lamp Les would still have

in the caretaker's house in the late 1980s. The lamp that Norm
has now. Which still throws good light.

Billy Maxwell had taken the lamp on the cart to use in camp
at night, bringing his baby son Les home; and on the last night
of that slow journey there had been storms and the road was
wet and the horses were slipping and Reedy Creek was running
high at the crossing and it was falling dark. Despite the rain and
the dark Billy Maxwell saw no point stopping this close to home,
so he found the lamp and lit the wick under the shelter of the
cart's canopy, and Olive held the lamp high to give them a little
light to see the road by.

ACCOUNTING

I have on my desk the diaries May kept, twenty pocket diaries,
each smaller than a packet of cigarettes, their plastic covers red
or blue or yellow or orange or green. There's nothing special in
these books, just a voice and a world that will never return; just
a couple of thousand of the works and days of the Kedumba,
hers within it, and her husband's.

Folded into the back of 1972, I find two sheets of paper.
One is her recipe for sweet and sour sauce; the other is a sheet
torn from a book of accounts, and on it May has made a table
of her Kedumba years. She made it, or she last added to it, in
1976, and why she made it and why she made it then and how
it ended up in 1972 are small and probably inconsequential
mysteries.

Herb Bowen died 1/25/65
Moved to Bowen's 3/14/65
Cancer operation 1/21/64
Norman and Franki married 10/31/64
VW 1500 station sedan 2/5/65

Returned to Camden 3/19/58

Les started wrk for Dan 3/20/58

I had a curette op. 12/17/63

Mervyn and Dot married 4/27/63

Camped at Caravan Kedumba Mountain 5/13/63

I got georm in bowel 9/21/65

I went to Dr. then hospital 10/11/65 Bad

Out of hospital 10/17/65

Went to hospital again 10/28/65 to 11/6

Les wnt into hospital 12/28/66 to 1/3/67

DAN CLEARY DIED 1/13/70

Les hernia operation 11/13/70

We married 2/2/1946

I entered hospital 1/23/71. Blood pressure high. To 1/29/71

Liver biopsy June 16, '69

4/23/71 I went to Katoomba hospital (slight stroke)

4/27/71 Returned home

2/3/71 Sent to hospital for 10 days

4/9/76 I got lower teeth

4/12/76 I went into hospital for op. on tongue

This is a memoir in free verse. It's a very brief life, slightly out of order, an audit of a life suffered in a valley.

KEEPING SCORE

The entries May made each day of each year tell a fuller story of a place and a woman and a man within it. But full isn't really the word. Her diaries are made of tight phrases, deft treatments of large-scale dramas; in her books, she abstracted into a sclerophyll vernacular her entire infinitesimal world as it made itself up and unmade itself again in its gargantuan and indifferent habitat. A real valley will never make it into a book, not even into twenty. Nor will a marriage. But it's astonishing how much does.

There's Les plowing paddocks and blasting stumps and mustering steers and chasing some that got away up on the flanks of Solitary and drenching heifers and calves and shearing sheep and slashing grass and raking branches off the airstrip; there's May shooting the snakes and parrots and rabbits and pigeons; there are the two of them down the Kedumba catching eight blackfish and twenty-seven trout and thirty-odd parrots, and there are her recipes for cooking eels; there's Les fencing and fencing again, and there he is leaving early on summer mornings to fight fires elsewhere in the plateau, and there he is clearing trees from the road after a storm and repairing pumps and other people's cars, and there he is endlessly making roads; and there they are losing pets and finding wild horses in the scrub and black snakes under the house and brown snakes in the kitchen; and there they are shooting wild dogs and kangaroos, everywhere but in the home paddocks; and there she is driving to town to perm her hair and pay her bills and shop at Fleming's and make her slow repayments on the VW and on her insurance and to accrete her small savings at the bank and to meet her friend Mary Greenwell; and there again she is planting seed and listening to the radio and sharing drinks with Les and with the boss Dan Cleary, whom she liked, and Cleary's son Bill, whom she didn't; she's mourning her mum; she's spending days in the garden; she's making wine; she's feeling crook and lonely and worried for Les dozing up there on the mountain again in the rain.

And what a price this place extorted from this woman and this man for making it so roughly their home; what revenge it took for what their love demanded of it. For they wasted the valley, and the valley wasted them right back.

THE LOW PRIESTS OF THE PLACE

The first time I came to the Kedumba, the first thing I heard was the friarbird.

Les, now that I think of it, was the friarbird. His face was long and his expression bashful, ironic, sad, and wary. All at once. He was tall and angular; in the end, he was stooped. The bird, though, is bald, and Les never was; until his death his hair grew long and wild, roughly swept back; first black and then gray. The bird, too, is black and gray. Les seemed always to bow his head and look out from under his high brow. His nose was long; his mouth thin and turned down at the corners. Like the bird, he was a sad kind of clown. And his hands, contorted by a lifetime at the crude and unforgiving controls of 'dozers, were claws.

The bird's voice can be harsh and guttural, but also rich and deep. It's intelligent but not quick. Les wasn't given to much speech or song—or speed, for that matter. But when he opened his mouth what came out seems to have been worth listening to. When he spoke, you could trust him because he never said anything he wasn't certain of, in the way the friarbird is certain, without either of them thinking much about it. What the bird says, according to my birdbooks, is "tobacco," "four o'clock," "poor soldier," and "yakob." Which you have to say with your mouth pretty well closed, the way Les used to speak. Les made more sense than that, but he spoke in short phrases like that, mellow, prosaic cadences.

The man's voice and his posture, like the bird's, were sepulchral. Sacerdotal.

Friarbirds are native to open forest, woodland, and watercourse. They live on nectar, as he lived on sweet sherry, and they speak of homely things.

May was the red-browed finch, which fusses roundly about and favors "grassy clearings in forests" and the garden.

THE SUBLIME

In May's books of days there is no birdsong. There is not the sweet metallic music of the magpies in the winter mornings. There are no trees or shadows or sounds of water in the creeks. There is no late afternoon light upon the sandstone walls, no silver wake of full moon upon the midnight grasses. Apart from the odd pet, there are no animals but those that she and Les murder or begrudge. But there is always weather. There are so many hot days and cold, so much wind and snow and storm and rain, so much frost and fire, humidity and fog, and just now and then a clear and sunny, beautiful day.

May's diaries are not a love song for a valley; they're a journal of exile.

Outside the weather and Les's work, her ill health is the rest of what she observed. It was her calling; it was her lifelong orphan practice.

Life and a valley taught May to pay attention, but not to beauty especially. Life and a valley taught her everything there is to know about the sublime except the words for it; they taught her that you suffer for what and where and whom you love; they taught her that there are many ways to sicken and die and many weathers to do it in; they taught her that things break and fall apart and you fix them and they fall apart again; they taught her a hundred ways to feel alone in a landscape that didn't care.

Saturday, December 30, 1972. Very hot. Trouble with pumps.
Terrible day. Les and Col went out for a beer, left me home and dam Hot.

Sunday, December 31, 1972. Cloudy and cool. Les Worked. I had
lonely day as usual.

SOME NOTES ON THE WEATHER

Jim Commens sits on the bench in the shed, and he studies
May's diaries, the two years I've brought with me. It's a Saturday
in April 2004. Jim pulls his feet back under the bench, and his
spurs rattle. He's taken off his soiled white hat, and he's thrown
it, crown down, on the gravel, where my boy, who's just learned
to crawl, discovers it, turns it over, tries its edge in his mouth,
and pulls a face.

Jim was mucking out the horses' yard when I arrived; the
girls finish up for him now, and they hustle the last of the horses
out into the afternoon. An easterly is piling a blue cloud against
the escarpment above, but the air in the valley is dry. The place
is heading back to drought. That's six years of it now, and Jim is
saying we may be looking back soon on the last two centuries as
a wet spell, the way things are going.

Fog at Blackheath is all this cloud will amount to tonight,
and down here it's just making the evening pretty. The last of the
daylight is yarded at the end of the valley among these sandstone
walls; it's caught beneath that patch of incompetent sky, and a
sad bright burnish settles upon everything—on the pale grasses,
the grey gums, the dirt road, the horses, the fences, and us.

Jim is reading 1967. "So she always wrote in these things?"
he asks. "These tiny books?" I nod. Every year the same kind of
diary; every year the same color ink. He shakes his head. For
twenty years Jim's kept a watch on the days himself, but he
puts his straight onto a computer. He flicks again through this
artifact I've put in his hands, this transcript of the neighboring
valley but one. He's looking back forty years—but it feels like
another geological era to him.

But look—here's some people he remembers, Mr. and Mrs. Hocking, and a place, "Carlooh Halt," just over the rise, and there's Les working it with Kevin Grady, digging a trench back in 1967. Kevin's son, says Jim, was here just a week ago. This is a world he lives in still; this is a world that's passed away.

Next he's reading the rain that fell in January and February and March that year—1,780 points of it, notes May, from Les's birthday, on January 23, to March 9. Jim's reading the shot horses and the mulberry wine and the grading of the mountain and the breaking of parts and the soreness of May's feet and the coldness of the nights and all the risen creeks and the fires that came to Narrowneck at Christmas. And now he's reading the rainstorms of early August, which almost carried the plateau away.

Jim looks out at the light, which is the color of dryness itself and which he knows, all the same, is a prayer answered. He looks back to me and says, "See, now there's another thing. It used to rain back in them days."

INUNDATION

In late July 1967 the weather ran cold, and nearly every day it rained, and May was feeling unwell again. Her tummy this time. Then her foot began to ache, and May blamed the weather.

The last day of July the sky cleared, and the rain pulled back, and the night was cold, and May woke to a valley white with frost. Cloud came in on Tuesday, August 1 and stayed all day; the frost held on till midday, and by evening the air still felt frosty, and still her tummy was crook. And so it was the next day. The winds blew on, as they will in August. Thursday started with frost, but the winds dropped, and the day grew warm, and May started feeling better. Friday morning Les left to work the Megalong road. Be gone for two days, he said.

Friday stayed warm until evening, when cold winds came down into the Kedumba and stayed. They drove May in from the garden, and she spent the night in the house alone, a night clangorous as a blacksmith's shop. It played itself out, hour on hour, beating out morning on the iron roof, and in her bed May felt every blow. She hardly slept. By first light her foot was throbbing.

Saturday, August 5. Freezing cold winds. My foot crook. Rain started in afternoon and teemed all night.

II

RIVER

THE RIVER I

Saturday, August 5, 1967, started out clear, but the winds rose through the morning. The sheoaks along the river keened and tossed their heads. Trees, as ever, in mourning.

They'd missed their train from Sydney and arrived late at Blackheath the night before, and it was after midnight in a heavy wind when they got to bed in the cabins. In the clean, cool air of Saturday morning they saddled up at Carlon's place on Galong Creek, and by eight they were riding over Carlon's Saddle headed for the river and the hut on the Kanangra Flats downstream. Twelve miles or so, a good day's ride. Overnight in the hut and back to Green Gully Sunday night. And back to work on Monday. That was the plan.

They were Oonagh, Clem, and Mark, colleagues from *Country Life* magazine, and their friends Lynne and Margaret. Oonagh was twenty-one and the oldest of them by two years; Clem came next. They all knew how to ride, but they didn't know the country. Only Clem had ridden the river before.

On five of Bert Carlon's horses and leading a packhorse, they dropped down to the river on Breakfast Creek, crossing and recrossing thirty times to find a track between the steep granite banks, their horses stepping gingerly among the stones in the creek. They made the Cox's River by one o'clock. Just below the junction, the riverbed is wide and sandy, the river running in braids, and they galloped their horses for a mile before the valley closed in on them and the sheoaks crowded about, and they slowed their horses again to a walk.

The wind was getting up. The big riveroaks swayed and rang with it, and the air was growing cold. It poured down the steep sides of Blue Dog on their left, down Scrubber's Hump and Mount O'Reilly on their right, and it found the narrow flats and it lunged and pawed at the horses, and it pushed the riders about in their saddles. In the billowing air, the manes and tails of the horses streamed like algae in a current. The day fell colder still. Around two o'clock, Oonagh looked up and saw that clouds had moved in above them—out of the west by the look of it, though it's hard to keep your bearings eight hundred meters down inside these mountains. And the clouds had a strange green hue she'd never seen in clouds before. They looked dense and grave. They looked like they meant business.

And then the rain began.

SATURDAY NIGHT IN THE KEDUMBA

Late Saturday, Les drove back to the valley in the rain, and the road from Mount Kedumba became a river behind him, all the crossings washed out, the creeks running hard, and he was lucky to get in. He knew he wasn't getting out again. Not soon.

HOW TO MAKE A PLATEAU

The plateau got here in a river.

It came in a river as wide, as inconstant, and complex as the rivers of the Channel Country in the continent's arid heart today. Go out there and see what the plateau looked like when it was first becoming itself.

The body of the plateau floated in as alluvium, washed off mountains to the north and, sometimes, the west, and right at the end, the south. The fragments that now compose the plateau were flushed out of rising uplands by rivers and carried by them and dropped by them into the sag between the New England Fold Belt north and the Lachlan Fold Belt west. That deposition is an epic story made of many episodes, some short, some long, some wide, but all of them fluvial.

The history of the mountains from which the plateau came, out of which the rivers ran, is longer, much longer, and far more complicated than the story of the laying down of the plateau. The mountains where the plateau was conceived were—their vestiges still are—old, old geology. The mountains that gave birth to the plateau out of their own suffering and demise, they truly were mountains.

The river that brought the plateau out of the mountains and laid it in the wide, bowed foredeep between them was a thousand small rivers; it was a complex, tangled braid of streams, falling slowly out of the distance, intergrading and coming apart and binding again like strands of a fraying rope. The river that carried the plateau in—these lithic and quartz sandstones of white and orange and brown, these conglomerates of large and tiny pebbles, these green, these brown, these red claystones, lapsed and disintegrated former volcanics, these siltstones—was a capillary bed. And it left behind the plateau— these hundreds of feet of abandoned sediment, of dropped, dried, stratigraphied blood; the blood of older mountains. The plateau is a mortified vascular system.

It has stayed where the rivers left it, pretty much. Over time, the ossified cortex that is the plateau was disturbed by volcanic episodes, never really enough to make it lose its form; enough to leave some mounds that today closely resemble mountains— Mount Hay, Mount Banks, Mount Bell, Mount Tomah, and some others in the south.

The plateau's eastern edge got dragged down at one stage, when the seabed stretched, when New Zealand migrated east and the Tasman Sea opened up. The western edge, the country in which my home sat, stayed roughly where it was during this subsiding out to sea, this stretching and pulling down; but from this geomorphological moment on, the surface of the plateau has sloped down from west to east at roughly three degrees.

Here and there, as at Wentworth Falls and Faulconbridge, some local folding steepened that tilt for short stretches. But not much else has happened. The plateau has stayed still and gently imploded for two hundred million years.

BENEATH

So the river's been running here from the start; it's worked its way down deep and made mountains rise about it.

Halfway up, the world invented plants. First cycads and ferns. Then rainforest, then conifers, and at last, the flowering trees—all these eucalypts, specifically. Higher up came the birds. Higher again came ice ages, and then came men and women. The river was here before all of us, before treefern, before fig and riveroak and wild apple, before white-faced heron, before eagle, before language, before wild dog, before heifer and horse, before pig and goat, before wandering jew and willow and thistle, before a young woman came on a horse with her friends.

The river is a snake—a red-belly black—moving with sly grace through the plateau, through everything the country remembers. The river is the plateau's reptilian mind. Its limbic system. It is where the plateau's instincts dwell—its grief, its deep but uneasy serenity, its gift for violence, its self-possession. The river is the plateau's unregenerate self.

When you find your way down to the river, to its bed in pink Carboniferous granite and gray granodiorite and coarse sands, down to its tannin waters, down to the sheoaks on its banks who will tell the water's secrets in oracular whisper, you will come as close as it's possible to come to the country's organizing principle. Here in the Cox's you'll find the plateau in somnambulant rehearsal—and sometimes in violent performance. For the river is the chord the sandstone country plays.

The river is the mind beneath the mind beneath the plateau.

FALLING SHORT

Oonagh and her friends, that August, rode a crescent of the river that lies just west of the plateau. Between Breakfast Creek and the Kanangra Junction, the river runs through granite that belongs to terrain that came before the plateau.

The river rises in what remains of the Lachlan Fold Belt, part of what we now call the Great Divide, north of Lithgow, and it runs south for a while between the divide and the serrated margins of the plateau. The girl and her friends rode down out of the paddocks of the Megalong and met the river where it slithers among the Wild Dogs. These are mountains of that older granite, which got shoved around, buckled and folded and intruded upon by the Kanimblan Orogeny. That was early in the Carboniferous, well before anyone had thought about setting up a plateau to their east.

The river does not escape the older geology, nor does it bend east and find the sandstones of the plateau, until it gets to the Kanangra Flats. That's where Oonagh was headed too.

THE RIVER II

Saturday, August 5, 1967. It had been raining hard since three o'clock. Now, in the winter darkness of the cleft of the valley at six in the evening, it was raining so hard it was difficult to breathe. Oonagh and her friends strung up a shelter in all the wind and rain—two groundsheets tied to two sheoak saplings—and under it, for a while, they kept a feeble fire going.

They were on a grassy flat, twelve feet or so above the river and a couple of miles below the Hornet's Nest, a pallid granite bluff where Heartbreaker Buttress reaches the river and the river bends around it. They were still a few miles short of the hut on the Kanangra Flats, and they knew they'd never make it in this weather. They hobbled the horses and drank some rum and lay down in their sleeping bags and tried to sleep.

It was raining all over the plateau. The creeks of every drainage were rising fast, and all of them were making their way in the dark to the Cox's.

In the morning, it was still raining, and two of the horses had got across the river in their hobbles and were grazing there. The water was still moving only placidly and had risen only slightly overnight, so Clem and Oonagh rode over and brought the horses back. They packed wet things on wet horses in the ceaseless rain. They had just made up their minds to forget the hut and head back upriver for home when the river came downstream.

The Cox's rises fast when it decides to rise; it draws itself together and it comes hard. And that's how the river came that Sunday morning—a muddy torrent banked up behind the rapid dam wall of it, taller than a woman on horseback. They heard it a few moments before they saw it. The roar of its coming, the drag of all this sudden water among the riveroaks and figs and bluffs, the clash of the freight of trees it tore loose and carried came down like God's own angry voice ahead of the water. Then the water arrived, and the river just below their camp was ten feet deep and fifty yards wide, and it kept coming fast, and the rain kept on falling.

They were on the wrong side of the river. It was rising between them and the way home. They tried—the first mad thing they tried—to lead their horses into the racing, teeming water. Oonagh thought it might be the last chance they'd get to cross to the homeward bank. But it was already too late. Only one of the horses would enter the water—Margaret's horse, Rebel. And the moment he stepped into the river the water swept the horse off his feet, and he was swimming for his life among the debris and the silt, and Margaret fell from her saddle and clung to the horse's mane, and like this they crossed the river, making land fifty yards downstream. That was when they all realized the river didn't mean to be crossed.

That's when they realized this was not the same river at all, but an older, more violent river, running wild again through the country it had made.

FLOOD SIGNS

It's not often it rains so prodigiously all over the catchment, especially in August. What happened that August to suck the heavens dry and pour them upon the plateau is mapped in the barometric charts.

On the Friday, the sky over Adelaide, a thousand miles southwest, had contracted itself into a tight and deep depression. A cold front, traveling much farther north than usual, was carrying that depression east. And in the north, the sky was slumped in a trough that ran from the Gulf of Carpentaria to the New South Wales–Queensland border. The trough was traveling east, and water from the Arafura Sea was flooding it and coming south along its reach. A cell of high pressure ahead of both these lows, circled placidly anticlockwise over May in the Kedumba

Valley and over Sydney, where the young people were still at work. But behind this stable basin the sky to the southwest and northwest was folding and faulting and coming this way, bringing two oceans with it.

On Saturday, as the kids rode down to the river, these two systems met. Rain came ahead of them and fell into the Cox's. The skies kept on coming, the depressions kept on deepening, and the rain fell harder down. Over Saturday night, while Oonagh and the others tried to sleep, the sky drew itself together into a double low; it drew a map of that, and dragged it south over the plateau and stretched it out to sea. As well as the wet air from the Southern Ocean, and the wet air from the Arafura, this isobaric double valley now drew to itself the waters of the Pacific.

There was nowhere for all that water to go but down. It circled clockwise, cyclonically, and fell to earth all over the plateau. There was not a place within two hundred kilometers of the Cox's that didn't get four or five inches from Saturday night to the middle of Monday. Some places got much more. Lithgow, where the Cox's rises, got six and a bit; Hartley Vale got seven. And Wentworth Falls, above the Kedumba, got nine and a half. It rained all over the catchment.

INUNDATION II

Saturday, August 5. Freezing cold / winds. My foot got / crook.
   Rain started / in afternoon and teemed all night.
Sunday, August 6. Still pouring / rain and wind. My / foot worse
   can't / walk. Rain stops at night.

THE RIVER III

Sunday, August 6, 1967. All morning Margaret led her horse upriver, keeping pace with the others, who were leading their

71

horses on the far bank. But then she hit a bluff she could not find her way over or around, nor could she lead Rebel past it. So she unsaddled the horse and carried the saddle and the bridle and her packs high up the rock to a small ledge, and then she went down and shooed the horse away. He stood there and looked at her and would not go, so she climbed the rock again as high as she could until she found a level bench of it. And the river climbed up after her.

On the far bank, her friends stopped for a while, seeing that Margaret was stuck. After a time Clem said he would stay and watch over Margaret, and Oonagh led the others upstream. They were forced by the swollen river to find their way forward through thick scrub and rock on steeply sloping ground, until they too decided to let their horses go. They left the leathers and the packs higher yet up the slope and went on.

The day rained on; the river rose; it drowned all sounds but its own. Margaret and Clem stayed and waited, but the day would not abate. By late afternoon, Clem made up his mind to leave Margaret, to go after the others and try, somehow, to cross the river for help. He gestured all this to Margaret, who understood nothing except that he was leaving, and then he left.

At last light she looked down and saw that her horse was no longer looking up at her.

Below her the river swelled and swelled. It had swallowed all the flats, and it had risen so high now it had swallowed the trees on what had been, before, its banks. It had taken all but the tallest riveroaks.

There she was, Sunday night fallen and the wind roaring and the water rising and its flotsam crashing into the banks and grating tree against tree, and she with no way up and no way back and all of them scattered now. She made of herself a fetus and lay like that on a ledge. She waited out the night and even slept a little. But the river rose in her dreams, and she woke again and again, sure she had fallen in. Sometime in the night the rain eased and stopped, and when morning came, the sky was clear. In the pale sunlight, she found a way down from the rock to a bench of gravel and sand.

There she stayed all Monday in the sun, while the river raged on and no one came. But she dried out, which was something, and late in the day, a horse whinnied behind her, which was something else. Rebel came to her from out of the timber where he had made his way around the bluff. The girl held the horse awhile, and the horse seemed happy to be held, each of them glad of the other's company, the warmth of another body. And then they got back to waiting for the river to decide something. The horse got on with grazing and the girl got on with worrying about her friends, and watching the bodies of trees race downstream. And the day got on with passing too.

THE RIVER IV

Monday, August 7, 1967. By morning, the river had swept away the shelter of ferns where they had bedded down. Mark and Lynne and Oonagh had heard the water rising in the night; they had abandoned the shelter to the river and moved to higher ground. In the dark, the rain had stopped, but not the river; it came and came. Then morning arrived clear and bright, and the wind pulled back to nothing. Lynne and Mark were wet through, underslept, and hungry. And when they woke Oonagh had disappeared.

They found her close by; she was sitting on a rock looking hard at the silt-brown river, which still ran thick with broken timber. She was looking at Breakfast Creek and the gully behind it, fierce with falling water, where they had come down to the river two days before. She had convinced herself that the river had calmed, that it had begun to drop, but it had not. The other two didn't like the stone-cold look that had come into her eyes. She turned to them and said, "I'm going to cross."

They told her it was madness. She told them it would be calmer upstream. "It won't," Mark said, but she wasn't listening. In her mind, she was already in the river; she was already going for help. She didn't have it in her to wait any longer.

All they had left was an orange and a can of rice pudding. But no one had a can opener, so they peeled the orange, broke it into segments and shared them.

At seven o'clock, in a light still pale, she took off her jumper and stumbled upstream high on the bank. "Don't follow me," she said. She climbed a tongue of sloping granite beyond where they'd camped and dropped out of sight beyond it.

THE RIVER V

Monday, August 7, 1967. Clem woke up high on the spine of Heartbreaker Buttress. He had not found the others, and the river was running so high at the Hornet's Nest when he reached it on Sunday afternoon that he had to climb well up the slope to find a way around. It grew dark before he found a way back down. He had no torch and no food, and he was tired, so he drew the groundsheet around him, found a level place, and lay down. But he didn't sleep.

Sometime in the night the rain had eased, and later it had stopped, and when Monday morning started coming up Clem felt like he was falling apart. When he could see properly, he pulled out his map. It was saturated; it was falling apart too. But he found his place on it and worked out a way down. He put the drowned map back in his Driza-Bone and set off. After half an hour he came to the river and after another hour and a half he stood and looked at the mouth of Breakfast Creek on the far bank. He'd hoped to find the others here, but there was no one.

Clem halted at the river and decided it was dropping. He walked upstream for over an hour more until he came to Harry's River. That would be far enough, he thought. The river was, he reckoned, two hundred yards wide at this point and running hard. He took off his riding boots. He couldn't swim in them, but he'd want them on the other side. He took off his belt and passed it through the bootpulls; he fastened the belt again and hung the lot around his neck. He walked gingerly on bare feet to the fierce edge of the water; he took two deep breaths and threw himself in.

The cold stole the breath straight back out of him. Then at once he was fighting to keep his head above the surface. The river rolled him and dumped him, and it held him under, and it let him rise to gasp air and water, and then it pulled him under again. It didn't take him long to feel sure he was going to die; it took him slightly longer to work out that it was the boots around his neck that were drowning him. Somehow he lost them—the river walked off in them—and after that he started winning. The flood seemed to abate now and then. In those stretches he could stop drowning for a bit and make his flagging arms strike out for the far bank. He and the river were racing along. He was halfway across. And then he was closer to the other side than the one he'd left, still speeding downstream. He saw the mouth of Breakfast Creek swim past, but by then he was close to the edge. His feet hit gravel and riverstone, and the river tipped him onto its new flanks among the broken riveroaks and the bracken.

After all that, baptized almost to death, his body disgorged bootless on solid ground, he worked back along the bank to Breakfast Creek, and he followed its savaged course up out of the valley, slipping and falling and rising again into the night.

Until the morning washed him up in Green Gully. And there, where they had begun, he found two stockmen saddling horses, making ready to ride out to find him and his friends, but by then all language had leaked out of him.

INUNDATION III

Monday, August 7. 9 and a half inches / at W. Falls. / All creeks up /
   high can't get out. / My foot worse. Les / couldn't work.
Tuesday, August 8. Les worked / till lunch clearing / creek crossings
   then / took me to Dr. he / said it was a / poisoned foot.

BEFORE IT'S TOO LATE

Forty years later, we came to the river on horses too. The men with me knew the river well. They'd ridden here since they could ride at all. So they came on horseback because this is the way they've always come to the river; I came with them because it was a chance to see the river that way, to follow on a horse the story of the young riders whom the rising river had caught down here forty years ago. It was a way of getting into the mind of the river, back into its banks of memory.

Three or four months before, Jim had ridden down from the Megalong to the river and it had got him thinking again about the story of the girl, and he'd been talking about it ever since. Following her path began to seem like a good excuse for a few days' riding, a thing I'd been thinking about for too long already and doing a whole lot too little about. And now it was March 2004, and we were riding down into the river the same way Oonagh had gone. If there are gods in the river, we were putting ourselves in their laps.

Once, riding along the river in the days when it was still legal to run your cattle there, Jim and Ron had come to the flats at Breakfast Creek and Ron stopped and pointed up to a rock outcrop twenty feet above the water and twenty feet back. "There's a plaque up there for the girl we found that time."

"Righto," said Jim, who was young. He'd never heard the story of the girl and didn't especially want to now. So they rode on. Just below the Hornet's Nest, Ron stopped again and pointed to a stand of trees in a sand island in the river. "That's where we found that girl, and I reckon that's the same tree the chopper pulled her out of."

Jim was getting more interested now, but not interested enough. He was a young man and he was down here to ride and maybe find some cattle and chase them out and get a little lunch at the end of it. And that was all Ron ever said about the girl in all the years Jim rode with him.

"I shoulda asked 'im more about it," said Jim now. "But when ya young ya never seem ta wanta ask what ya oughta ask when ya oughta ask it, and by the time ya getting interested the old blokes've gone."

THAT REAL GOOD LIFE

"Coupla years before 'e died, Dad decided ta back outta the sheep an' get more inta some cattle. That was when Ron come on the scene. When I was twelve, maybe thirteen, Dad started ta buy all these young calves, day-olds, week-olds, and bring 'em up. Idea was ta fatten 'em and sell 'em as vealers when they stopped bein' calves, an' it was a pretty good idea, but it seemed like Lach an' me got most a the hard work to do, an' then Dad was never a cattleman, so when the calves got ta breedin' age, 'e didn't really know what 'e was doing, an' that's where Ron Flynn come in. Somehow Dad got onto 'im and 'e just pretty much come in an' took over the yardin' and brandin' an' truckin'.

"So when Dad died, Ron was just 'ere. 'E lived in Megalong in them days, an' 'e 'ad a wife, name of Val, but they never 'ad any children, an' one day, two days a week 'e'd ride over or truck 'is horse over an' get into it. An' for a few years, with Lach an' I takin' turns with the fencin' an' the rest of it, we run the property with Ron.

"An' Lach an' I spent a lot a time with ol' Ron, an' not just 'ere, helpin' 'im do different things on 'is place an' down the river. A lot of it was chasin' cattle, 'specially me, 'cause Lach became more of a tractor man, a chainsaw man, an' even ta this day Lach gets me ta bring 'is cows in 'cause 'e doesn't want anything ta do with ridin' a horse. So I rode out an' about with Ron Flynn, round Kanimbla, up an' down Megalong, all along the Cox's River for years, an' Lach tended ta stay an' run things 'ere. An' I'd be doin' more an' more work with Ron, cattle work an' workin' dogs with movin' cattle around an' that sorta thing. Did that for a good number a years.

"An' then a course when I met Judith an' then we got married, all that real good life pretty much come to an end, 'cause ya knew ya couldn't keep on with it, all that ridin' about an' stayin' away an' earnin' bugger all. I wouldn't a got paid for a lot a that work for years. I didn't need the money, so I jus' did it. But then when ya start ta get married an' all that sorta thing, well I 'ad ta find some kinda work that paid the bills, an' eventually that led me down the coal mine."

THE RIVER VI

Tuesday, August 8, 1967. The two stockmen, Ron Flynn and Gordon Brewer, took three hours to ride down Breakfast Creek. The creek was still running hard, but they could see how much higher it had worked the day before. Where it met the Cox's, bark and broken saplings hung from the oaks twenty feet up, and everything was gone at the junction with the river but the tallest trees, and they looked like they'd been rasped. But the weather was clear now, and the water was no longer rising.

Ron and Gordon worked their horses downstream along the ruined banks and the fallen timber, wrack fifteen feet above their heads and the river falling fast. In an hour they came to the bluff opposite the Hornet's Nest. There the country got too steep to take the horses farther, and they tethered them on the flats, and they walked on, climbing uphill around the granite outcrops. They were looking for the girl Clem told them about, and just on dusk they found her. Her horse beside her.

Margaret had woken that morning to a fallen river, to a valley edging back toward normal. She thought she had woken alone, but when she tested the morning with a cry, she got an answer, and she looked and saw Mark and Lynne jumping and waving on the far bank where they had spent the night. The river's noise drowned conversation, so they gave it up. What Mark and Lynne were trying to tell was how they'd got sick of waiting at Breakfast Creek for Oonagh to return and they'd walked back downstream late in the afternoon to find Clem and the extra supplies, and that they hadn't found Clem but they'd found the supplies, and then night had fallen and they'd stayed.

Now Mark and Lynne ate a little. They spread out the wet gear to dry, and they lay down in the sun and slept. Margaret stayed awake, waiting on the river, watching it fall, wondering what to do next, but knowing better than to move.

And so Ron and Gordon found her at the end of the day. She showed them where the other two were over the river. The men gave Margaret the food they'd brought, and they told her that Clem had swum the river and found them. Margaret told them what she knew: that Clem had stayed and then left, that Oonagh and Mark and Lynne had left but only Mark and Lynne had come back.

Tuesday night closed in and Ron got a fire going. Margaret

drew herself close to it and slept, and later the men slept. On the far bank, Mark and Lynne spent the night in a cave.

SUCH A SMALL THING

Jim had met me at Blackheath, two of his horses on the back of his truck, and I drove behind him to the Carlon's place in the Megalong. Dave had floated two mares in from Lithgow, and he was there saddling them up when we pulled in. By ten we'd left Carlon's paddocks and entered the timber, and we walked the horses through gray box and yellow gums, tacking down the flint slopes to Green Gully.

We stopped by the kicking yard where Oonagh's party had saddled up. Oonagh and the others had gone by Breakfast Creek, but we rode down to the river by Ironpot Ridge, for Breakfast Creek was dry and its gully now is deep and difficult to take on horseback, and we arrived at the river in the early afternoon, a mile or two upstream from Harry's River.

The river is such a small thing, after all this riding down to it through gray box and ironbark, wild apple and tea tree and kurrajong. You'd think that so much mountain would make a bit more river. And sometimes it does. But today the river was running in slow channels along a sandy bed, braiding and unbraiding, going about as fast as it could. Behind it, west, reared Black Harry—the Black Range—and Cronje Mountain, steep country named for wild horses and the cracking of whips.

We rode our horses into the water. The river was the color of tea, and it was running low after five seasons of drought. My horse drank, and Dave's two mares—the Arab he rode and the young gray packhorse he led—drank until Dave had to pull their heads from the water, but Jim's horse just sniffed at the water. "Ol' Russell's a bit fussy about who 'e shares a drink with," Jim said and turned him toward the bank.

We tied the horses to some sheoaks on the flats. Then we pulled up logs and gathered sticks, and Jim made a fire, and we sat in the afternoon and ate sandwiches and biscuits and drank tea.

When we got on our horses again and rode downriver among the oaks, it turned out it wasn't the same river at all. Not the same one Oonagh rode anyway, even before the flood. Where Jim remembered great runs of coarse sand, thinly timbered— where he reminded Dave they used to let their horses run in a flat gallop—the riverbed had grown up with young oaks, and it was choking with weed. So we didn't gallop; we picked our way through weeds.

We rode down the left bank for a time, and when it grew too steep we crossed to the other. A bit later we crossed back. And in this way, we walked our horses down the disheveled, pretty river, sometimes on one bank, sometimes on the other, sometimes in the sand between the channels. In deeper crossings, the horses lurched among the river stones and it would have been easy to fall but none of us did. At one bend black ducks fled from us, and just past the mouth of Harry's River we rode up a white-faced heron from the shallows. An eagle dived and caught a snake and flew downriver, the snake writhing in its claws.

We picked our way among thick stands of sheoaks, among lantana and wandering jew, blackberries and agricultural weeds, among ground disturbed by pigs, down a river much diminished from what it was when Oonagh took it.

Somewhere we passed through a gate, and Jim said, "Well, you're breakin' the law now, Mark." But it didn't seem like much of a crime to me. I looked around and tried to imagine the kind of damage our horses might do that pigs and weeds and diminished flows weren't doing much more of already. Jim and

Dave rode in, and I followed them, all of us outlaws now.

THE WORST THING

"So I was about twenty when Judith an' I got married an' we rented a house in Blackheath, kept a few horses up there, an' I went ta work in the mine. The Clarence Colliery, out Chifley Road. The actual colliery didn't start for another two years after that, but I was on the site, an' then once it started I went underground.

"It must've been a bit of a lazy period a me life, 'cause that's all I did was the pit work, an' then I used ta go down the river with Dave an' some other blokes, go down chasin' brumbies in the Grose Valley, ride all over the joint. An' down the Cox's River.

"Course it was about then that Ron got shafted from the Cox's 'cause of the National Park comin' in, and 'e 'ad ta pull 'is cattle out, an' it's occurred ta me more than once that if that 'adn't 'appened, I might a bullshitted meself that there coulda been a grazin' career in the area. Bein' around those coupla blokes they mighta said ya could run fifty in there, 'undred down there on that flat, an' that mighta been the worst thing that could ever've 'appened to me."

A FRIDAY JOB

"Ron always 'ad a finger in the pie pretty much everywhere. Instead of us payin' 'im any actual money for 'is work 'ere, we gave 'im the run a these back paddocks. This paddock we're sittin' in right now, this was Ron's paddock, an' 'e run 'is cattle in 'ere. An' 'e 'ad a coupla those little deals happenin' elsewhere.

"'E 'ad 'is own property, coupla hundred acres at Megalong, an' 'e woulda had two or three hundred head in the river, an' then 'e had another coupla thirty-, forty-acre blocks about the Megalong, an' then when 'e had ta start bringin' 'is cattle

82

outa the river 'e began ta migrate out ta Mudgee. A bit later on 'e got onto a good deal on a big property out there. Got half the property to run the other half, and I used ta go over there and help 'im quite a bit before I went down the mine.

"An' that was the downfall a Ron. 'E just wouldn't stop. An' one day 'e run into a bloody tree at bloody six o'clock in the mornin' drivin' out ta Mudgee. 'E woulda been dead but the next car along 'ad a doctor in it. The doctor pulled over an' Ron was bleedin' from the ears an' the eyes an' the nose an' just about everywhere else an' whatever that doctor did it saved Ron's life. This woulda been in, I s'pose, seventy-eight, an' 'e stayed in a coma for two or three months.

"After the accident an' before I left here for the mines, I begun doin' this other bit of a Friday job. I'd ride across ta Ron's place in Megalong every Friday after lunch ta check 'is stock. Judith got caught up in that one for a while there, too. You'd ride out across De Losas' then straight through Mansfields', then through what's McGills' now an' on down Peach Tree Road for two or three ks an' you'd come ta Ron's property, an' then you'd ride another one, two ks down to 'is back paddocks an' you'd check the stock an' feed the dogs. I did that Fridays. Other people were doin' it other days. An' that lasted for eighteen months, let's say, till I started workin' up at the mine. Ron was back then, an' a bit better, but 'e never did come back to a fit 'ealthy workin' man after the accident. Even when I was ridin' with 'im down the Kedumba catchin' Dan Cleary's cattle, Ron was only forty percent of what 'e once was, which was still more of a man and more of a rider than most men get to be."

THE RIVER VII

Wednesday, August 9, 1967. The river was almost calm now, and Ron made himself heard above it. He called across to Lynne and

Mark to head upriver as far as Breakfast Creek and to stay there. He knew that Bert Carlon and anyone Bert brought with him would come down to the river at Breakfast Creek.

Mark and Lynne carried what they could—a can of soup, a billy, a blanket, a groundsheet—and reached the Hornet's Nest by mid-morning. Across the river, they could see the men's horses tethered on the flat, and after a time they saw Ron emerge from the timber. He was helping Margaret. The other man came along soon after, leading Margaret's horse.

Mark and Lynne went on then past the Hornet's Nest, finding a way near the feet of the fig that grows against the face of white granite there. They took the bend in the river west and south. The river must have run hard here, for the trees, they noticed, looking up, had been stripped of their bark and most of their foliage, and their shattered crowns were draped and flagged with debris, and among that flotsam they saw their friend Oonagh wedged between the upper limbs of a watergum and a boulder it grew from, out in the middle of the swollen river.

They went on upriver. They did not know what else to do, and Margaret and the men had fallen behind on the other side. Mark and Lynne had gone a mile or so when they saw men and horses across the water—other men—coming downriver. Mark shouted across that they had found their friend and that she was dead. Someone else threw matches and some packets of food across the waning water and told them to wait and that someone would come over and get them.

They made a fire and cooked some food and made some tea and did not know what to say to each other about Oonagh, so they said nothing, and by late afternoon, three men found them. Two of them went on downriver and stayed with the body of the girl, and one man walked with Mark and Lynne to the bank opposite Breakfast Creek.

On the other bank and a little downstream, a party of police and rescuers ran into Ron and Gordon and Margaret and their horses coming slowly upriver, and together they returned to Breakfast Creek. Someone pointed out to Ron, as they went, where the body of the girl was lodged, but Margaret didn't see her friend there in the tree in the river and she didn't understand the gestures the others were making.

At Breakfast Creek, someone brought her tea in an enamel mug, and she sat on the wet ground in her woolen coat and sipped it. She let the steam of it warm her face. A policeman came over to where she sat. He dropped to his haunches and said nothing. He picked leaves and twigs from her duffle coat and asked her how she was. He told her she had been brave, and then he told her her friend was dead.

INUNDATION IV

There were no mobile phones then, of course, but there were radios, and the various frequencies of rumor, and so it was that later that night May was writing into her diary the story of what had happened on the river, along with everything else that mattered.

Wednesday, August 9. Foot much / easier. I walked at / 3.30. 4
    horse riders / still stranded. 1 girl / drowned in Cox's River. /
    Dan called with hose.

THE STARS AT NIGHT, 2004

About four in the afternoon we arrived at the Breakfast Creek junction. We came at it across the river from the west bank, and I would have missed it on my own. No water flowed out of the creek's mouth. A bed of gray riverstones alluded sparely to the creek that should have been entering the river here.

Jim climbed about on the ledge above the junction, and after a while he found the plaque. The copper is turning green, and there are pink lichens on the stone it's fixed into. *Here it was*, the letters say, *that Miss Oonagh Kennedy passed to higher service, helping others*. She'd been the Akela of a cub pack, the 2nd Marsfield; it was her troop who put the plaque here.

Something must have knocked the girl out that day, before she drowned and snagged. Something took her mind from her before the river took her life, and so she didn't get to experience her own drowning. She'd floated among the teeming freight of the river, just as inanimate, past her friends while they sat on the far bank wishing one of them had brought a can opener and hoping she hadn't jumped in.

We pushed on, and the day began to lose its color, and Jim led us to a bench a hundred feet back from the river and thirty feet above it, where the river used to run in another life. Dave pulled some beers out of the packsaddle, where they'd been in ice and they were still half-frozen and I don't remember ever drinking anything so cold as that beer. Dave ran a white tape around a wide swath of grass, a rough enclosure for the horses. The scene of a crime. We rode down to the river and watered the horses and led them back. We unsaddled them and let them graze a while. Later, we hobbled them. Jim made a fire, we rolled out swags before it was too dark to see where the rocks were, and Jim and I talked while Dave made a curry over the fire. We ate it, and drank some wine and then some rum, and we talked on in the darkness by the fire till it was late.

The stars rose. Saturn came along. Orion, the Southern Cross, and some other bright constellations. We were so deep in the cleft the river made in these mountains that the stars, when they came, seemed to come down closer than I've known stars to come. And they gave off their white and their pink and their yellow light so brilliantly out of the pitch-black canopy that the horses cast shadows, and even I cast a pale shadow upon the earth.

Before I slept, an owl called out, and its mate called back from the slope behind us. Five or six times after falling asleep I woke to their *oogh-oogh, oogh-oogh*. And I woke to the clink of the horses' hobbles, and I woke to the light the stars were singing down. And every time I woke, I was looking at a different sky.

Later, when the moon got up, I woke to it, too. And each time I woke, the moon had traveled a few degrees more, until it was gone into the west. Before it was light, I watched a shoal of cloud swim in from the southeast, drowning the stars, and when the morning came, the sky was gray. Only then did the earth on which I lay stand still. Only then did the sky go quiet, and a light wind came down from the mountains to the river.

WILD DOGS

I hauled myself out of the swag into the slow light of dawn.

"How'd ya sleep?" said Jim.

"The bits of it I can't remember were good," I said.

"Yeah?"

"The hobbles kept me awake." I didn't think I'd mention the stars.

"It's when I can't hear the hobbles I wake up," said Jim.

And then the morning started singing.

Dave had water boiling in the billy and bacon spitting in the pan, and the dingoes must have noticed because just then they started up somewhere across the river. Dingoes in their dissonant chorus. They make a sound like wild dogs everywhere, like wolves and coyotes, yet they howl their own distinctive elegy. It said, specifically, *We're here, we're hungry, we're always hungry, this place is*

ours, we're alone in it together—and who in hell are you? This morning
it also said *Whatever that is you're eating, we want some of it.*

Here we were, camped between the feet of Blue Dog and
her Pups, among these hills, these Wild Dog Mountains. Wild
enough yet for dogs to cry the mornings up.

We got ourselves on the horses eventually. We found the
river and rode on down it.

Before Blue Dog Bend sweeps the river northeast and
then south again, around the tip of Heartbreaker Buttress, we
stopped, got down from our horses and tied them, and for an
hour Jim looked for the tree. But the river had changed beyond
recognition; it had become a forest. And if Oonagh's tree was
there, it never found us.

We rode on around the Hornet's Nest, and something stung
Dave on the ear and he yelled and his horse jumped and we all
jumped. We sat back in our saddles then and rode on farther,
and about then I was looking up at some figs growing on the
ridge when a watergum caught me in the chest. I pulled on the
reins to keep my seat, and my horse lurched forward. For a
moment I wondered if my back would break, or the branch, but
neither did, and then I was under the branch and I snapped back
up straight and reined in my horse and stopped, and I can still
feel that moment in the base of my spine. I got down from the
horse onto the sand and led him back to pick up my hat. As I
swung back up, I looked and Jim was looking back at me.

"Ya right there, Mark?"

"Just lost my hat."

"Righto," he called, and I knew he'd seen the whole thing,
and he sat and waited for me to catch them. And we rode on
downriver, Brindle Pup Ridge and then Yellow Dog rising before
us in the east, and we passed Merrigal Creek and other creeks,
all of them dry, coming in from left and right, until, just past

Queahgong Creek, on a narrow grassy flat, we stopped at about two o'clock for lunch.

We weren't thinking of it at the time, but we had chosen the very place Oonagh and the others had made camp on the Saturday night when it all began. This is where the river arrived ten feet taller in the morning than it had been the night before.

But today the river was a mirror sliding past, bearing the sky away; and we sat with tea while the blue smoke from Jim's fire played itself out among the riveroaks before us, and the horses stood, half-asleep in the shuttered afternoon light, tethered to the branches of those trees. All the morning's cloud had gone and left the sky bereft; and so we had what one has endlessly in a time of drought—dry air flooded, down here, with bronze light, the shadows sharp on the ground. The stark and lovely days the river's losing patience with.

We lay against the saddlebags and Jim and Dave spoke of all their old falls and all their old wounds from the days when the cattle still herded the rivers and young men still herded the cattle. These men are storytellers, but they need to be near horses and they need to be inside the only country they've ever known for their stories to come out and for their stories to be true. And one of these stories was just about to happen.

THE RIVER VIII

Thursday, August 10, 1967. Mark and Lynne woke on the western bank of the river, and Margaret woke on the east, and it was raining again.

The morning was good for grief, but not so good for rescue. In this weather, all the same, Mark and Lynne came across the slate-brown water on a flying fox someone had strung up in the dawn. They met Margaret on the other side, and they cried together a while.

Mid-morning, they heard an engine and then a sound no one had heard down here before—the flailing of a helicopter's blades. The horses stamped and stirred and pulled at their tethers. The young people and these men—stockmen and police—turned and watched a dark-blue RAAF helicopter fly low down the river past them. It pivoted and slowed above them, gathered pitiably on the stony flat in the gray morning. Then it continued downriver. They heard it slow some more downstream, hover a while, and put down.

Word came upriver to clear ground for the chopper to land. Ron and the other men slashed the few remaining saplings and pulled away the fallen timber. And then they heard the helicopter's propellers beat hard; they heard the machine rise; they heard it turn and beat the air harder as it tilted its bulk and came upriver; they heard it put on speed. And then they saw it come and slow again and begin to feel its way down. Its landing—the storm of wind and noise it rained upon them—panicked the horses and had them all clutching their hats to their heads and their coats to their chests.

When the chopper landed, Margaret and Lynne and Mark ducked under the swath of its blades and got aboard and sat within its enormous vibration. Shortly, the helicopter took heavily to the air, beating straight up until the slopes drew back and gave it room to turn and pick up speed. And soon the river, such a small thing now, was falling away beneath them, and in ten minutes, they were landing on the roof of the plateau. Within the hour they were in the hospital, their families about them.

The chopper went back for their friend.

THE STORY

Just before you reach the Kanangra Flats, the track leaves the river and takes you a little way up Konangaroo Gully and out of it and over one more spur and down through a dry woodland of yellow box and white gum and ironbark to the clearing. We rode there in an hour after lunch.

The stockman's hut Clem had hoped they'd reach that night has been done up now. These few acres, the only cleared ground in this mountainous reach of the river, have fallen into the hands of a big landholder from the Megalong Valley. A patch of lonely freehold in the middle of a National Park.

It's a pretty bit of land, just a triangle of grasses and sedges and wombat holes, ironbark fences and the encroaching forest. Here, where the Kanangra flows down out of the hard country behind and meets the Cox's, here at this remote meeting of the waters, miles and miles from anywhere or anyone, William Maxwell's friend Thomas Brennan had settled himself in 1862 and claimed and cleared these forty acres and built the hut.

Here on the Kanangra Flats the mountains crowd you in. In front of you Yellow Pup and Dingo Mountain; Heartbreaker to the north; Cloudmaker and the Gangerangs to the southeast; behind you is Konangaroo, and behind that, all the others with their dark and rainy names—Paralyser, Storm-breaker, Guouogang, Cyclops, Thurat.

There's a quiet here, but it's not a peaceful quiet. You're set down on a small stage, overwhelmed by rock and timber, an unsympathetic crowd waiting for you to fail. I can't imagine Brennan stayed here for long stretches.

We tied our horses to some trees and walked through the gate to the hut, and now we sat outside it on a bench. And there we sat in the one place in all this timber where we might have been seen, when the sound of a helicopter came downriver, the machine-gun sputter of its blades.

There was only one place it was likely to be headed, and we were in the middle of it.

"Run," said Jim.

I ran across the clearing. I untied my horse and mounted and turned him at a gallop for the trees. Jim came after me. Dave, leading the packhorse, came last of all, his young mares distressed and fighting him, and well before we made the cover of the trees, a helicopter rounded the bend in the river and came down on top of us. We kept on riding into deeper cover, but there was no doubt we'd been seen. We rode on and waited. The chopper flew circles over the clearing, passing over us several times, making a small cyclone in the trees. Jim looked up hard and defiant through the canopy.

There weren't too many people it might have been: the owner of the flats or the park rangers. Neither would have liked what they saw. We thought for a while they were putting down, and we wondered where we'd head if they did and came looking for us. But after buzzing us a few more times, the chopper picked up altitude again, flying larger and larger circles until it headed off southeast and was gone.

We rode down to the river and along the sand and across the mouth of the Kanangra. They'd seen us, but there was no way they could know who we were. And riding off, back in the trees, free of them, we were our own men. Jim and Dave were telling stories again about camps down here, a dog lost in the river and found again. We walked the horses across the Cox's, which was a wide and shallow expanse here below the junction. The horses' hooves made the sound that river stones make when the current rolls them one over the other. And the horses drank a little. Coming out on the far bank, we disturbed a red-belly black snake, and it slid off fast for the trees.

We rode the toes of Yellow Pup and crossed the river again to find a flat that Jim had in mind for a camp. The grass was strewn with weathered logs the river had rolled in. We strung up a blue tarp; the sky was clouding up, and we thought that it might rain. We unsaddled the horses and hobbled them and left them to graze. We made a fire, and we rolled out our swags under the tarp, and Dave dug out some crackers and cheese, and we were lying back in the dusk against one of the fallen trees, sipping port, when we heard the chopper coming back.

It flew low and slow above us, and it turned and came back even lower. Then it turned again and put down on the stony flats across the river.

THE MORAL

It felt like we were leaving the river forever.

An officer from National Parks had our names. He'd had Jim's before. Now we were halfway up Yellow Pup, the horses laboring, and back in Oberon someone was writing up a report about three men they'd found with horses in a wilderness area.

It turned out the chopper that had come upon us on the Kanangra Flats was carrying the owner of the land and some rangers. That one had flown down to Sydney, but it had radioed another crew in the Kowmung working on weed reduction, who flew up and found us.

And what all this proved was that this country had been taken from these men. It was not theirs to ride anymore. They'd known that before in their heads, but not lower down, in their hearts. That's where the ranger had brought it home. And I know that Jim and Dave had gone to sleep beneath the tarp that night knowing that they might never sleep down here, their horses grazing, hobbled, close by, again. Feeling in their stomachs that they had just been banished. The rum helped, but not much.

We got up in the morning and cooked breakfast and caught the horses and left without saying much more about it, and we started up Yellow Pup for the plateau.

And now the river dwindled from us at about the pace at which a horse can take a grade as steep as this. And at the same pace, the whole country to the south composed itself. You never saw such country. I think you had to see it this way—on horseback over your left shoulder, riding out forever—to really see it: mountains, translucent with morning, sparsely timbered, lifting themselves up out of a small river.

This was an orogeny of exile—the past lives of these mountains reenacted, rising below us into their present tense as if for the first time, raised up by means of our own rising for the last time from the same river. They were coming into being again because we were passing from them. The river was cutting down between us so that we could see each other separate and entire: these mountains, these men, each other's witness. And maybe the mountains saw us go; I can't be sure of that. Their intelligence and their noticing work differently from ours. A slower kind of witness.

As we rose higher I saw the river herself, a thin shining strand, sinking back within everything she had ever conceived; and she runs on, now in drought, soon enough in flood again, carrying the mountains away to the plateau and the plateau away to the sea.

The river has been here from the beginning, and the mountains are what it's been thinking about all this time. The mountains, and also the plateau. Into which we came again by lunchtime, back into its soaks and caves and scarps.

THE SALT OF THE EARTH

Later. I'm standing at the rails with Jim. We've fed and watered the horses and watched them file down toward the dam, evenly spaced, Benson at the front, the new horse, Shadow, at the tail.

"I guess they talked about that spacin' before they left the shed," says Jim.

It has been a warm day. Late October. A front blew in while we rode. A single drop of rain fell onto my arm just as we passed the paperbark in Potter's paddock, a massive tree that never looked so parched in all its two hundred years.

"Mum does mention the fact," says Jim, "that the droughts used ta force the family outa here every now an' then when the creek dried up an' there was no water. Tank water'd run out, they'd pack up, go ta Blackheath, an' stop with someone up there. An' that happened most prob'ly once every five, ten, twelve years, dependin'. I s'pose the drought frequency'd be about the same now, but with warmin' a the planet, who knows what we can expect.

"I was readin' in one o' the science magazines" he goes on, "where they've found evidence of a drought that went on for five 'undred years somewhere 'ere in Australia. Now that'd be a drought."

The horses are making for the ridge. For night pastures. Pastures stripped a little too bare of trees a little too fast, and pocked with dams. Pastures that are pulling up Precambrian salts from beneath the skin of the earth. Salt that's running now in the river, which is running low, in a drought that's growing long. I look into the coming night, and I grieve at what we've done shaping country as beautiful as this.

III

CATCHMENT

WHERE THE TREES GO WHEN THEY SLEEP

On a night of high wind and cold stars, a night like many on the
Dargan Ridge, Henryk is woken by a forest of iron figures, which
lean toward him in his sleep, clashing their heads in the west
wind. The assembly is so loud and real it wakes him to the blind
dark at five in the morning.

Visions come to him like this, from somewhere, from
outside, from down in the valley of Monkey Creek. They come
on the wind. This is how sculptures come. He lies in the dark
figuring how to give body to the dream. It is only a matter, now
the idea has dawned, of technique. He doesn't bother to get up
and draw a picture; he leaves the figures in his memory, where
he knows they will not fade. For weeks he will carry them there,
and then one day in the shop, between jobs, when he has the
right steel, he'll begin to work them into life. Land transmuted
thus to dream, woken into memory, becoming art.

In the morning, when Henryk steps onto the balcony in the
gray light and the flagging wind, it is casuarinas and petrophiles
that lean toward him out of the gusty world. And mallee gums.
Trying to become dreams.

HENRYK

Henryk was the first person I met in the mountains, and he became my closest friend.

His is another kind of belonging altogether. He comes from another world. He came to this continent under duress and up to the plateau against his better judgment, and half his life lies elsewhere, forgetting itself in a foreign tongue. But he has worked himself down deep into the plateau in the years he's been here, so that it's hard to tell any longer just where he ends and where the plateau begins.

Before I met Henryk, and before I came to the plateau, though not long before, I met his work. Which seems right. In a store in Sydney just before we left the city, M. saw some shelves that turned out to be his. The store wasn't selling the shelves; it was selling what was on them. The owner gave us the name of the man who'd made them and his number, but he said it mightn't do us much good because the guy lived up in the mountains. I said I didn't think that would be such a problem, and on our second or third weekend in the house, Henryk drove across and measured up, and two weeks later we had the shelves. He made us many things after that, and they furnished our dwelling in the plateau, but that is only the start of it.

MURDER

"So, the first thing I do in this new country, first proper job I get, is I start poisoning trees.

"After refugee hostel in Perth and some time in Sydney working in factories, Peter and I headed out to bush. And we ended up on this crew clearing scrub for farmers in north of Queensland.

"Was hardest thing I have ever done in my life. We did it with axes and poison. A bulldozer would have done this job better, but we were cheaper. We would start at four a.m. to beat the heat, three or four, and work till eleven and then have siesta, and start again at three, four. Another few hours, then sleep. Living in middle of the bush in tents.

"After two days my right hand was raw. I couldn't hold a spoon, not to mention an axe. The men knew that I was struggling and that Peter was struggling even more. We would work in line, two kind of wings, and these guys would close ranks, like they would narrow our bit, so at some point I was left with two meters to clear in front of me and they, the guys on side of me, would take, you know, five of my meters on one side and five on the other. Average you were meant to have was about fifteen meters. And as I got progressively better they would spread out, and after three weeks I could keep up with what I had to do, but Peter sort of stuck to his two meters. And after two weeks, he was told, you know, look Peter, sorry. And he went, but I stayed.

"These people were mostly, you know, crims. Good to me, but bad hard men. There was murderer there. Killed his wife ten years before. And for ten years he worked for this crew. He was cook. He had big chest where he kept the food, and his first thing, I never forget it, his first thing in the morning was to get the snakes out. He'd go 'Browns,' just like that. Bang a great pan on the tree. And there were always two, three, in the food chest, every morning, no failing.

"But worst thing was heat. That's what pushed me out. I remember temperatures of forty-seven °C in shade. And it would be forty at night. And you just work all day and you get totally dehydrated and then you can't sleep. And then mozzies came, just before Christmas. I had bite on bite on bite, over my whole body. We worked practically stripped. And no matter what I put on, what sort of repellents, they just did nothing. And these other guys didn't put anything on and had maybe, one, two bites. Maybe you build up immunity because, ever since, mozzies don't come near me. Never.

"But back there mozzies were killing me. I had to leave because of them. I remember night when I left the camp. They drove me to main road, which was about ten ks away. And bus was supposed to arrive at seven. But bus was late. And then it became eight o'clock, nine, ten o'clock, and I was stuck there. I couldn't walk back to the camp because I had no torch, nothing. And I was sitting there and I had two blankets, and I covered myself in blankets to keep the mosquitoes off, and they were getting through the fabric and had just about killed me when bus finally came. And that was my farewell."

THE LAY OF THE CLIFF MALLEE ASH

In behind the Three Sisters, half a mile from where I lived, you'll find a tree that lives nowhere else on earth. Of the eight hundred eucalypts, this tree, a mallee ash, has the smallest leaves of all. I have one of her leaves in my hand. It's as long as my little finger; it's curved and slender; it has a crimson hook on the end, good for fishing drops of water from the clouds.

Here's a plant exquisitely adapted to the site of the Three Sisters, one of the most visited places on the continent, and yet here is a plant that botany only properly identified thirty years ago. One day in the 1950s on a botanizing walk, a local minister named Burgess got to thinking that perhaps this small-leaved cliff-dwelling gum might not be the same tree as another similar mallee he knew from elsewhere on the top of the scarps (*Eucalyptus stellulata*). When Burgess spoke with the experts and they came and looked, they agreed with him and they gave the tree a name, *E. rubicola* (cliff dweller).

But it turned out that a specimen of this very same tree had been sitting in the herbarium at the Royal Botanic Gardens since 1822, collected and sent there by Allan Cunningham and named by him *E. microphylla* (small-leaved). The Australian botanist Ian Brooker happened upon that specimen in 1980, recognized it as his friend Burgess's cliff dweller, and renamed it, as botany obliged him to, for the man who'd found it first (hence *E. cunninghamii*).

For four years I had never noticed the mallee ash until one September I went walking the Prince Henry Track with Brooker, whom I'd met three years before when he came along to a writing class. No one knows more about the genus *Eucalyptus* than Dr. Brooker. It took us two hours to walk from my place to the Three Sisters, no more than a fifteen-minute wander normally, so often did he stop to touch the peppermints and ashes, the smooth and scribbled and the stringybarks; to look up into the canopies for the color and form and drape of leaf; to kneel on the orange ground and pick up the fallen seed cases of the four or five species that grow in this kilometer of escarpment's edge—*oreades, piperita, sieberi, stricta, racemosa*.

There were individual gums here Brooker couldn't be sure of. They hybridize; they alter as they age; they sculpt and color themselves to suit the place and survive the weather and lose themselves among their colleagues. They reveal their names and natures cryptically. Brooker takes his time among the eucalypts. He's smart enough to know that the trees deceive, that they are careless of our taxonomies. A lifetime in the field with the gums has not made him their master; it's been about long enough, he says, to make him a half-decent student.

As we came close to the sisters that day, he grew excited; he had remembered the cliff mallee ash. We hurried then, and he found some right in behind the Three Sisters, where they've always been.

Why does the eucalypt with the smallest leaf choose to live here, in all this wind, in this sparing rain, on the threshold of this vast amplitude? Why does it not manage anywhere else? It has what it takes for this place, and only for this place. It is more finely calibrated to these facts of life than any others anywhere. Like the pink flannel flower, like the clumpy conifer *Microstrobos fitzgeraldii*, which you'll find on ledges beside seven waterfalls that give themselves up above the valley of the Kedumba, like the seven stone sisters, only three of which remain here, the cliff mallee ash is a place tragic, it is a heroine of the eaves of the plateau.

But if you came to this precipice to find this tree, you might easily miss her. She's so much a part of the place and the wind she almost disappears into them. So let me tell you what she's like.

Brooker's book calls the tree a "small, densely foliaged mallee." Her bark is smooth. It starts out creamy, but it grows dark purple-brown over the year, and it sheds and falls in April. And she's a mallee—a multi-stemmed shrub. She splays herself against the sandstone. She fragments herself better to fraction the winds.

The flowers of the cliff mallee ash come from buds that cluster on short stalks that grow in the angle between the leaf and the stem. Each stalk puts out seven buds, and those buds look like small, yellow clubs. Inside the conical head of the bud, the stamens, each topped with its sac of pollen (the anther), are twisted and bent so that the anthers are gathered against the central column—the style. Every stamen is fertile. Every anther is shaped like a kidney, and it opens to release its pollen, once the lid of the bud is shed, through slits that slope away from a point at one end of the anther. When the club head splits and the anthers emerge thus, what you see in March and April is a cream-white flower. And if a honeyeater, let's say, carries the pollen from one flower of the little tree to the stigma of another flower of the same tree, or another cliff mallee ash, fruit may set, in which the pyramid-shaped seeds of a new tree will form.

These fruit of the cliff mallee ash—what's left of the flower once it's dried—cluster like small brown grapes. The fruits grow in these small communities of seven from a common stalk, and each one of them is the shape of a barrel. The rim of the fruit is thin and sharp, and the remains of the tissue that, in the bud, lay as a disc between the feet of the stamen and the roof of the ovaries will, unusually for eucalypts, hang below that rim.

Not that the cliff mallee ash ever lost any sleep waiting for science to give it a name, to compare and anatomize it. It just carried on, as it had done for ages at the top of these cliffs, known since the Oligocene to the sandstones and ironstones at its feet and to the long generations of honeyeaters and native bees, known since the dreaming to the cliff-tops' first people.

THE DOOR TO THE WILD

It's fallen dark outside. Sitting against pillows on my bed, I read to my son, and he leans against me. Together over many months we have been reading this book.

My son is nearly ten. When I was just a bit older than that, I first picked up this book, and I have read it many times since. Long gaps stretch between our readings. He goes ahead on his own without me. One time, a year back, he got three chapters ahead. Together again, I said, "Do you want me to pick it up where you got to?" "No," he said, "I want to read that bit again in your voice."

Tonight we're reading the first part of the second volume of this book, *The Lord of the Rings*. The Fellowship has been broken, and the two young hobbits have come upon the ent, Treebeard, at the edge of a remnant of ancient forest. The ents may be Tolkien's most beautiful creation. They speak for the intelligence of trees and of the land's consciousness, its integrity. They embody the animation of the whole world—a thing we remember, in modern times, mostly in our dreams.

Ents are lively trees; they are trees that sing and remember; they are trees that grieve. They are trees that walk and fight and love. They stand for the magic of creation, the long sad history of a world in which the woods have steadily withered and life itself has diminished. In Tolkien's ents lives a heavy sorrow for all the departed woods, for all the old wildness. The ents have grown still with grief and time.

I was led to Tolkien for the reasons that brought me to the plateau. Landscape is alive in his books, and people move inside it, shaping, destroying, redeeming themselves and their places. People grow from places; places make them. Places in Tolkien are particular; they're defined by the pattern of trees, grasses, rivers, weathers, and mountains that compose them; and they are shaped in Tolkien's characters' hearts and minds by the languages that have also sprung from those places, like trees.

Places not so inhabited are where all the trouble comes from. Doom in Tolkien is the time when there are "no more songs" and when the woods have all withered. Home is a place well enough known and loved to be defended fiercely and hopelessly against placelessness and abstraction.

Tolkien and Treebeard opened the door to the wild for me. They carried me out into the forest and put me down. And here I am still, reading to my son inside a timber cottage. Outside, the moon, nearing full, is up in the branches of the cypress.

There is a tree growing in my name, and in my son's. I wonder where its roots lie; I wonder where its branches reach and who has nested in them. I wonder what stories—of weather endured, of leaves fleshed out, of seasons of rest and renewal—are written in the rings of its body.

The tree I have in mind is the prefix to my surname, and my son's: *Tre*. What this *Tre* means is *place*. It's a Cornish beginning, a Celtic syllable. In Celtic culture every place was animate, of course, and some, including home, were holy.

What I am called, calls *me*. I speak the word *place*, with all its mystery, longing, and possibility whenever I speak my name. I say my name, and I speak the tree that grows there, a rooted but animate thing, a placed life, three letters spelling home. I carry a place; it carries me. I carry a tree; it carries me, too.

My mind has wandered back among these deep roots, and my son is looking up at me, waiting for the next sentence of our book. This story enchants him; it tells me part of who I am and why. Reading this book, I am again the twelve-year-old boy who first read it, with his griefs and worries, and with wild and difficult roads all to come; I am a man in the middle of his days, who sees now how this book foretold me as I would come my long round spiralling way to this place in this house beside my son; and I am my son, whose own path this also, inevitably, foretells. We are two small beings on the shoulders of these moving trees.

When the hobbits first ask Treebeard to tell them his name, he tells them he can't. It would take too long to say, he says. He has lived near on forever and seen everything. His name has lived and grown with him and includes the stories of everything he has seen, all that he has done.

What is true of ents may be true for all of us: our true names, the only proper way to describe ourselves, are all the storylines we carry, of places and peoples, of histories, cultural and natural. Who we are is where we are and where we have been—in dream and in story and in waking life—and it is whom we have been there with. Who we are is too much to tell, and most of it has little to do with anything we've achieved. To know ourselves and name ourselves we're going to need a literacy that is ebbing: words and songs for landforms and lifeforms, for clouds and watercourses, for family history and places on maps, for love and grief. And we are going to need time. We are too hasty. Treebeard says: "Real names tell you the story of the things they belong to, in my language. . . . [Ours] is a lovely language, but it takes a very long time to say anything in it, because we do not say anything in it, unless it is worth taking a long time to say."

My son is looking up at me. "Dad?" he says. "Do you want me to read the next bit?"

"Yeah," I say, "you take it from here, son."

WHAT THE PLATEAU BELONGS TO

This is how you'd say *forest* in the plateau, if you had the time. It's a way of saying what the plateau belongs to. It's how the plateau might tell you its real name.

Tribes

Escarpment Complex, Megalong Forest, Camden White Gum Forest, River Oak Forest, Blue Mountains Sandstone Plateau Forest, Sydney Sandstone Complex (woodland), Sydney Sandstone Complex (open forest), Gully Forest, Yellow Box Woodland, Shale Cap Forest, Newnes Plateau Shrub Swamps, Kowmung Wilderness Complex, Burragorang Ironbark Woodland, Snow Gum Woodland, Tablelands Grassy Woodland Complex, Montane Woodland, Cox's River Swamps, Black Range Scrub, Jenolan Granite Woodland, Montane Heath, Pagoda Rock

Complex, Sedge Swamps, Boyd Plateau Bogs, Pastures

Realms

I. Woodland—Ridgetop and scarps and a little way down

Blue Mountains ash, black ash, piperita, scribbly gum, yellow bloodwood, red bloodwood, ironbark, smooth-barked apple, grasstree, *Grevillea laurifolia*, black sheoak, false sarsaparilla, lomandra, *Banksia serrata* (old man banksia), *Banksia marginata*, hairpin banksia, petrophile, isopogon, mountain devil, soft geebung, broad-leafed geebung, blackwattle, spike wattle, sunshine wattle, sweet wattle, prickly moses, hakea, flannel flower, cliff mallee ash, *Eucalyptus stricta*, kangaroo grass, white dogwood, epacris, correa, dracophyllum, eggs and bacon, pultenaea, devil's twine, tea tree

II. Open Forest—below the cliffs and on the valley floors

Sweet pittosporum, turpentine, deanei, oreades, ribbon gum, grey gum, yellow box, brittlejack, wild apple, stringybark, ironbark, Camden white gum, white mahogany, *Telopia speciossisima*, blackwood, riveroak, paperbark, hakea, blaxlandia, fastigata, kurrajong, wonga wonga vine, clematis, common ground fern, climbing guinea flower, sweet mardenia, spreading fan fern, *Indigofera australis*, *Pultenaea flexilis*, white paper daisy, blueberry ash, grasses

III. Rainforest—narrow places in the shade that mostly escape the fire

Coachwood, sassafras, treefern, possumwood, lillypilly, broadleaf bramble, rock felt fern, kangaroo fern, strap water fern, hard water fern, pepperbush, cedar wattle

IV. Heath—dry ridgetops where the wind rules

Callitris, *Casuarina nana*, *Casuarina distyla*, privet-leaved stringybark, heath banksia, coral heath, *Epacris rigida*, pink flannel flower, mountain baeckea, *Darwina taxifolia*, isopogon, petrophile

V. Swamp—headwater valleys, wet heaths, valley bottoms

Buttongrass, snow in summer, sword grass, dagger hakea, *Banksia oblongifolia*, *Grevillea acanthifolia*, coral fern, *Acacia ptychoclada*, swamp heath, pink swamp heath, blunt-leaf heath, rush lily, veined sun orchid, sundew, Christmas bell, bladderwort

And that's not all of it, but that will do. And each name tells a long story, if you listen, of frogs and birds and snakes and possums, the nearness of streams and the angle of repose and the coming of moths and the falling of bark and the setting of seed. But only the plateau has time to listen to them all.

BENTHAM'S GUM

There is a gum as loyal to the Valley, to the Cox's and its tributaries, as the cliff mallee ash is to the ridge. The Gundungurra call it *Durrum-by-ang*; no one is sure what that means. It is *Eucalyptus benthamii*, Bentham's gum, the Camden white gum.

Bentham's gum is a forest tree, but it likes the ground where the rivers flood their banks and deposit the ruins of the plateau all about. The tree grows tall and fairly straight. You'll know it by its leanness and its pallor. When it sheds its creamy-white bark in long ribbons in the summer, it drapes them almost to the ground. And out steps this tall ghost, paler yet than the tree it was, astonished at the world it enters—a tree nourished by the broken bones of the sandstone country.

The white men got to know the Bentham's gum around Camden. And when they got to the Burragorang, they found it growing there, too, right up and down the river. This was its country. They used its timber in their houses. They enjoyed its company.

But most of the trees are drowned now, lost beneath the Big Water. It grew right up the Kedumba, though, and you'll find it there still, a tree in exile.

Les used to say the Bentham's gums up the Kedumba hadn't got there by themselves. He reckoned his grandfather brought some up with him and planted them, meaning, I guess, to farm them. The tree grows slowly, though, so if old William planted the trees, he never got to harvest them. Maybe Billy cut some down; maybe he built with them; maybe he sold some off. But by the 1970s there were big white gums growing alongside the blue gums and the white mahoganies. And in the eighties KPC had Les take out as many as he could find—which was most of them. Cleary was bargaining with the Waterboard then. He was making what he could from the valley, while he could. He was giving the Waterboard the hurry-up. Periodically, through that decade, the long pale bodies of Bentham's gums were being hauled up the Kedumba Walls and off to the mills. The result was that most of the Bentham's gums were gone when the Waterboard moved in.

But twenty years has been enough, through fire and the odd flood, to raise a new generation of the white gums. Along by Reedy Creek you'll find a callow forest of them.

Sometime in the midnineties, a fire went through the valley, along Reedy Creek and the white gums. It took out Smith's hut, the place the Maxwells' neighbors built in the twenties from Bentham's gum. What was left of the hut was dangerous, so the Waterboard dismantled it. All that's there now is a stolid chimney made of stone. Terry, the Waterboard ranger, says it was the old lunatic who started the fire. There were from time to time men who made their way into the Kedumba, seeking some kind of refuge there, mad enough to find it in the valley. It was a few years after Les had gone that this particular lunatic got loose down there with his matches. He set fire to the grasstrees, just to see them explode. Terry came across him one time, standing stark naked in the elbow of Waterfall Creek. The lunatic had all his clothes off, drying them on strings he'd hitched around a fire. Scared the hell out of each other.

The fire he started this particular time burned through the Benthams, and Terry and the national parks people thought it would kill the trees. That was the received wisdom about the Bentham's gums. But it turns out the trees enjoy a burn. The bigger trees made it and stand in the valley still. The saplings the fire gave rise to are swarming the old airstrip paddock now, and they've taken Reedy Creek for their own.

WATERCOURSE 101

Down in the Kanimbla, Jim Commens makes fast the wire gate, swings back up onto Russell, and trots up beside me. It's winter, mild, and four o'clock. We're moving west into an antique light. We're riding beside a creek that runs beneath a broken ridge of sandstone holed like honeycomb. The afternoon falls still and cool about us, and we ride through long shadows thrown on the grass and gravel by stringybarks and brittlejacks.

Jim spurs his horse and draws up to my shoulder. I'm riding the bay stockhorse. I point at the creek, and I ask Jim, "What would you call that?" Little rain falls here in the winter, nor further west, nor anywhere from the east coast to the western plains. This winter has been drier than most, and the creek bed below is about as empty as you'd expect.

Jim looks at me from under his hat, which is the same color and wears the same kinds of ancient stains as the cliff beyond the creek. Jim looks at me hard as we trot.

"That'd be a dry creek bed."

"Got any other names for it?"

"Few other names, I suppose, depending on how much water's running in 'er," says Jim. "Like creek, or maybe even flood."

"I have a friend in the States," I say, "who's putting together an encyclopedia of geographic terms. In different places over there they'd have a bunch of different words for a creek like this: arroyo, draw, wash, gulch, that sort of thing. Anyway, my friend Barry was asking me the other day, when we were talking on the phone, what we'd call a creek bed dry of water, like the Todd River in Alice Springs. I told him I thought we'd probably just call it a dry creek bed down here, but I thought I'd check."

"Righto," says Jim. "Well, you can tell 'im you got that one right. But make sure you say we only call 'em dry when there's no water in 'em."

CATCHMENT II

"Come on," Jim calls out to my children, who've let their horses carry them on ahead of us, up this long paddock. "Turn 'em round. We'll head up 'ere." Up the open ridge, he means, away from the creek. He puts his heels to Russell, the red Arab, and I follow him at a canter on Stock, up the flinty face of the ridge. A path the cattle and horses have made threads through young gums over crumbled shale. We ride a sclerophyll hill, which is here, I reflect—leaning forward in the saddle as we shatter the shale even further—because the so-called stream below has sometimes worked a lot harder than it's working today. Nearer the top, there is yellow tussock grass, bracken and lomandra, tea tree and taller eucalypts. The ground is brittle with fallen bark and leaves.

We reach the crown of the hill and sit our horses and wait for the children to catch us. We look back at the river and the broken ridge beyond.

"You know the word *catchment*," I say.

"Sure," he says. "The Cox, the Grose, the Murray-Darling. The country a river drains."

"Right. Well you know in America they call that the watershed."

"Is that right?"

"Yeah. But we use *watershed* for the high ground that divides the catchments. Right?"

"That or *divide*," says Jim. He's getting into this.

I look down at the parsimonious stream, and I look up and greet my children, who've made it now to the top. Stones fall down the hill behind them. For a moment that's the valley's only sound—that and the breathing of the horses.

Then we turn and ride east along the ridgetop. The ground falls away steeply on the southern flank of the hill. The wide valley of the Cox's River lies out there, surrendering its heat, falling into shadow. The sky is turning yellow above it.

"Interesting," Jim says now, as we walk the horses through the pale timber along the slender ridge and look out on all this darkening country, "when you think of it, that we'd speak about the pattern of rivers in a valley—you know, the catchment—in terms of the water the place catches. While the Americans talk about the water it sheds."

He is beside me, as he says this, riding among the trees and long shadows, picking through some deadfall, and he doesn't look up. And I ask him, "What do you think that says?"

"I don't s'pose we like to think of wasting anything here," says Jim. "Specifically water. We'd rather catch than shed."

What I'm thinking is that catchment is a word about water without any actual water in it—a word adapted to scarcity; a sclerophyll word apt for a sclerophyll landscape.

"Makes me thirsty," says Jim, "all this talk of water and so little of it about." He looks toward the Cox's. "Goes on like this, we'll be getting fires before Christmas."

READING THE SIGNS

Along the Darling Causeway on the way to Henryk's you pass a road sign, and it says "Flood Sign." There's got to be a reason why that sign is there, but I never worked it out.

The causeway is a divide, you see—a watershed. Shedding—not gathering—water is what it does, and it does that fairly fast. West of it runs the Cox's; east of it runs the Grose. The rock and the road upon it run about ten ks from Mount Victoria to Bell, and when you get there, you're looking north into the Wollangambe wilderness. It's a hell of a drive, all that scarp and heath and canyon on the right, and all this stone sculpture and woodland on the left, and, way down deep, the pretty paddocks of Hartley Vale.

But you see my problem with the flood sign? You're driving a thousand meters in the air. You're driving along a narrow ridge from which every drop of water falls into one of these river systems or the other, all of them finding, in the end, the same river and the same sea.

They call the road a causeway, so you'd expect water. But all you'll ever find is all this rock and amplitude and light.

Just short of the flood sign one day late, when sunset was flooding the scribbly gums pink, Henryk got to thinking some thoughts about belonging he knew he shouldn't think. He was nearly home, and he would have been traveling; Henryk never learned the English word for *slow*. In Poland one had no prospect of ever owning a car, he told me, and there were none worth owning even if you did, so you never learned to drive. Here, Henryk took to driving as though it were the very enactment of freedom—a thing best taken at speed.

I know the bend where he thought these thoughts. It's where those scribblies stand, forlornly waiting there for something; maybe it's redemption, maybe it's a yellow Suzuki. They plead, mutely, pale as death, looking into the west. So I can understand what came over Henryk. Which was this: *I know I'm s'posed to think the country doesn't need me, but it's telling me it does. I can feel it leaning my way. It's asking me to heed it, to remember it, to make something of it. Love is what it wants. Or something.*

When Henryk told me this later, I knew he was deadly serious. I think I've heard the trees say something similar. What the country wants is for us to let it in—into who we are and what we're doing and what we know of eternity. It needs us, and it wants to tell us something. That's why it's leaning our way. It wants us to listen, too; it wants us to know who it is, which is not what we've thought it, at all.

CATCHMENT III

Think about catchments long enough, and your mind will travel through all the country that houses you, to its outstretched fingers and back to its heart, running like blood down every gully and along every butte and spine, slowly descending all the time, deepening even as the country shallows, until it carries you—that river, your mind—to the sea. And back. The mind, too, is a country of rivers.

REFUSE

It was raining lightly, and we'd decided to pull the swags inside. We were in the shearing shed at Duddawarra. One winter, in the middle of my days in the plateau. My brother's school leases the shed and a few acres around it from the Commenses—the Presbyterian Commenses—who still own it. The other side of Jim's family.

I'd stayed here now and then to get some writing done, and I'd come this time with my older children and with Henryk and his children. I sat with my son by the furnace in the middle of the long tin shed on a wooden floor dark with decades of soil and lanolin and sweat. A light wind carried in the smell of the river and the smell of rain and the smell of the cow shit. Henryk had put his girls to sleep and he was sitting with us, drinking red wine and talking mordantly.

Outside, it was midnight on the paddocks, on the rising river and on the wooded, blackberried, tired and trafficked, steep-flanked hills of the upper Cox's. Inside, it was early afternoon in southern Poland.

When he was a boy, Henryk used to go in the holidays to stay with his grandparents at the foot of the Carpathians. His grandparents ran pigs and milk cows on a farm that felt like *Fiddler on the Roof* without the singing. Once, when Henryk was maybe six or seven, he'd walked himself into the sluice, sank above his head and nearly drowned in swill. My son and I thought that sounded quite funny, but you can imagine how such a thing might put you off agriculture for a bit. How the smell of cow shit might sink you back into bad memories.

Years after he'd grown up and left for the new world, Henryk's granddad hanged himself one day in the barn. A man of ninety-two. He left his wife of sixty-something years a note to say that lately he hadn't been so happy in the marriage. A man with exacting standards in matrimony.

A year or two later, his widow, at eighty-seven, set the farmhouse alight and sat in the middle of the living room and let the fire burn the house and herself to the ground. Everything had got too much for her, too, though it had taken nearly a century.

Why both of his grandparents, and then each of their five children, the children of that beautiful country there under the mountains, should take their lives, Henryk still can't say. "My mother had horrible life," he says; "so, with her, I wasn't surprised. But all the others . . ." He shakes his head. It was like they were following a pattern that had nothing to do with the state of their actual lives, which were reasonably happy. As though they had to do it, following each other in a dance of death.

It's a hell of an inheritance. A line of family business you might want to turn your back on. "Don't worry, mate," he tells me. "I'm not going that way. Not now."

But he was maudlin this night, and there's enough in his past to fuel his gloom whenever he cares to give himself over to it. This night, he seemed to have caught the weather, and it felt to him like the weather of the whole first half of his life.

After my son fell asleep, Henryk told me about his first love affair. It was with an older woman in Warsaw. She was very beautiful, and she was spoken for, and you can imagine how happily that came out.

KARMA

The next night I drove back from Duddawarra, and the sky was low, and the road was lost in it. I rounded the bend on Kurrawan, taking it easy because it's hard to see when the sky is turbid and you're driving at the bottom of it, and my lights picked out a shape on the tarmac. A shape that said: lump of wood. I pulled alongside it. Thinking cat or possum. But it was a frogmouth, playing chicken.

I wound my window down, and she turned her amber eyes on me without moving her head. She'd heard the car and seen the lights, and made of herself a broken branch. This is how frogmouths disappear: they raise their beak and petrify.

"I'd move, if I were you," I said.

And she did. Without a sound, the branch took flight. I lost her in a moment.

Three hours later, after getting in and making dinner and sharing it with the kids, I went outside near midnight to haul the rubbish up to the street. The sky was still the sea, and the night was still the bottom of it, and at the top of the drive I looked up and saw through the mist something roosting on my mailbox. Broken branch with yellow eyes. It stopped me dead. It was the bird, returned. I stepped closer; she stayed where she was, and she stayed calm. She sat and looked at me. And I've got to tell you it felt like thanks she'd come to observe; it felt like a blessing she'd come to bestow. If there are angels, she was one, and I knew it was I who'd been saved.

DRAWING A TAPER

The sound gave birth to a dance. It's a steady, high-pitched hammering, starting out slow and picking up speed as it goes. Men and women learned Flamenco to this beat—a hammer beating down upon an anvil. The surface of the anvil has been made to bear the blows and hold its form and sing. It rings like a bell under the hammer, and each bell holds its note for a full three seconds, so that the beating becomes percussion beneath a sustained note, high in the register.

The surface of the anvil is made, Henryk has told me, from chunks of steel, forged, beaten with hammers like this one, quenched in water, heated again and beaten flat, and quenched again, and in this way tempered, until they become a hard, shining surface fit for the blacksmith's work that will be practiced upon it.

Henryk is drawing a taper in the blue workshop on the Dargan Ridge. It is winter. The day is cold and damp, and outside the shed the trunks of the mountain ashes are black; the scribblies are purple and gray. Henryk has taken this length of ten-mil mild steel from the forge, white hot. He holds it in his right hand at the cold end, and with his left he beats the soft end with an antique hammer, which is an extension of his personality. He is drawing the steel flat and long and bringing it to a point. He tries to get a rough taper in one go, starting with this hammer and moving to a lighter one, which he brings down at a faster tempo, tidying up the blemishes of his heavier strokes. He returns the rod to the forge, then cranks the blower, and takes another rod and does the same with it, drawing a taper, tapping out this music he says he hates, but doesn't.

He's not doing this for fun; it's not that kind of a dance. He's not interested in being a blacksmith, though he's getting good enough. He makes stools and tables, shelves and stands; he makes gates and towel racks and balustrades; he makes sculptures from ideas that come to him in the night; he makes spiders that Philippa has sketched to furnish a park in Fairfield. Today he's making some sort of boot rack for a client. And this business with the firebox and the hammer and the anvil and the vice is what you have to do to make steel take certain forms. He does what he can at the bench vise. But you can't make the knots he's doing now that way; you can't hammer cold steel into the furled fronds of a fern; you can't roll it into a ball for the head of a bollard.

Henryk works fast. He jogs from forge to anvil and back, and over to the vise. Most of the work he does, including the way he runs with hot metal in his hands, is a matter of rhythm and feel and balance. You have to be strong, but mostly you don't need to prove it. It's that kind of dance.

He's always losing hammers. He lets them lie where they fall when he finishes beating, and when he brings out the next length, sometimes it grows cool while he hunts for the hammer he dropped a moment ago. He swears at himself in Polish and English, and he finds the hammers and puts them where he'll find them again, and he takes the steel back to the furnace and pulls out another rod.

Henryk looks like he's been working this way—his body taut, his movements only as large as they need to be—all his life. But he hasn't. In Poland he was a student and then he was a teacher for a while and then he left. He never had to work this way before he came to Australia, but he's been working this way ever since. It's how he makes a living; it's how he does belonging. To this rhythm. It's that kind of dance.

Henryk has the forge set out in the open, on the concrete slab between Philippa's studio and the workshop. It's out here so it can vent into the open air. It's undercover but open to the north. Henryk carries a tapered rod back to the forge now. He cranks the blower hard and enjoys the warmth the forge exhales, and he looks out at the light.

Color is the blacksmith's key. The color of the flame in the firebox tells you when the fire's hot enough; the color of the steel tells you if it's soft enough or too far gone to work. And the color of the afternoon has suddenly changed. The sun has found its way under the canopy of low gray cloud. It's thinking hard about setting, but it hangs on a moment. Rain falls on the tin roof and on the trees outside, but between the trunks Henryk can make out where the sun has fallen from the cloud and turned the horizon the color of the coke in the firebox. The afternoon glows vermilion and draws itself to a taper.

REFUGE

Home is not always where you come from. Home is where
you arrive.

It's where you arrive at who you are, and know it. It's where
you become real. That could be the place you start from; but it
doesn't have to be. It's perfectly possible never to come true
where you came into the world. There's no guarantee. Home
could happen anywhere; it could happen many places. It could
happen on the other side of the earth, for instance, quite against
your will.

Henryk left home because he had a home that needed
leaving. He had a life that needed finding. Australia was where
he landed and where the finding began. The plateau, specifically,
is where home started happening for him.

Home is where you start to breathe, and where you look
out on a ridge and see hope, for the first time, embodied. It
is the space in which you are born again—that sky, that air,
that sandstone, those gums. It is where you find out that who
you are stretches out far beyond your skin and bones and the
gloom they contain like a toxin. Home is a place whose trees
you hate at first almost as much as the demoralized country you
left behind—it's the same trees, these bloody eucalypts—that
twenty years later, when you return to the land you were born in
the first time, you miss so much that you start to count the days
till you return to them.

Home is where you know that where you are is enough, and
always will have been, no matter where you go from here. That
having been here, you have really lived.

And maybe you have to surrender something to find your
way home; there is a world of other places you might be,

including the place you were born. You may even need to lose a home to find one. Maybe it doesn't have to be a whole country you lose, but if it is, imagine how much deeper into you your sense of home, your newfound place, will sink. And part of what home feels like will always be the ache—that never goes—of exile from wherever it is that you are not and cannot now be again.

ASYLUM

"So, I was refugee. Things were changing in Poland, but way too slow. And I was involved in these protests and marches and people wanted me to become leader, all that sort of thing, but most of the people behind protests seemed to be the same old people who would have sold your soul to the government two years before, but now they'd crossed over because power had shifted and they wanted it.

"So one day I left Poland with my friend Peter, I caught train to Austria on some kind of day pass, but when we arrived at Vienna Bahnhof, we went for beer and then after a few we approached cop on the street and we said 'Asylum, asylum' and he took us and put us in a quarantine, they called it. We spent two weeks in a room with hundreds of other males, lots of crims. Every morning policeman would walk in and throw a bag full of rolls on the floor, some rolls would just spill out, and that was breakfast.

"I landed in Perth. And they sent us to migrant hostel. It wasn't detention in those days. We had own room, and it was free, and you were free to come and go. They gave you money to get started, I think five hundred bucks. Plus your dole, plus food in canteen, plus English lessons, really well taught. But every night there were knife fights, all kinds of petty violence, between Asians and Whites mostly, people got badly hurt.

"So I left after four weeks and rented an apartment. And three days after I left there was a huge fight between hundreds of Asians and hundreds of Polish bastards. Poles got huge beating.

"Peter left for Sydney. He got job in factory, somewhere in Cronulla. And he said 'Come over, I fix a job for you.' I got that job, but I lasted about a week. They were punching out metal bits with these old machines, completely unsafe, and I will never forget, I was chatting up this girl, really pretty girl, and she brushed her hair back like this and I saw she had two fingers missing. And that was it. I dragged Peter out, and we went up to Queensland."

FORGERY

"I came back to Sydney out of the brigalow and one of my friends got job at this foundry and they were wanting people, so I went to work there. Place was in Alexandria, and this was 1985. I worked there seven years. What they do is they melt metals and mix them to make different alloys, like bronze out of copper and tin and lead with bit of arsenic, and they pour them into casts to make machine parts, sheet steel and things. So, it was where I learned to work with metal.

"While I was there I also went to uni again. I was doing BA in French at Sydney Uni. Would go to my lectures and tutes in the day and go to factory and do eight hours nightshift. That was my life for seven years.

"Place was run by unions. They ran it into ground in the end. But it meant I had a quota each shift, and I'd do it in three hours, once I got used to things, and then either go to sleep sitting on my chair or do my assignments.

"Owner of the business was lovely gentle man. He took care of his people, and they just took advantage of him. He used to come onto floor, and I would be asleep—he knew the situation—or reading newspaper or a book and he would come and chat, and you know he was a multimillionaire, and he would still take time to talk to people. He was a lovely man, and later died of a heart attack at the age of fifty-five because union-wise things got so bad that they were losing a fortune trying to just keep afloat.

"Before then, ironic thing, unions made it too expensive to cast these alloys anymore, so this man, the owner, resorted to importing billets, ready-made chunks of alloys, just to fit straight into the furnace, importing them from Poland. From Poland, of all bloody places, where I left because everything was crap. And within three or four years all factories closed all over this country, six thousand people were out of work."

DISCOUNT GIACOMETTI

"Meeting Philippa was the turnaround in my life. Like, I was doing uni, right on the way to become teacher again. I taught in a secondary school in Poland for six months and I absolutely hated it. Polish language and German and Russian and Polish literature. And I hated it. They were all disgruntled, you know, partly alcoholic, partly bashed wife. Victims of system.

"But then ten years later in Australia, I found myself going down same path. And in my second year I met Philippa. She was doing prehistory. We started going out. She was always headed into art, she was always drawing and doing stuff, and talking about it, and she encouraged me to do some, gave me clay to play with, and I started to enjoy it.

"Beginning of third year, I was sitting in this tutorial and I thought shit, what am I doing here? I just walked out, and everything changed. I was still working at the foundry, and I started to make clay figures and sculptures and making molds and casting them. It was great. I could just go to these furnaces and cast my sculptures, and pay for this stuff on the way out, five, six dollars. Where normally to cast that size sculpture costs you fifteen hundred dollars.

"So I was on my way to become another Giacometti, at discount price. And then Philippa gave up prehistory, probably three months before final exams. I was trying hard to make her finish. I don't know why she stopped. But then we both started doing part-time art course at the East Sydney Tech. She was doing painting, and I was doing sculpture, and we both completed it after a while. And got our studio going. Started making toys, selling toys, which was a bastard of a business. This was in flat we bought at Bondi. Our sunroom was workshop. But after I got big bench saw and started to cut stuff at night, there was flood of complaints, because whole unit was shaking. So we had to stop.

"And then we thought what do we do? Do we buy another unit somewhere in Sydney or buy in the country and build studio? And that's what happened."

STARTING TOMORROW

It's September 2002, not even a year after the whole plateau went up, and it's burning again. And near midnight, when Henryk walks down the front steps of his house, the ridge south glows with the fire behind Lithgow, and beyond the darkness of the Wollangambe the northern horizon looks like a length of fired steel. A big fire at Cessnock. And the wind is getting up. Henryk shakes his head. This bloody country. What can you do?

What he does is join the Rural Fire Service. He gets two days' training in mid-October, and at the end of it he asks when he might be called up. The manual says six months; the man from the RFS says, "If we've got a fire and a spare pair of overalls, you start tomorrow."

123

He's out by two weeks. At the end of October, Henryk
is standing in orange overalls on the Shipley Plateau at
nine o'clock at night, burning a containment line along the
Megalong Road. He's shocked at how cold it is. But the sky in
fire weather is big and clear and dry, and the wind is coming up
hard out of the valley, and Henryk sets the bracken alight by
the road, shivering.

Bending to shift a hose, he sees the tarmac turbid with
beetles and lizards. An exodus from the big fire, which is
climbing out of Blackheath Glen in the dark.

Henryk's mob holds the road that night, but the next
afternoon, in wild weather, the fire takes the back off the Hydro
Majestic at Medlow Bath, improving the place, some say, and
falls back into the valley.

THE PRESENT

Eight days after Christmas, on the way to Henryk and
Philippa's, I pull over at Mount Boyce and look down into the
Valley. The day is warm. There's a lot of sky below me, and
a lot of it above, and all of it is drenched in summer. At the
bottom of all this saturated cyan and magenta light lie the
grasses of the Kanimbla, and it takes me a full minute to work
out I'm looking down at Jim's place, his big green shed, the
yards beside it and the new house behind. The plateau goes on
baffling me. It changes its shape. The world is not the place I
thought I knew.

At Henryk and Philippa's, there's grass two meters tall
standing in the shed. There's an owl as big as a man roosting
in the rafters. There's a monarch butterfly with text all over
her back, fallen on the concrete floor. They're pieces for a new
library in Narellan, all forged and blacksmithed and fabricated
over the past two weeks. Narellan was once called Cowpastures,

and the sculptures are for the town's celebration of 150 years since white men discovered the cattle who discovered the place that had been turned to pasture by the people the place discovered, once when the world was just awake. So there will be cows, too, when Henryk and Philippa get to them. Which will have to be soon.

Preparing, instead, for my birthday, Philippa has sat in the brown armchair in the window and painted me a card. She's painted what the heath and scribbly gums mean to her. She's painted who she is because of where she lives among these white and yellow trees. She's painted what it means to them that I am their friend. She's taken the time to do this even though she doesn't have the time to take: the owl and the butterfly and the grasses and the cattle and a dozen so far unfabricated human figures must be on the ground in Narellan by the end of the month, and the month doesn't really hold enough days to get them there.

THE BELLS

It's after midnight, and Henryk is running home. He's running steady along the Bells Line of Road, and above him there is a bright moon waning into the Wollangambe, and beside him there are these heathlands, these captured valleys and their seeping swamps, and about him are the broken heads of the basalt gods of the Bell Range, and below him there are chasms cold with the night.

The Suzuki ran out of petrol at Mount Tomah. He let it roll until it stopped where the road rises at the gates of the botanical gardens, and he left it there. He'd been thinking, right when the engine died, how fatigued he felt from turning out bollards all day in the shed and from losing a volleyball final all night at Penrith, and when he started running he saw that he was right. But the running and the winter woke him. They brought his mind back to his body, they got his heart working properly again, and they gave him back to this high country road he recalled now how much he loved.

If he'd had a phone he might have called Philippa. But then the girls would be long asleep, and how could he ask her to leave them in the house and drive the thirty ks here and back, just because he'd let the tank run dry? So he leaves the car and sets off running the Bells Line home.

It's something you might do if you wanted to feel how undulant the Bell Range is, how the road upon this narrow remnant of the plateau ravels, how it dips and bends, how it rises again as you go—Mount Tomah, Mount Bell, Mount Charles, Range Hill, Mount Banks, Oronga Ridge, Mount Hay to the south on the other side of the chasm, Mount Wilson to the north, and Watertrough Hill close to home. You can feel that in a car; but you'll feel it better on your feet. You'll feel how the broken plateau slumps both sides of you and leaves you there alone under heaven. This is the third leg of some divine comedy, Henryk thinks, as he pounds the road. And it is kind of funny. This is paradise he's regaining: the stars, the sky, the ruined ceiling of the plateau, the whole enacted tragedy.

It's something you might try, but don't—unless you're as lean and crazy as this man. He goes on, making for home, among the hanging, quaking canopies of the eucalypts, shining with the moon, and, nearing one, he makes the railway station at Bell. He's almost home, but he stops and calls ahead from the stationmaster's office. He really is shot now, breathing hard, and she answers at the second ring. She's not asleep. That's the problem.

"You've run this far. You can run the rest. I'm going to bed," she says. And then he loses her and starts running again. She will forgive him; her anger is just the way her love comes out, and he can understand it, under the circumstances. He runs on. The wind gets up. The trees toss and rattle. Henryk's in his various elements: the night, the wind, the wild, the wood. There are stars, and he's wide awake under them. There are fugitive trees, and he's running for home among them, never looking back.

IV

ESCARPMENT

LITHOLOGY

Sooner or later I want the rocks in my head. I need to know the story of the ground I stand on, the lithology of home. I've always been this way. And how could I not have been so in the plateau, a landscape profound with geology?

Geology divines the past life of a piece of ground. There is another world, wrote the poet Éluard; and it is within this one. That is the world, a world very largely lived before men, before this incarnation of the earth and sky, before most of the plants and all of the animals, before language—that is the world the geologist imagines, hears as an undertone in the bits of broken music stilled in the rocks that remain. And it lies—that former world, that deeper music—within this one. It is not gone, or not all of it. This plateau, for instance, is made out of it.

What the geologist wants is the oldest poem in the world. The poem beneath the poem beneath our feet.

A geologist will hold the plateau's hand and read its fortune backward. Tell me who you were, she says, and how it came to this.

It's hard to teach the stones to talk, and when they speak,

if they ever do, long silences stretch between their words; they seem to last for ages. There are gaps in their stories. For the stones speak in fragments, and they never seem to finish their sentences. What they utter is incoherent, muffled, deep, suggestive, cryptic—just about as clear as mud. Only harder. And to me that opacity, that embodied mystery, that densely clustered secrecy is unaccountably compelling.

WHAT REMAINS

Most of the plateau isn't here anymore. It took the form by which we know it—turned itself into itself, this dominion of scarps, this kingdom of valleys and ridges—by ceasing to be what it was. A terrain is only what weather and the larger movements of the earth leave behind. A landscape, like a work of art, is what remains of a larger work. And even what remains is already on its way out; it's on its way to becoming somewhere else.

Creation is only half the geological story of a place. The other half—the much longer part here in the plateau—is the fall. But here's another thing about the narrative arc of stone: Just exactly how a plateau got here—how long it took, what kind of rivers brought it, how rapidly and from where—will determine the way it disappears. And conversely, it's not till a plateau falls apart that you can work out—from the particular way it falls— how it came together in the first place.

Les looked for nearly eighty years, on and off, at the escarpment of the Kedumba Walls. Passing his eyes or driving the Holden from top to bottom, he was traveling backward from the middle of one geological era—the Triassic—to the tail end of the one before it—the Permian. This is what fifty million years of country-making and then two hundred million years of unmaking feel like. This is how time and its particular music became flesh, became stone, here. And this is how they have come undone.

If you sit where Les and May lived, you're nearly three hundred million years back in time, on the rubble of the eroding scarps and upon the unsteady Permian foundations of the plateau—sandstones, mudstones, shales, and coal measures, softer, all of them, than the ground above, and the reason why so little of the ground above is left. And down in the creek, you could catch eels and trout and blackfish swimming in Devonian time, hiding out among stones the river has dislodged from the tilted and folded bedrock of the plateau, four hundred million years old—rocks from time's basement.

And if you sit where Les sat and look east at the scarp, you'll see orange cliffs that rise sheer out of a skirted talus, dense with eucalypts. You'll see cliffs in retreat. It looks simple, but it wasn't.

People always talk about the scarps, but the slopes below them are most of what you see inside the plateau. They are where the plateau loses most of its height; the scarps are just there for decoration. So stay down on the slopes a moment. Under the scree fallen from the sandstone scarps, you'll find the unreliable Permian rocks that are the plateau's foundation. The scarps above are all that's left of the great sedimentary basin, and right above the tree line, you enter the earliest episodes of the Narrabeen deposition, forty meters or so of the Caley Formation, a zone of intercalated fine and coarse sediments. Sitting on that, going straight up, the next one hundred meters is Burra Moko sandstone, tough rock made of coarse grains, the gift of strong-willed rivers. This ends in a band of red claystone, fourteen meters thick, named for Mount York. You can make it out because it supports a narrow community of eucalypts and angophoras. Tough life, theirs.

Above the claystones, sandstone resumes, fuller of quartz than the Burra Moko slab below, a sign that the sediment-bearing streams were slowing and meandering and coming in, at that point, from the mountains to the west. This is Banks Wall sandstone. They end in a band of claystones ten meters thick, a very late event in the Narrabeen deposition. The sand-carrying currents from the north and west petered out and clays and silts came instead, borne on slow, mature streams out of the west by northwest. The sands that came after from the southwest and capped the plateau slip easily off the claystones and slide into the valleys, and water seeps down into them.

And so, if you look, you'll find hanging swamps in the sandstones of the summit. You'll come, there, into headwater valleys. Nott's Swamp on the Kedumba Walls is one. Here—in these upland depressions—is where the waters start that fall into the valleys and sustain all this endless sculpture going on below. Swamps form up where the creeks saunter on flat beds and languish in the softer stones until they find the edge, and then they plummet to the bench made by the lower band of claystones and then they plummet again into the Permian and run on into the creeks, like the Kedumba, which have found their way down here long before.

Because of this sequence of rocks, small rivers cutting down from above into the joints within the sandstone have caused a plateau to fall into itself, leaving, here in the western regions, these steep, benched escarpments. The sandstones fall in great blocks from their footings in the softer stone; water gets into the claystones and washes them out, undermining the sandstone structures above. Which fall away in slabs, as though chiseled. The stone that falls makes the slopes below the scarps. And those debris-slopes are on the move, too. As they roll away, in an avalanche or a slow subsidence, and find the rivers, they expose the scarps to further erosion. The Permian footings go on failing the harder rock above; and, higher up, the claystones go on letting down the sandstones. Soft, as ever, conquers hard; water, as ever, defeats rock. It's been going on like this for some time; and so it will carry on until there is no plateau left, nor any valleys, but just a great plain.

SLOW TIME

You can't begin to imagine how long the plateau has taken to get all this done, to make this emaciated sculpture of itself.

The plateau, for all its mass and plunge and drama, is an essay in slowness. What you feel when you sit and study the scarps, what you taste when you breathe the valleys in, is the weight of a longtime's passing. Fifty million years the rivers spent carrying the country in; and fifty million years they've spent carrying it out again. In between, the plateau slept. For two hundred million years, the rocks lay down and slept.

To rise to your elbow, then, and shed three-quarters of your self in the following fifty million years is slick, by comparison. But it's still a pretty stately kind of degradation—a ponderous sort of weight loss—when you set it alongside, say, the carving out of the Grand Canyon by the Colorado, work that got done in only ten million years. That kind of erosion is an essay in drama.

By contrast, it is persistence, it is patience, that the canyons of the plateau want to tell you about. They observe the slowest meditation, upon the theme of staying put. Their metric is grave; this is how eternity moves. You can enter—you can *almost* enter—deep time in the plateau.

What you might learn here is that, in the face of all the evidence, nothing lasts, no matter how still it lies—or how long. You might learn how to wait. How to stick to your task. Maybe that's what Les learned. You might almost get used to a different order of time, a larger sense of yourself, a feeling for the way that endings are only another kind of beginning.

Or, depending on your mind's lithology, these scarps could tempt you to plunge, as they sometimes do themselves, straight down into geologic time. For the valleys seduce. They can convince you you're already moving in eternity, so that it would be nothing, really, to leave the edge, to abandon time completely and fall into all that dreaming.

FALLEN BOY

The first time I came to the valley, I woke with a child on my chest. I woke with a start from a dream, and in the dream I lay in the elbow of a creek, and a boy lay asleep in my arms.

It was the morning after we had driven in, and I had slept all night in my swag among the riveroaks on Waterfall Creek, for that is where we were camped. When I woke, Norm's son Ross was kicking the fire back to life; Jim Commens was snoring close by in his swag; and there was no one resting on my chest. But the warmth of the breath of the boy in my dream and the press of his small body on my chest were so real that, when I woke, I looked beside me at once, expecting to find him fallen there. I found no one. But all morning I felt bereft.

KEEPING YOUR FEET ON THE GROUND

I drop in on Jim one day with a tape recorder; he's going to tell me more of the plateau's life story and a bit more of his own. While he makes tea, he asks me how I'm going with the book, and I tell him that the more I write, the less I realize I know about the plateau and about writing and about anything of much use at all.

"Yeah," says Jim, "yeah. But that seems to be the case with a lot of subjects, not just the plateau, isn't it? I'd been around horses twenty-odd years before I started the natural horsemanship, and it was only then I discovered I didn't know anything about horses at all." He pours us both tea. He adds milk to both mugs and two sugars to his and stirs.

"It's funny," he goes on. "You advance a little bit more and you think, well, at least I know enough now to know I still don't know nothing about horses. But you can't let that overawe you. Otherwise you'll be too worried about makin' a mistake you won't do anythin'. This Ronnie Flynn had a bit of a sayin' like that. 'E said you ever come onto someone says they never made a mistake—they never done nothin' at all."

Then I tell Jim I'm reading from my book up at Wentworth Falls this Friday night, part of a festival that's on up top, and he says, "Anyone turn up?"

"Even you."

"I might just do that. Where's it at?"

I tell him and he says, "I'll put that down in me little book."

"I should warn you," I say, "you might hear your name being read out."

He writes it in his book anyway.

"I guess I'll have to change my copy now," I say.

"Take all the swear words out."

"That sort of thing."

THE FALL

Les Maxwell worked the scarp; his terrain was the Valley's walls.

Back when he lived in the valley with his parents, he'd taken the Kedumba Pass, a steep and narrow bridle track, up out of the valley to collect the mail, to get stores, or to get away, at least as far as Katoomba. "Better be sure you walk to one side comin' down," Les used to say, "so's your packhorse don't collect you when she slips."

In the midthirties, Les ran the mail up and out of the Valley three times a week. Then the war came, and Les spent it moving earth around Camden, and after that he spent two years driving up and down the escarpment again, ferrying holidaymakers into the Lower Burragorang, and then for a while Les went out west. But in 1953 the Clearys called him back to make their road into the valley, and he was there doing that when the escarpment let them down in November.

When he was getting on and they'd taken him out of the Kedumba and put him in the old people's home at Katoomba, Les got famous. Suddenly he was a relic. He was an endangered species and people came to see him before it was too late and the past was lost. One man who talked to him often, knowing the value of everything Les might remember, was James Smith, a historian, a folklorist, curator of the plateau's secrets. Smith once told me that no matter what topic he embarked on with Les—his family, his religion, his parents, his childhood in the valley—Les ended up talking roads.

But none of the curious and adoring, none of the people from the social history unit on the radio, nor any of the pretty nurses, could get him to say a word about what happened that day on the Kedumba Walls when the boy fell.

On November 16, 1953, Les Maxwell and Ken Cleary, Dan's son, were cutting a road across the escarpment. They were bullying and insisting with gelignite; they were scouring a jagged and ingenious way across the sandstone wall, and they were making the mountain bear it. Les and Ken were making a road a car could take, and a truck full of steers or loaded with timber, up and across the Walls to Wentworth Falls—the only way out of the valley now that the dam was filling downstream.

Concreted into the rock near the lookout on Mount Kedumba, there's a plaque that remembers the day. It says that Ken was twenty-one. Some of the other words soldered onto the metal plate mention that the Clearys were the valley's pioneers. Nothing about the Maxwells. Less about the Gundungurra. History is written, often badly, by the winners; but the valley never cared much for winners.

Next to the plaque, if plaque is quite the word, the valley's pioneers have rammed into the sandstone the front end of one of the little 'dozers that wrote the road on the scarp.

But Les did speak once about what happened that day. He mentioned it one night to Jim. He said Ken had been driving the 'dozer but was off it at the time, or on its roof, he couldn't quite think now, when the cliff-face gave. They were jackhammering. They were as sure as you can ever be that the cliff above them would hold, but this time they got it wrong. A slab of escarpment snapped above them. Les saw Ken sway and drop his drill and cover his head with his arms and a few thousand tons of sandstone coming down fast. Les covered his head then, too, and he heard Ken cry out, but he didn't see the rocks collect Ken and carry him over the edge. Les looked up when he realized he still could, and by then Ken and the rocks were way below him, falling. They fell a long way and a long time. Half a minute later—an eternity under the circumstances—Ken lay way down among the timber near the bank of shale where Les, years later, was going to roll the 'dozer. Smaller rocks went on spilling down the scree slope for the next minute, before the amplitude of the valley closed over everything again like water. Les was left standing with the churn of the 'dozer's motor and the whir of the 'hammer's generator and the wider silence of the valley, which had known so much rockfall it paid no attention and got on again with the business of geological time. And Les was left alone on the mountain, mortified by what he had now to do, which was to go down and find what was left of his friend and carry his death to Camden.

Think about being Dan Cleary. You lose one of your two boys making your road. What do you do? The valley has made you pay for your ambition. It will never let you forget what you gave away to force your way in—or was it out? And every time you drive past the spot, you suffer the indescribable pain of the parent who lives on when their child is taken. So, in time, you put up a plaque that will still be here when the road is gone, and you are gone, and the valley herself has forgotten what you had in mind for her.

Think about being Les Maxwell after this. You live with that death, which you alone saw performed, every day you make that road and make it better ten years later, and keep on making it endlessly all the years ahead, like some kind of penance. And you look up at the scarp every night, and every night, when the rocks light up at dusk, you see Ken's fall, and hear his brief cry, the long storm of rockfall, and the longer silence that follows. Ken is always the twenty-one-year-old he was, the rich boy who was your friend; and you are always growing older and no dearer to that boy's father, who blames you because you were there and did not die and did not save his son. Here you are, happening again and again every day, and Ken is not. He got turned to stone and then later to myth. And you look at the scarp every night and know it might have been you.

Think about being Ken, felled in a second by a rock he was trying to fell. Here was a boy who'd taken twenty-one years to know how to fashion a cliff-face into a road—and here was rock that had taken two hundred million years to turn from the sediment of a slow stream into a rock waiting to fall on a boy like this. Think about being dead all those millions of years and then being suddenly alive. Think about being a rock face and then cutting loose and becoming an accident and then a talus slope, just like that. And think about being alive, like Ken, eternal as all young men are, and then falling like a stone— being dead, like a stone, only more so.

LIFE ON THE EDGE

Les spent the best years of his life poised between heaven and earth, his bottom on the seat of a small bulldozer, his hands on the levers, scraping progress across the face of the stone. His life's major work.

And even when that work was done, when he had cut as many miles of track in the plateau as there is road between Sydney and Brisbane, still the escarpment was not finished with him. The Kedumba Mountain Road, once made, had to be made again and again—every storm some of it fell off the mountain, and it was Les who had to put it back again.

That road was his destiny, and it looks on the map and on the scarp like the trail left by the larvae of moths, making their angular escape from the flesh of scribbly gums, feeding on what had housed them.

EXIT WOUNDS

Later, someone shows me on the flesh of a scribbly gum how the larvae always turn back before they go. What calls them home, no one knows, but you can see their recursion traced on the yellowed parchment of the gums, a brown calligraphy of hesitant departure. Sophisticated exit wounds. A loop at the end of a rope. Some of the larvae journey halfway back again, but something always makes them choose the world and break the skin of home and fly loose. Escape is a noose from which you slip, alive long enough if you're lucky, to fall and land and fly and couple and carry on this cycle of endless return, and die.

STUCK IN THE MIDDLE TRIASSIC

Somebody was always getting stuck on Red Corner: Les himself, Bill Cleary or his wife, one of the men (Barry or Kevin or Mack), some tourist. May mostly got around because she drove the VW, its motor mounted above the rear axle, but Les was up there every time it rained, dragging someone out of the end of that episode of the middle Narrabeen deposition. That's where people always got bogged—in Mount Wilson claystone, halfway up the scarp.

Les called the corner Red for the color of the clay it turned into in the rain. You'd have called it a dumb place to cut a switchback if it hadn't been the only place you could. The cliff-face benched right there and made a decent platform for a corner. And the bench was here because, in ages past, the sandstone above had been undercut along this bed of clay and tumbled into the Kedumba. That stone fell, and this bench formed, and this corner became impassable in the weather, all for the same reason: this is stone in love with water.

So Les was eternally hauling gravel to Red Corner, trying to make the claystone stay. He was a minor geomorphic force, that man. And in the end, he turned this claystone bend into a kind of conglomerate. In gluing the road to the cliff-face like that, in coagulating the claystone, he may have added a hundred years to the life of the scarp just there.

HOW TO MAKE A ROAD

The thing about cutting a road across a cliff-face, Jim Commens had to tell me, is that you have to start a long way from where you want to end up.

I had, till he told me otherwise, an image in mind of a man on a bull-dozer finding a bit of a ledge and scraping it wider with the blade. I pictured someone reading a contour more or

139

less as it appeared on the map; he'd follow that line and carve it into the cliff, articulating thus the stratigraphy of the mountain as he went. You wrote contour lines on the rock. You made over a bit of the scarp to resemble the map.

Les knew it didn't work like that; so did Jim, who's made the odd road himself. You can't start where you mean to end up. You read the contours, sure. You elaborate with steel a line you feel out in the rock. But first you've got to plane the cliff-face back so that when you expose your contour, there'll be room for you and your road. You whittle the rock; you chisel and shave it away, until what you're left with resembles a road across a scarp. Les would have had to start exploding and 'dozing away rock sixty feet or more up from where he imagined the road—sixty feet up and quite a way back. The making of the road was a controlled and incremental plunge to a place on the scarp where the rock, you hoped, would hold. It was a frame-by-frame dive in a 'dozer through rock and space. Where you hit some kind of bottom, a sound kind of stratum, that was your road.

Les was a sculptor on a tractor—an artist on a grand scale. He was a force of nature. He was erosion itself; the hand of god. He was the chisel—he and his 'dozer. With each blow he might have fallen. But he never did. There's the miracle.

Take the road down to the Kedumba and you'll get a feel for the man's gift for reading rock and wrangling machines, for whispering a 'dozer down a mountain, for keeping his balance.

THE WAY BACK

The first time I came into the valley it was late September. The weather was warm, the winds were bated, and the sky was becalmed in the latitudes just north of winter and just south of summer. The winter had been dry again, and none of the creeks we crossed on the way in were running. The Waterfall and the

Kedumba creeks on the valley's floor were lower and quieter than any of these men had ever seen them. And emptier of fish.

I drove down the road Les had made. May wrote her diaries; Les wrote this road; and I drove down it with Norm, and with Ross, Norm's son, and with Jim Commens and Dave. In three four-wheel-drives, we went the way Norm had gone most weekends for nearly thirty years, the way Ross went most of the weekends of his childhood and youth, down six hundred meters from heath to valley floor in two deft zigs and three deft zags. They came to see Les; they came to shoot and fish; they came with different women over time, most of whom never came again to this piece of an unforgiving former world.

But all that had stopped thirteen years before. When the Waterboard locked the gate, they didn't give Norm a key, and he never thought to ask.

But I had a key. Writers sometimes get keys. They get to visit; it's an aspect of witness, which is their work. Since the only claim a writer makes on a place is imaginative, the people who run places sometimes let them in. And so here was Norm, this Tuesday morning in late September, an exile pardoned, leading me down to Les's valley. For Jim and Dave, too, this was a kind of coming home; and it was a return they never thought they'd make. For five good years before the gate got locked they camped with their families where we would camp tonight, where I would wake the next morning at the bend in Waterfall Creek, a dream upon my chest as light as a woken child, as heavy as grief.

CREATURES OF THE NIGHT

The evening of the day we drove down into the valley, Jim made a fire on the ground beside a rough iron table and chairs he'd welded together when he worked at the colliery. We made a circle with our chairs around the fire. Darkness fell, and stars gathered in it, as thick as thieves, as white as lies, and it was like being at the bottom of a well.

I don't think I'd fathomed, till the darkness fell and the fire rose and the beers flowed and these tough small men began speaking in the savage diction men keep for each other in places and moments such as these, how deep the valley had cut into their souls. I'd come to find Les's valley; what I found was the childhood country of these two men, a hard and lovely refuge, where they had learned who they really were. It has burned in them every night since, and they were as grateful to be down here again as men are for a miracle, if they get one. They drank more, they remembered more, they thanked me on and on, until I grew embarrassed and told them to stop, and they didn't stop till they slept.

But before that, coming on ten, Ross saw a pig among the trees. He spotted the oaks with his torch and reckoned he could make out eyes. He wandered off to hunt.

Now Ross is a man who's shot himself plenty of pigs here, so I wasn't going to tell him he was wrong. Not even when he came back and said he'd lost him. He and his father were so convinced of the dangers of the valley they weren't sleeping on the ground tonight. Norm told us, as we were slipping into our swags, how he'd saved some girls, once, who'd come down to the valley with his boys and insisted on sleeping out; one of the girls woke in the pitch-black midnight, looking into the red eyes of a boar. Norm had some more stories about wild dogs and wild horses and giant goannas, all of them true, or near enough, but I found myself thinking a bit later, when I should have been thinking about falling asleep, that maybe Norm's and Ross's world requires such wildness in a valley to justify the kind of order they want to bring to it with guns and roads and shelters. If it moves, shoot it; if it's standing, cut it down. That's the kind of ethic these men inherit, along with a deeper, better love of country than I will ever know.

Ross was still up sharing a drink with the fire when I fell asleep. And, when I opened my eyes at dawn, he was there kicking the fire awake. So who's to say he wasn't there all night keeping the valley from my throat?

A SEDIMENTARY CHILDHOOD

There are things I learned growing up in sandstone. I wasn't born among these valleys; I grew up among sediments laid down farther east in the same vast sag where the plateau grew. Gullies and railway cuttings, the massive incisions made in my lifetime to put in freeways out of the city, and promontories enclosing yellow beaches—these were the rocks of my childhood.

My strata floated in from the southwest; they are yellow and orange and gray. Hawkesbury sandstones—quartzites banded with vivid clays and powdery dull shales—gave me the ground and the groundsmells, sustained the timbers and grasses of my childhood. And, still, I am most at home in sedimentary rock, wherever I find it. I seem to guess what sandstone knows.

Yet as a young man I longed for granite; my terrain was an afterthought of creation, and I wanted the origins of things. Maybe that longing is one of the gifts of the sandstone. For sandstone is an abandoned child. There is a feeling my sandstones gave off—the sadness of exile, the yearning to find where you came from, the knowledge you weren't on original ground—and I think as a child I caught it. Sandstone is given to going away. It's an exile and a nomad; it has a journey to take to somewhere else that, who knows, might feel like home.

And this is what the stone has made me, too: a nomad, a seeker after home, who ends up belonging best where he began, in sandstone terrains, those outcast and restless geologies.

But I learned some other things in sandstone. I learned that even the densest things, the rocks, are porous. They carry within them light and water and sometimes fire. Sandstone breathes and it sweats; it weeps; sometimes it seems to glow. It weathers, it discolors, and it breaks. It's never the same rock twice. It was hard for me to avoid feeling that the very earth one walked on was alive and transitory. Continuity was a dream; nothing but change could be depended upon to last.

Growing up in light-filled, watercoursed rocks, I saw that dignity—and truth, for that matter—consisted of both lightness and gravity. I came to aspire to the same kind of presence upon the earth, the same poised state of being, that sandstone practices, that simultaneous standing firm and giving ground that sandstone has to master. Sandstone country teaches you, too, that water comes first and last. This stone is birthed and carried to the next world in water. I let it convince me that soft things outlast hard; I let it persuade me that the real world is a work in progress, always dying and always giving birth, always becoming, never quite become. I let it teach me what water had taught it.

LENT

It's March 1962, and in a suburb on the Cumberland Plain, I am two months old. Up on the plateau, Les Maxwell has been working a road down off the Shipley into the Kanimbla. And down in the Kanimbla, Jim Commens is four going on five.

For the last few months, May and Les have been camped in the caravan at the top of Mount Kedumba, returning at weekends to Camden. May's diary for late February is a chronicle of afternoon rain and wind and sudden cold and then the heat again, and she's thinking she picked a bad time to paint the caravan. But, between the chapters of the weather, she's nearly got it done. Then they move. They pull the van to Shipley at the start of March, so that Les can put in a last burst on the Kanimbla road, and she finishes the painting there.

Five years before, some of the fiercest fires the plateau has known had swarmed these valleys—Kanimbla, Kedumba, and Megalong—and over the Shipley ridge. May notices pink flannel flowers blooming where the fire burned the heath black. She notices them about the caravan, like splashes of paint, like spots of blood coughed onto a handkerchief.

Les was only finishing a road other men had begun. The road off the Shipley got started in the Depression. Jim knows an old bloke who worked on it and saw a man killed when they cut a tree to clear their way, and it rolled on him. There were other deaths; the going was hard and the tools rudimentary. With picks, a gang of jobless men carved a road through the rocks, heading it southeast with the mountain's contour and then switching it back northwest above the gorge where Blackheath Creek gathers the waters shed by the Shipley. They pushed on, sculpting a nice road in the sandstone until the ground leveled out near the foot of the scarp. There the Depression ended; and there the road stayed, still a difficult mile short of Centennial Glen. And that was where Les picked it up, working on it in fits and starts from 1958, shaping it against the toes of Mount Blackheath until in March 1962 he coupled it up to Kanimbla Drive, which came in from the Cox's River, and cut twenty minutes off the Commenses' journey to Blackheath.

And, in 1962, it's the start of Lent, and at the sharp end of the Kanimbla things are poised just short of a new beginning.

Saturday, March 3. Much better. Les / Worked on jeep, we / went to B. Heath in / afternoon. / Bill moved caravan / to Shipley.

Sunday, March 4. (Quinquagesima) Les worked on jeep / again brake trouble. / We went down Megalong / fishing Les got 1 eel. / Lovely day.

Monday, March 5. Nice day. Les went to / work with Kevin. I / went to B. Heath & got / Master Cylinder for jeep / fixed.

Tuesday, March 6. (Shrove Tuesday) Finished painting caravan.

Wednesday, March 7. (Ash Wednesday) Les had starter / trouble with jeep. / I went to Bullaburra. / Rain at night.

Thursday, March 8. Les & Kevin went to / Kedumba to search / for missing boy. / No luck. / Rain in afternoon & / all night. Cold.

Friday, March 9. Misty showers. / We went home late. / Mervyn & Dot called.

Saturday, March 10. Went to Dr Palmer. / Good news. / We won 2 chooks / at Narellan. / Rain at night.

Sunday, March 11. (Quadragesima; 1st in Lent) We returned to / Shipley.

Monday, March 12. Tractor breakdown. / Fuel line? I went to B. Heath—parts / for jeep.

Tuesday, March 13. (New moon) Cold day I took Les / to work, went B. Heath / for jeep parts. / Rain at night.

Wednesday, March 14. Still raining. / Cold misty day. / Les finished Kanimbla / Mtn Rd.

The nights of early March that year are wet and cool, and there is no moon. May has got the van painted, and her health has lifted again. The road is done. And somewhere in the valleys below Katoomba, somewhere on the way to Easter, a boy has gone missing. Les goes looking for him on a Thursday; he looks for a boy in the valley where Les himself left his childhood; and he finds neither. And on the first Sunday of Lent the boy stays lost.

David C. is seventeen when he disappears from the cliffs

near Leura. He's a prefect at Katoomba High, and he's working up to his leaving certificate at the end of the year. He's a quiet boy, a conscientious student, according to the school's magazine. The Lithgow *Mercury* calls him a keen bushwalker, which makes you wonder why he left his home in Commonwealth Street, Katoomba, that first lovely Sunday, in March, headed for the cliff walk in plastic sandals.

The Sunday Les was fixing his jeep and throwing a line into the afternoon on Megalong Creek, David C. was walking past the house that later became mine and getting himself lost in the valley.

May's diary says no more about the boy. From the beginning it seems most likely David fell, exploring the cliffs between the Gordon and the Leura falls. Someone finds tracks on the path between those falls, left by his plastic sandals, and someone finds a brand-new handkerchief. David had recently been given a box of handkerchiefs, his father tells police. People search for him under the cliffs and find no trace. Midweek comes, and his family and the police begin to hope that David may not have fallen but wandered farther into the Kedumba and got lost. That's when Les goes after him, too.

But what would a boy be doing, mid-term, wandering in a valley in sandals? A week after he disappeared, the police look again, harder this time, under the cliffs and find him—no longer a boy, but the broken form a boy leaves behind when he ceases on a valley floor beneath a waterfall. And the coroner returns a verdict of accidental death.

The rain goes on. The days of March improve. On the second Sunday in Lent, May and Les and Norm and his wife Frankie take a heavy toll on the parrots in the apple orchards of the Shipley Plateau. May takes a few of the parrots and cooks them up that night in the pressure cooker. The birds might have been fifty years old, but May turns them out as tender as corn-fed chicken, and their flesh tastes of apples.

CHRISTMAS

On Sunday morning, December 10, 2006, David I., a boy of seventeen from a private school in Sydney, left Katoomba with two friends headed for the Kedumba River and the Kings Tableland beyond. They'd planned the walk as a three-day trek, a dry run for a Duke of Edinburgh event in the valley the coming February, and each boy carried food and clothing in a backpack, a tent on top, and water. Each of them carried tablets to purify the water from the creeks if they ran through the water they carried, and they took the iron stairs down the escarpment and followed the track along the valley floor in fine warm weather, and on the first night they camped on the slopes of Mount Solitary. A change blew in overnight, bringing a light rain. On the morning of the second day, in cooler weather, the boys found the road on the Kedumba's floor that takes you down to the river and on to the Kedumba Valley Drive up and out of the valley.

Many times both days, David left the other boys, saying he would wait for them ahead, and each time they found him later, sitting by the track. Just after midday on Monday, David walked ahead again. This time he said they'd find him at the river, but when they reached the Kedumba an hour later, he was not there.

During the afternoon, David made three triple O calls from his mobile. "I'm lost," he said very calmly; he told them he was trying to find the Kedumba River.

For nine days, seventy searchers—police from the city and the mountains, some of them on mountain bikes, some of them in helicopters; volunteers from the Rural Fire Service, the Volunteer Rescue Association, the Wilderness Rescue, and the Blue Mountains Climbers Rescue Group—looked for David along the river and up every damp and stone-dry watercourse, and they covered as many of the hundreds of criss-crossing animal trails and four-wheel-drive tracks as they could find, and they looked for the boy up and down the rocky, thickly timbered slopes on the ground between the mountain and the river and even beyond it, and after two days someone found a red-and-white first aid kit that might have been David's but proved not to be, and until just after midday on December 19, no one found him. At 12:45 that day, searchers, returning to a slope they'd scoured days earlier, found a boy dressed in clothes that sounded like the clothes David had been wearing when he went on ahead of his friends for the last time.

The boy was lying dead, caught between a boulder and some trees just a hundred meters off the road to the river near the bottom of a rocky slope, and who knows how long he had wandered lost and how many nights he lay down somewhere scared and when he stopped calling out and just when he lost his feet and landed here and at what moment and by what means he died.

If I could tell you the days were very hot or the nights improbably cold or that it rained heavily and made the ground treacherous, you, like me, might find David's death easier to fathom. The plateau got quite a bit of rain late in the week David disappeared, but the days were, if anything, cooler than normal in mid-December, and there's nothing at all in the charts to explain the boy's death.

David left, his father said, a huge hole in the family, and one can only imagine how deep, for each family grieves after its own fashion, and every child's death is a loss never put right.

THE PRACTICE OF BELONGING

There is a practice of belonging, and it starts with forgetfulness of self. This thought came to me one afternoon along the track above the valley, and I walked it home and wrote it down. Don't come to the plateau to find yourself, I wrote; come to find the plateau. Come to know oneself, after a time, as one is known by the plateau, as one figures in geological time, in the pattern of the seasons and the rivers. That would be a self worth finding; that would be a life worth living. Of course, it might take about forever, and you'd have to do a lot of listening; it could be hardish work.

I feel less certain now about what I wrote then. Belonging is a practice, not a birthright; this I still believe. Attachment grows if you abandon yourself, if you let a place in, and if you're lucky. It may happen fast if you are porous to places; it may never happen if you're impregnable to the world, and many of us are. But it is performed best, this practice, when it's an accident of one's being and staying somewhere, making some kind of a life and some kind of a living from the country. And then there are some kinds of belonging that can kill you—the ultimate loss of self. Memories of these children lost in the plateau and so many hard lives lived there make my own practice, my pursuit of emplacement, seem to me now a soft and self-indulgent hobby, though it mattered to me then. The best kind of belonging is unself-conscious; I was always trying too hard to find it.

Still, to aim to understand yourself from a plateau's point of view—that, I think, is a worthy and perhaps even a useful aspiration. It engenders modesty; it puts the world first and yourself within it second; and I worked at it for years. And now I see how the working at it was the problem.

Yet, in the middle of writing this book, as I passed forty, I had a dream in my house in the plateau. And in the dream I was there in the cottage, and I knew that I shared it with a snake, a giant red-belly black, which lived where it had always lived beneath the floorboards. I was not, in the dream, afraid of it, and yet one afternoon after lunch I took an axe and I went down there, and I killed it. As it slept, I lifted the axe a hundred times and I brought it down hard a hundred times and I sliced the snake into as many pieces.

But when I had finished I watched each piece of the disarticulated snake become a snake itself and slide into the timber behind the house. Night came in my dream, and I took myself to the bedroom and lay down to sleep on a mat on the timber floor. And as I settled, I realized that the fragments of the snake had formed themselves into a broken circle beneath the blanket and made of themselves a bed, into which I sank. The snake was not whole, and yet it was somehow alive, the tip of its tail nearly in its mouth. And it held me, and in my dream I fell asleep on the blanket within the broken circle of the snake, and I felt at peace as I have rarely felt in waking hours, as though I had been forgiven everything. As though my life had come together at last.

When I woke in the room in the house in that plateau of reconstituted mountains, I felt like I'd arrived somewhere older than myself.

V

PASTURE

NOWHERE ELSE . . .

Jim, on the other hand, has been in the right place from the start. Where he is—in these paddocks his grandfather claimed as forest and swamp and his father opened up, down here between Mount Blackheath and the Camel's Hump—is where he's always wanted to be. He was born in the Kanimbla, in country drained by the Cox's River, in a flange the Valley presses into the side of the plateau, and this is pretty much where he'd like to stay. For Jim, there really isn't anywhere else. It's a lucky man who inherits such country, but liking it's the easy part, even if it's prone to frost and drought and fire. Making it work for you—that's the hard part.

It hasn't always gone smoothly for him in the Kanimbla. Some of his luck has been bad. But a life is what you do with your luck, and he's done pretty well with his.

. . . BUT HERE

From Blackheath, a thin promontory juts into the valley of the Cox's River, like Italy into the Mediterranean. This is the Shipley Plateau. South of it lies the Megalong Valley, north and west of it the Kanimbla. Up in the webbing between Mount Blackheath and Mount Victoria, the scarp piled up behind it like a coming storm, is a cluster of cottages, stables and woolsheds, set down on the soft thin shalestones and the blond grasses. These are the pastures, this is the home, Jim Commens shares with his brothers and his mother.

Jim's house and his stables sit right below Mount Blackheath. When he speaks of the mountain, this is the one he means, its tall purple and ocher bluff, the blue-black blaze of heath up top, the blue-gray scrub on the talus below, which is taking back a lot of the ground Jim's father took from it. The home Jim's built just recently, and the small village of used shipping containers arranged inside the great green Colorbond shed in which they lived before that, face west toward the river, the granite roils of its valley, the lowly Great Divide and the inland. Behind the house the plateau is a steep and enormous amphitheater. Sugarloaf Peak, Mount Tosh, Mount Kitosh, Mount Blackheath, Mount Boyce, Hornes Point, Mount Piddington, Pulpit Rock, Sunset Rock, Mitchells Ridge, Mount Victoria, and Camels Hump arc around Jim's paddocks, from south to north.

You're down in an earthenware pot. One side's smashed and fallen away. The other side's good, but the rim is chipped and fractured, somewhat less than true. It's all over the place. And here's Jim, where he's always been, the cliffs at his back the color of fired clay that's sat in the weather too long, the soils at his feet meager, the grasses dry and the dams empty.

COMING INTO THE COUNTRY

"Julia Grady 'er name was. She's the one started the Commens family off 'ere in Kanimbla. Bloke called George William Commens, that was me grandfather. 'E married Julia. They used ta call 'er Nan, but 'er name was Julia, an' 'er family come from over at Boggy Creek over on the Jenolan Caves Road.

"Now marryin' a Grady 'ere, see that's a bit of a worry. 'Cause ya get ta the Gradys, yer pretty much related t'everyone in the mountains. The Gradys, that's a huge family, pioneer family, I'd 'magine. They coulda been out there for another generation before old George William's people arrived, though 'is lot come pretty early on too. George William come from a family at Duddawarra on the Cox's River, Hartley way, an' 'is father was John Stephen Commens an 'is mother was Elizabeth.

"Jus' when me grandfather first come in here, that's a little bit foggy. I think 'e come in originally around about 1895 or 1898. An' 'e most prob'ly just bought a single little block ta start with. At the end of 'is life 'e 'ad a 'uge holdin'. 'E pulled that together over 'is life here. But the five thousand acres was all just scrub, an' the only bit that was cleared was round the house—Mum's house as it is there now.

"An' the other thing we know, the oldest bit of that shearin' shed that's still there over by Mum's, 'e built that in 1925. So 'e cleared the paddocks, got some sheep started, an' then it was a good twenty years before 'e got around ta buildin' a shearin' shed. I s'pose before that they woulda most prob'ly shorn 'em under a tree. But 'e finally got this shed up, and then, not long after that, 'e died. 'E was only in 'is forties still. An' left Julia with five girls an' me dad, the youngest. 'E was called George William, too.

"Now, you were askin' me if me granddad would've found much of the valley cleared, fired by the Gundungurra, when 'e first come in. There'd 'a been some. Must 'a been—name like Kanimbla, meanin' battleground; be hard ta have much of a fight in the thick a the trees—but I don't know there was much. Mosta these paddocks 'ere got ringbarked an' cleared by me grandad an' me ol' man over sixty years. You can see it in the old photos, all this standin' dead timber where there's grasses now. There's swamp, though. That swamp there, y' know, where Potter's is now, old George William 'e's responsible f' drainin' the greater part a that.

"The story goes that when me granddad got around ta drainin' it, it come down an' washed the orchard out, an' the orchard was on the creek flat below the house. Can't 'ave pleased old Julia very much, you'd think."

FARMING TREES

Clearing has been the great Australian project. And in the valleys below the cliffs where the mallee ash and the clumpy conifer hang out, farming the trees was a way of making a living. When you cleared, you left standing the marketable trees. When your cattle money was not enough, or when the price of wool dropped too low, you could harvest those trees and sell the timber. You could push the forest further up the slopes.

This is what Jim's father did in the 1950s and 1960s. The pointy end of the Kanimbla became a timber operation. Jim, on a Clydesdale, helped his father snig grey gums and boxes felled by the hired men out of the thinning woods on the slopes and down to the mill near the house, where the swamp used to be.

The coal mines at Lithgow always wanted timber—lining for the shafts. Most of Katoomba, including my place, was built with timber cut in these valleys. The building slowed down mid-century; fibro (God help us) and brick took over from timber, but there was always someone wanting flooring or frames or trusses. There was always someone wanting to make tables and chairs. Then timber went out of fashion and plastic came in, about the time Jim's father decided to clear the rest of his land and sell the timber. So his timing wasn't great. But there were always people who wanted good wood for yards and fences and sheds. And in winter the towns on the plateau sat low in woodsmoke; they were burning the forests of the valleys in their stoves.

Then in the 1970s Jim's father picked up the contract for the new high school buildings at Katoomba, and that kept the Commenses clearing and milling for years. Jim Commens grew up in a timber operation, really.

This is the way the Kanimbla, and for that matter the Kedumba too, came to be the valleys I knew.

But stop cutting long enough, let the ground lie as Jim is now letting it, and watch the timber return. Given time, the war against the forest is sure to be lost.

THE OLD BASTARD

"I wondered for a long time why it took me granddad so long ta get around ta puttin' up the woolshed. I mean what was 'e doin' for thirty years? Apart from accumulatin' land, which might almost explain it. What it turned out to be was 'e was a builder, a pisé house builder. That's what 'e was doin' all them years, buildin' everybody else's houses down 'ere. And I don't know 'ow many houses 'e built, but it seems like it mighta been quite a lot. Even runnin' round the place now, in Megalong there'd be three, four pisé homes that 'e woulda built still standin'. 'E built one 'ere for me neighbors, Guy Teseirero's people, an' there's a nice pisé house out on Collinses' land on the Cox's River Road there. An' scattered right throughout the valley there's a lot a pisé places yet.

"An' in that Cullenbenbong book ya brought along 'ere that first day, he's made mention of: George Commens, the bush carpenter. 'E 'ad a reputation for bein' a cranky ol' bastard. 'The old bugger,' or whatever they called 'im. That's in the book, I think. That's me granddad.

156

"Anyhow, the pisé house, let's say somethin' useful about that. It's about a two-foot-thick earthen wall. Rammed earth. They'd board up a frame, an' generally shovel in soil from the side, from the ground right there, ya know, dig it on site an' dump it straight into the frame, an' form it up, ram it, and jus' go straight up from there. Then they'd put logs around the windows for window-frames. Then they'd sit the big logs on the top to nail the roof to. An' you'd get a bit of an awnin' happenin' to keep the weather off the walls. Then they'd whitewash the walls to seal 'em, but one a the biggest problems with pisé houses, see, grandfather didn't seem ta know 'e was dealin' with quite a bit a weight. We're not talkin' about a bush hut. Some a them got quite substantial. An' most of the pisé houses have failed over the years 'cause the foundations were no good. See, that was a lot a weight, an' granddad oughta 'ave dug some deep foundations and got some footin's down, but I don't think 'e took that much trouble.

"What's Mum's house now, it's a pisé house, a course, an' she'd been ironin' shirts for us this one day when we were bits a kids, an' she walked in an' put Chris's ironed shirt on 'is bed in 'is room. An' then she thought twice about it, I s'pose, thinkin' I won't put it on the bed, 'cause 'e'll come in an' sit on it, an' she went ta pick it up ta hang it in the wardrobe, an' as she walked away with it, the whole bloody wall come crashin' down on the bed, dust and crap everywhere. If she'd lingered that little bit longer we'd a had ta just leave 'er there, dead and buried all at once in 'er very own house."

HARD LANDING

"So George William come over from Duddawarra, an' I think 'is lot were Presbyterians, an' fairly strictly so, an' there's George William goin' an' marryin' an Irish Catholic girl, an' that's got a lot ta do, you'd think, with why 'e 'ad ta leave the Cox's River an' start on 'is own over 'ere.

"Seems there wasn't a lot a good feelin's for a bit. It didn't lead ta hangin's or shootin's or any murderin's, but I think it did lead ta George William being I s'pose ostracized t'a fair extent. Don't think 'e got too many visitors from Duddawarra at all over the years, though we talk t'our cousins over there nicely enough these days.

"But me grandad an' Julia got thrown on the place pretty hard, an' they got thrown inta the church pretty hard too, as a consequence, which they all took ta quite a bit. Quite a few a me old man's sisters entered the church, became sisters or whatever."

GRADY BOYS

"Julia 'ad these brothers, three a them, an' the story is they were bits a rogues these blokes. They used ta just take whatever they thought was necessary, an' they got by, 'parently. They were livin' on Boggy Creek, an' while the old man, that's me grandfather, was alive, the story goes he kept them all in check, but as soon as granddad died they all moved in 'ere ta take care of the sister, and made 'er life fairly hard. They weren't inclined ta work all that hard, an' in the end she was feedin' the lot a them.

"But Julia, she musta had some kinda business sense 'cause she started off an orphanage in the house. Children come 'ere out a the city, a gov'ment-sponsored thing, if they 'ad asthma an' that kinda thing, an' they weren't doin' well down there. They did their schoolin' 'ere too, with Julia I s'pose, and visitin' teachers an' nuns. They lived 'ere in the house, most prob'ly on the veranda. An' that lasted a good number a years.

"When we were over there near Mum's with the ridin' school, before Judith an' I put up the shed, you'd get these old blokes gettin' out a the car an' old women an' next thing they'd come in an' say, 'I was 'ere for seven years.' 'Appened a lot."

TRYING TOO HARD

Very often, on a horse in Jim's valley, I felt I'd come all the way home. I felt it more strongly there than in my own house up on the escarpment. I recognized his valley, and also the Kedumba sometimes, as though I'd lived in these grasslands in a life before this one, as though they were a childhood I'd once had. But no amount of coming and going and longing could make them mine—could make me theirs, I really mean. And they baffled me; I rode in the valleys and I walked, and now and then I slept in them, and I could feel myself reaching for them, but they never did take me in.

My belonging in the plateau, most specifically in its valleys, was a project, not an inheritance or even a sentence; living there, putting myself about in the valleys on horseback, was an essay I was trying to write home, and I never could get to the end of it. I willed the plateau to own me, but I'm sure it never did.

AT A HUNDRED PACES

Three or four years, for instance, after I've first ridden out with Jim and he's started telling me the place—describing at a trot its natural history and at a canter his own place within it—he leads me one Saturday afternoon down to the paddock beneath the shed to find my mount, a stockhorse he calls Stock, whom I've ridden already a dozen times by then.

Jim carries a blue halter; he'll be doing the catching, and I'll be doing the watching. We walk toward twenty horses grazing together, one of them Stock, and Jim calls to him, and Stock lifts his head and takes some steps our way, and that is the moment I recognize him. "You know Mark," Jim says to the horse, and the horse bows into the blue halter, and Jim motions me to grab hold and lead him back to the shed. I stroke Stock's long face, and the horse looks at me with that infinite gentleness of his tribe, with the kindness of his particular nature, with the trust Jim awakens. And we walk back into the yard and into the shed, where Jim saddles Stock neatly while I bridle him badly.

I can barely tell one horse from another; I can scarcely name one hill or creek with certainty; I get lost on these rides. Jim's ease with leathers, his picking one brown horse from another at a hundred paces, his quiet assurance in landscape—these are skills I aspire to and envy, but they are not my career. I do them part time and I do them ineptly. I just can't see yet what Jim sees here, what Les saw in the Kedumba. Most of the plateau is lost on me. I could lose my way and die here as easily as any careless and cynical stranger, in country I think of as sweeter than heaven.

I am daunted by all that escapes me and does not escape Jim. If there are things I know that Jim does not, skills I have that he does not, I can't think of one of them down here; I can't remember why they'd matter more than how to sit a horse well and find my way home on it out of Blackheath Creek in under a day. I'd like to recognize a horse I love at a hundred paces. A horse who, come to think of it, would be the one who'd be finding my way home for me—another sure-footed local, more at home than I'll ever be in this landscape.

ONE OF THE PRETTY HORSES

Way back, when William Maxwell was living down at Black Gooler, before he got around to settling the Kedumba, he was indicted for stealing a horse. The horse in question was a chestnut filly, raised by Timothy Lacey on his station on the Wollondilly in Central Burragorang. Lacey was a landlord, mostly absent. He lived in town, up at The Oaks, and he left his lands by Lacey's Creek and his horses, his sheep, and his cattle in the care of hired men.

Let's say this filly wandered when Lacey's station hand wasn't looking at her hard enough, and found her way north to the Cox's River and then out of the scrub to William Maxwell's plot. Such things happen. It's also possible Maxwell came downriver and saw her and took her when Lacey's man was looking the other way; but you didn't hear that from me: up in The Oaks at that time, Maxwell and his father-in-law had a reputation for horse rustling, though no one ever got anything to stick.

The filly can't have been branded, or the matter would have been simple. Anyway, Maxwell had sold her to another man, Grundy, a farmer at Brownlow Hill. And it was on Grundy's land that Lacey next saw his horse—saw it one day as he rode past, two years after he'd last seen the beast. And that, I suppose, is my point.

Timothy Lacey recognized his filly at a canter; he knew her at a hundred paces. He rode in and confronted Grundy, who told Lacey that the horse had strayed across his land one day and that he decided to keep her. When Lacey insisted the horse was his, Grundy gave her up. Lacey had an idea that young Maxwell was involved, so he took his horse home and later on he rode up and found Maxwell and asked him if he'd known the horse was Lacey's when he took him, and Maxwell said he'd never taken the filly and had only found out she'd been Lacey's when he'd sold her on to Grundy, and Lacey didn't believe him and took the matter to court.

But Lacey couldn't lead enough evidence, and the judge in Campbelltown Quarter Sessions wasn't happy to back a hunch, no matter how widely shared and plausible, and there was Lacey with his pretty horse back already, so the case was dismissed and Maxwell got off.

MUSTERING THE SKY I

The heads of thirty kangaroos poked from the grasses bunched by Potter's Cottages. The animals held themselves as still as holy men, if nowhere near as calm. They stood in a sustained and perfect vigil of alarm, and we were what alarmed them: two men on horses, crossing their ancestral grasslands.

But Jim wasn't looking at the roos. He was pointing at the fox stealing through the grasses away from us. "Knows 'is way around these tussocks," Jim said, and steered his horse after the fox. "The old bugger. Ya see 'im? There 'e goes." I turned my horse after Jim, but I lost the fox at once.

Veering thus from our slow straight line, we tipped the roos from the precarious meridian they'd been holding; they gave up, in an instant, the hope of not being seen, and they bolted for the timber. Jim nudged his horse. I pressed my heels to Stock's sides, drew the reins tight, and we turned our horses after the roos, and the tall grasses crowded about us, so many clustered bristles on the head of a broom. We were the afternoon's breath. We were passing among these grasses like a thought through someone's mind.

If you'd asked the roos, whose elegant panic had carried them already into the brittlejacks, they might have said the thought we embodied was threat or nuisance, just plain trouble. And they might have been right. What the fox spells—for animals with a far longer lineage in this valley than the fox, for young kangaroos and smaller marsupials—is death. If Jim had a rifle he'd have been firing it, but not at the roos.

Jim's palomino side-stepped sharply round a strand of blackberry in the tussocks as though it was barbed wire, and Jim

rode the swerve and got himself straight in the saddle again, and
our horses broke into a run for the ridge.

If it had not been so much like riding through belly-high
grass toward the trees, I would tell you that this metrical rise
and fall, this rapid rolling stress and unstress, felt like cantering
in dactyls through cloud.

MUSTERING THE SKY II

I'm describing an afternoon in early June one year. At three
o'clock, as we set out to look over some of the horses Jim agists,
he'd pointed to the sky. "It's two years since I saw a cloud like
that," he said. A skein of high cirrus, fraying and bone white,
was drawn taut across the blue sky, north to south—ice, braided
by wind. Up there the winds were screaming; down here in the
grasses of the Kanimbla, sunlight pooled, and the air was very
still. "I wonder what shapes a cloud just that way, every other
year," Jim said. Two years earlier, one afternoon in winter,
the quality of the light and the mood of the wind high above
these dry paddocks had been just the same, and way up in the
troposphere the air had been as fierce and cold.

To remember this, to be fluent in the language of the sky, to
recall the figures it recites and repeats, is to belong, I thought
then, to a valley as the roos belong to it.

MUSTERING THE SKY III

Halfway round the horses, we stopped by Jim's mother's house,
and Jim's twin Lachlan was there working in the yard. The sky
that morning had been full of clouds, and Lachlan reckoned
they were an odd color; he reckoned they were stained with dust
blown all the way from South Australia and all the dry country
in between; and he reckoned the dust was still in the air. The
afternoon was now so clear—just that rope of cloud, as pellucid

as optic fiber—I found it hard to see how the sky could be steeped thus in drought. But as afternoon wore on, and we rode among the horses, the cirrus rolled east, and the sun fell west and as it fell discovered filaments the sky remembered, all of a sudden, from the morning. The droughty sky flared pink, and evening made a sunset out of all that desert overhead.

MUSTERING THE SKY IV

Jim looks at a horse the way some men look at a car. He loves it, if it's any good—sometimes even if it isn't. He knows its sins, its signature moves, the way it breaks his heart; he works with it; he enjoys the way it carries him across the ground; and when it breaks or grows too old, he lets it go. He sells it or—speaking of horses exclusively now—he puts it down.

"Ya dig a hole till ya find rock," said Jim as we rode on toward that sunset. "Then ya lay the horse on the rock an' backfill. Ya make a mound over it, an' ya let it settle flat. Ya need ta dig down ta rock—ya need it deep or the dogs'll get at it. No one wants that. 'Cept the dogs, a course.

"People get sentimental about animals," Jim went on. Among the agisted horses that afternoon was a white mare, twenty-eight years old, three-quarters blind. She had to come up close to find out what we were, and we watched as she made her way off through the paddock, head lowered, walking half-steps, feeling out the terrain. She came up too close to a pony and shied. "An' that one's over thirty," said Jim.

Another old limping mare belonged to a woman who'd moved to Tasmania three years back. "She rings me one night," Jim said. "'How much would it cost to ship her down?' she asks. To Tasmania. A horse thirty years old. 'More than it's worth,' I tell her. So she asked me ta keep the horse here. She shoulda put the mare down. But I couldn't bring meself ta say it. A thousand dollars a year is a lot ta spend ta keep a lame horse alive, though I'm 'appy ta take it.

"An' look at this old thing . . ."

Our ride among the elderly continued. But these horses didn't look old to me, and if they were suffering they weren't showing it. Or was it just the kindness of the light they grazed in?

It had been months since I'd ridden, and we pushed the horses along, for the afternoon was failing, and we still had a way to go. I was thinking how sore I'd be tomorrow or the next day, and how this was the widest I had been awake for weeks, out here in the air on a horse in a valley. We moved at a steady canter past the old woolshed, and we were talking as we rode, and I was thinking how smart that felt, when Jim's mobile phone rang. It made a sound like a frog in a swamp, a frog in some agony. At a canter, Jim pulled the phone from his belt and held it up and looked at the number on the screen and pressed the talk button and asked, "What's 'appenin'?" This is what cowboys do these days.

"Righto," Jim said to the phone. "Won't be long," and I guessed then it was Judith. This particular cowboy had just turned forty-five, and Judith had a party organized for him up on Camel's Hump that night, though Jim thought at that stage it was just a barbeque with a couple of friends. Jim clipped the phone back onto his belt, still at a canter, and we pressed on.

"The wind's gettin' up," Jim said, "an' it blows like buggery on that ridge." And he didn't know it yet, but fifty people would be up there later freezing with him in the wind and letting him know he'd be out to pasture soon himself.

At Potter's, we had trouble with the gate. The post, which was new, had shrunk in the dry weather and pulled the chain taut so that Jim had to take pliers, from his belt beside the phone, and bend the hook so it cleared the eye. He got that done, and we rode through and I shut the gate behind us, and that was when we became two doubts in the minds of a mob of kangaroos.

MUSTERING THE SKY V

We slowed the horses to a walk and came down off the ridge through the evening timber, and Jim said, "I guess it's what ya grow up with.

"When we were kids an' Dad come in an' said there's an old cow or some bloody thing that needed a bullet, there'd be a fight f' the job. You know, Lach'd be goin' Jim shot the last one an' it was 'is turn an' I'd be runnin' ta get there first. It wasn't that we liked the killin'. I don't think we were 'specially cruel. It was just a job with a gun, an' that made it one a the good jobs."

MUSTERING THE SKY VI

I looked up at the sky again and the darkening scarps as we rode through the home paddock, and I decided I'd been wrong earlier about the light. It wasn't kind; it was, as ever, simply true. It touched the grasses and it brought out the drought in the clouds, and it didn't care. It knew nothing about pity. But it seemed to me that we should. We need to be careful, though, whom our pity serves. Are we sparing ourselves or an animal? What is right, I was thinking, is what has about it the quality of this light; whatever helps to keep such stern beauty alive.

MUSTERING THE SKY VII

As we rode past Jim's new house Judith came out and waved and called, "We won't have any horses ridden through here, thanks," and Jim sang out "Did ya drench the horses?" and she said she had. "But get a move on down there, you boys," she added.

By the shed, a fire still smoked in a big circle of rocks Jim had built there for the tourists. There was a billy hanging in the smoke. "Now wouldn't it be nice ta sit an' drink some tea right now," said Jim. But we didn't have time, and he knew it. We unsaddled the horses, and hung the leathers in the container where they were stored. Jim fixed the horses' feed in a couple of buckets, molasses and oats, and stirred water into it under the tap.

We waited till the horses had eaten. Then we opened the gate to the yard and let them water at the trough. They stood a bit in the last of the daylight, and each of them looked out across the paddocks for his mob. It must have felt good—it felt good just to watch them—to look out at the evening, fed and watered and done carrying men, done spooking at blackberry and chasing roos, ready to find your mates and graze with them while night fell.

Then Judith came down and hurried Jim away, and he sauntered to the house flicking through a book I'd given him. A book about a meadow, a place not unlike this one, but at the mercy of a different sky. And I walked to my jeep, and turned it around, and I waved at Jim and drove away. Halfway up out of the valley, a lyrebird crossed in front of me and carried his furled tail into the bracken by the road. A shadow puppet on the gray backlit screen of the night. And then it was night entirely, and I let the jeep peer ahead astigmatically into the darkness and take me home along another road Les Maxwell had made.

THE QUALITY OF MERCY

"Dad seemed to be sick pretty much all me life. 'E 'ad 'yper-tension. 'E 'ad it when 'e was as young as sixteen or somethin' an' by the time 'e become thirty an' forty a lot of 'is organs were playin' up. 'E died when 'e was only forty-seven, forty-eight. 'Im an' 'is dad, 'e died of 'ypertension of some description 'bout the same age. I'd better watch me step.

"Chris, me elder brother, 'ad a bit of a 'andicap, an' 'e spent a lot of 'is time livin' with mum, an' then later 'e left mum's an' stayed in a nursin' home f' 'andicapped type people in Blackheath, an' two years ago 'e 'ad a stroke up there an' died two days later. The family never talked about it too much, but Chris 'ad a 'ard birth an' 'e was never quite right from the start. 'E never talked prop'ly or learned ta write, but 'e was still quite bright, ya know, do all sorts a work. One of 'is arms was a bit withered, an' then 'e walked with, not a limp, but one leg wasn't as good as the other. I can remember 'im speakin' quite a bit when we were kids, an' apparently 'e did speak quite a bit up until the old man started ta get seriously ill. An' then, he musta just withdrew into 'imself, an' when Dad died, Chris 'ad stopped speakin' completely. An' that was it. Not another word out of 'im."

LETTING IT SLIP

"How me parents met, that'd be through Mum's brother Colin. Mum's family was in the mountains right back in the early days. 'Er roots come from a family called Phillipses, who were pretty much the first people who lived in Blackheath. But Mum's family, her mother an' her father, 'ad moved away ta Sydney an' then f' some reason Colin come back an' when 'e come 'e met the ol' man, an' Colin an' the ol' man got to be some sorta drinkin' partners. An' through that, Mum met George, me ol' man. She's Helen. Name was Underhill before she married the ol' man.

"An' in between the stage of me grandfather dyin' an' me mother comin' on the scene there was bugger all done at the property. When she first saw the place there was blackberry bushes everywhere an' off the veranda there was a pile a bottles ya couldn' see the other side of.

"When me grandfather died me dad was still only eight but somehow the property come to 'im. An' as a boy the ol' man used ta take a lot a notice of the Grady boys, an' they thought they knew 'ow 'e should run it, which was pretty much inta the ground. But when Dad finally grew up an' 'specially once Mum was on the scene, 'e began ta sort a lot a things out and get the place movin'. Mostly 'e realised 'e could make some money by g'ttin' out a the sheep an' cuttin' down the timber, millin' it 'ere an' sellin' it. 'E turned the place into a timber operation over the years. It was only near the end 'e got into a few cattle.

"When Dad died, an' it come ta splittin' up between Mum an' us kids, most a the land granddad 'ad pulled together, that was already gone. See, there's a bit of a blank there. I dunno what 'appened. Might a had somethin' to do with them Grady boys, I dunno. Story goes, there was five thousand acres once from 'ere ta the highway out at Camels Hump. But when Dad started gettin' round an' runnin' the place, I s'pose 'e might've sold it off bit by bit. Pay some debts from all those years of doin' nothin' much down 'ere, t' afford some sheep, t' pay for some saws an' teams an' tackle for the mill, I guess that'd account for it. But I know that it all got broken up an' Mum ended up with just these few 'undred acres up this end."

HOW IT REALLY GOES

The time I rode Stock and he and I chased Lach's bull around a bit and got him in the end into the top paddock; the time M. rode the black thoroughbred Tsar, who wasn't that interested in helping corner an animal the color of a golden retriever and the size of a small whale, and Jim rode Tallis, who wasn't that interested either, so that Stock had to show me how to do what had to be done, and somehow we did it; the time the other two watched while Stock and I pushed the heifers into the yards down the bottom by Helen's house; the time the six o'clock sun steeped everything the color of billy tea as Jim and M. and I rode home after all that through Potter's fields, Jim cantered up beside Stock and said this: "Once when I was beginnin' ta get on better with the Potter bloke who moved in 'ere, I was walkin' with 'im through this paddock, an' 'e says, 'You ever noticed how many shades of green there are in each of these tussocks?' An' I said I never 'ad, an' I looked at them 'ard, an' ya know, 'e was right. Each one's got about fifty colors in it, 'ardly any a them green. Been muckin' about 'ere all me life, takes someone from the outside ta show me what I been lookin' at all this time."

We left the flat then and rode up into the second-growth timber, where the grass gives out completely and the ground is flint, and the horses stepped between the slender standing stringybarks and the deadfall, and a big gray kangaroo bounded from us as we topped the ridge, and we rode out of the timber then and back into Jim's own paddocks.

"Take a look at Tsar," said Jim, "walkin' along like we're all lookin' at 'im. Pickin' up each foot, all delicate, an' puttin' it down again. There's Stock just gettin' on with it, but that's nowhere near good enough for our Tsar. Gotta' go about it like 'e's on parade at the Royal bloody Easter Show."

VI

FIRE

WHAT THE VALLEY TAKES

There were plenty of days, through winter, when ice still hung from the eaves at midday. Les was rarely there to see that—he was out on the tractor or the 'dozer, out on the bike chasing cattle, mending fence or fixing somebody's car—but May saw it often through July and August.

Some days the valley could be an ocean of cloud till late morning. Those days, you couldn't see farther than your outstretched hand. The valley is slender, you see, and the scarps about it are high. So everything gets stuck here in its season—heat or cold, cloud or wind; people, sometimes. It's not an easy place to get into, and it's even harder to get out.

When the wind was up, Norm tells me, the valley was awash with it. They come in, the winds, and they can't get out, and they fling themselves from cliff to cliff, and they scream and roar like demented children. "Wildest place in a wind I ever knew," says Norm. Once, at night, the winds tore the roof clean off the Cleary house and carried it in one piece over Les's and dropped it just beyond the hedge. Les slept right through it. It was a Saturday, and Norm was there, too. Not sleeping. Listening to the loudest and most sustained roaring he ever heard. And when they went outside at first light to look at what the night had done, they saw Cleary's roof lying where it had landed in the paddock; and they saw that they'd lost their own chimney, and that they were lucky that was all.

Norm remembers days of cloud when the nothingness about him, an absence of color and distance rather than the presence of anything, stirred endlessly, if nothingness can stir. Such days were a weird and restless congregation. A wind would press down and the mass of blind air would sway and race like water under a current. And it was cold.

Other days, cloud poured off the Walls or Solitary like white-water that never reached the valley floor. Some days the clouds looked like smoke, only slower and cooler than smoke and whiter, seeping down from behind Sunset Hill or Dawson's Wold. And other days it was smoke.

The valley is a woman who likes a bath, and she likes to smoke while she lies there. She breathes down the sky, and she lets it travel through her body, and she holds it a long time, and then she breathes it out again, heavy with desire and complaint. The sky above the valley is a memoir, once you learn to read it.

GAUGING THE RAIN

As the sixties became the seventies and May worried with growing cause over her health and consoled herself among her lettuces and tomatoes, her parsley and onions and beetroot and roses, the watch May kept on the sky became a stricter observance. Whatever the sky let slip she caught in her diary. At the back of the blue Collins diary for 1974, May gathered the daily rainfall into months and made a table.

Rainfall 1974	Points
Jan	936
Feb	462
Mar	836
April	1048
May	848
June	678
July	62
August	347
Sept	55
Oct	325
Nov	286
Dec	None

A year in the pluvial life of the valley. There are always storms in January, and it looks like were plenty in 1974. But April's not normally so wet. Things were as lean as ever around the middle months, and September was the leanest of them all, which is usually the way it goes about it. December, though, you'd have expected something. But for the rains of the first half of the year, there'd have been fires at Christmas for sure.

THE NURSERY OF FIRES

The plateau is a nursery of fires. It's built to burn. If it didn't burn, it wouldn't be the plateau, but that doesn't make it any easier to bear. Anyone who lives here needs to reconcile themselves with fire; and the drier we get, the more reconciling we're going to have to do.

Fire will find you in the end, in the valley or on the ridge, and not only in the summer. You'd better be ready to flee or fight; you'd better get ready to grieve.

Though historically the real fire season happens from

September, fire often visits the plateau around Christmas. And one particular Christmas, our fourth in Katoomba, as the plateau entered its fifth year of drought and M. the tenth week of her first pregnancy, we stayed in our timber cottage, tiny in the plateau's womb, and watched it birth and fledge a hundred fires around us.

FIRE HISTORY

Eucalypts harvest fire. Had this continent of astringent soils not slipped steadily north into warmer latitudes over the millennia and made itself a lightning rod, the place would still have been covered, when Europeans found it—even when it found the indigenous peoples long before that—with rainforests. But it did drift north; it still does. It warmed and got itself becalmed in the driest latitudes on earth. Where fire destroys a rainforest, it only encourages eucalypts—trees that love to burn.

So it was sclerophyll country that birthed the first peoples; it was eucalypts the first people's fire-farming encouraged; it was eucalypts the white men found. In the plateau, and nearly everywhere else.

Gums are fire specialists. They seek out fire-prone country and make it more fire-prone, and when fire comes they proliferate. They've taken hold of the continent and made it, wherever they grow, a paradise of flames. The plateau is one such paradise.

Though it still rains in the plateau and waters run and the air is often cool, there are days in early summer when, after winters that are habitually dry, the wind blows from the northwest out of the stark arid inland, and it finds the dry-leafed forests poised for conflagration. All it takes then is a half-hearted storm to send some lightning down, and the bush burns. A storm will do it, or an idiot with a match.

Fires like those that took the plateau on Christmas Eve 2001 burned in the mountains in 1814 and 1843 and 1849 and 1875 and 1888 and 1895 and 1900 and again in 1904. These past hundred years the plateau has gone up a dozen times, most savagely three times in the 1950s. In 1965 parts of the valley below me burned; they've not burned since; they're overdue. In 1968 half the mountains went up. Before the fires of Christmas 2001, the last big fires burned in 1994.

So there we were that Christmas inside the latest chapter in the long fire history of the plateau. A history that's getting faster and hotter.

EXPECTANCY

In the middle of a mild Friday, four days after Christmas, I walk with M. along the Prince Henry track to the amphitheater above the Leura Forest. We go easy. Smoke is seeping into the Kedumba, spilling over the sunlit cliffs of the Kings Tableland. It streams down the face of the sandstone and insinuates itself among the promontories below. As we watch, it effaces the scarp completely, and the valley is gone.

Huge fires burn up in Bulga and Mount Yengo, down along the Nattai, and on the south shore of the Burragorang. Wiseman's Ferry is burning too. My country is on fire.

We walk home above the stolen valley. Around the cottage, the afternoon light, trapped in the smoke and refracted, sepias the silvertop ash at my window. By evening, everything has disappeared. The moon, when it rises as if from nowhere, looks diseased.

Nine o'clock comes and darkness falls. The wind has turned and pulled the smoke back to the sea, and the night air smells like penitence, like eucalypts and charcoal. It carries the last thoughts of savaged trees, the intelligence of lives violently felled. Most of them will rise again, but that doesn't make them smell less ruined.

IT'S MARK YOU MOURN FOR

Saturday. Five days after Christmas. Nine-thirty, and the moon, just shy of full, is white tonight, and it swims in an estuary of cloud.

The wind is coming out of the north, and it's rising. Everyone, from the fire commissioner to the premier, speaks grimly on the late news. We are prey to the weather. What worries us is the fire at Spencer near Wiseman's Ferry, and its coming south on tomorrow's winds; what worries us are the fires in the Shoalhaven; what worries us are these untamed blazes on the eastern escarpment of the main ridge; and the fire at Burragorang, which might jump the dam again and join smaller blazes in the Wollondilly, and the one in the Nattai.

Here's what's coming tomorrow: the temperatures will approach forty degrees; the sky will be a desert; the morning will bring fierce winds, northwesterlies, fire-stokers; and the afternoon will bring storms from the south, colder air but little rain, and lightning strikes. The state faces the worst threat it's stared down in thirty years.

But right now the night has fallen still. It's about as warm as it ever gets in Katoomba. The night is a kiln, and someone's stoking it.

The house fills with smoke. I leave my study, and the smell of the burned peppers meets me at the door. M. has opened the oven just in time on the red bell peppers she's roasting for tomorrow's soup.

I throw open a window in the kitchen, and a big gray moth flies in and follows the light into the bathroom and lands on the wooden frame of the mirror. From there it watches M. let herself slenderly down into the bath again, and I watch too, and I think about joining this woman in the water, but I content myself with kissing her mouth and one nipple of a floating breast, with resting my left hand on her belly, the coming child, and I leave them to the water and go back to the study to think. What I think about is growing old—my fortieth birthday falls the day after the day after tomorrow—and I think about the fire out there biding its time in the dark.

Death is as natural as night or fire or a long tepid bath or a coming child, I say to myself, and the forests need this kind of dying, and I need to grow old to live, and then I need to die. There's no stopping any of it. But it doesn't make you want it—the fire and death, the aging and declining—anymore than you should.

LIVING WITH FIRE

On the third day of January, the weather eases. The winds back to the south and then shift to the east. The seabreeze submerges the Kedumba again in smoke and carries ash to Honeymoon Lookout, where I stand at ten o'clock in the darkness.

On the fourth, the fire of the eastern escarpment moves northwest ahead of a steady wind. It rushes up gullies at Faulconbridge, at Hazelbrook and Woodford and has to be wrestled back south of the highway. It presses toward Lawson and Bullaburra. It's coming our way, up the gradient of the tilted table of the plateau. Then the winds drop back to nothing, and the fire tenders burn a break on the Kings Tableland, and smoke falls over Wentworth Falls and Katoomba and stays the night.

Two hundred thousand hectares of forest is burning, half of it out of control. A change due late on Sunday may ease the temperatures. But no one's foretelling rain. No one presumes to know when this will end. In October 1957, a famous mountain fire that got going in the Megalong climbed Narrowneck and burned in the Kedumba for three weeks.

This is what it is to live in country fashioned and nourished by fire.

I should live like a migratory bird, but I am a man, and a man's belonging wants a roof, the same one most of the time. At the center of my sense of place, even of my sense of self, stands a house. There, most of my belonging rests: in its rooms, the memories that inhabit them, the books that live there, the visiting voices of my older children, the work I've done, the love I've made. Most of my belonging? No, most of my belonging stretches out over a sandstone plateau that's on fire, but it likes a cottage to come home to and sleep.

That kind of belonging may be too heavy and too slow up in the plateau. That's what these fires tell me. To live here like this, to want so to belong, is to lie prone in the path of fire.

THE QUICK AND THE DEAD

Billy Maxwell told Les a story about fire in the valley, and Les told it once to Jim. This story started with a big fire—Les called it the red steer—that got loose in the Kedumba in the summer of 1904–1905. That fire, too, came after years of heat and drought, and that summer all the valleys at the plateau's western edge went up.

One day in January in the middle of all that, the red steer came up the valley toward the Maxwell place, running hard. When they were certain it wasn't going to miss them, Billy climbed up a ladder and helped his father lift the roof from his father's hut. The roof was covered in stringybark, and if the fire got into it, they'd lose the whole hut. So they got up there and took it down. It was built in one piece on an A-frame, and they lifted it and dropped it to the ground, and they dragged it down to the creek. They drenched the house in water from the creek, and they stood with the boy's mother on the banks and waited.

When the fire got close to the house, it slowed in the grasses and garden plants and lost its way. Then a wind kicked in and the fire billowed and it swept right over the hut, and the three of them watched it run north at speed and beat itself out against the escarpment. Their slab hut stood intact. Beside it Mary's rose garden and a year's worth of vegetables lay charred in the black earth. The men carried the roof back to the hut, and they set it on top, and they knelt down and prayed.

But you're usually only that lucky once, no matter how hard you pray.

One summer in the early 1930s, long after William Maxwell was dead, when Les himself was fifteen or sixteen, the steer came back and took the hut his grandfather had made and Billy had helped him save from the big fire of 1904–1905. Having failed to save their grandfather's place a second time, Les and Jimmy and their father soaked the ground around their own home at the meeting of the creeks, and they drenched the timber walls and the veranda of the house itself, carrying water in buckets up the hill from Waterfall Creek until the fire was almost too close, and then they climbed a ladder and stood together, their mother with them, on the tin roof and fought the red steer back.

They won that fight, and that's where Billy's fire story stopped. But Les lived to see its epilogue. In 1965 the red steer came back. Though it burned out most of the Kedumba Valley, the fire spared the caretaker's cottage, and it left alone the slab hut Les had abandoned to the past across the creek. It burned through the home paddocks and the forest below the Kedumba Walls, and it burned to the ground the timber cross that marked the place where Les's grandfather, William Maxwell, pioneer of the valley, lay. A retrospective cremation; a day, perhaps, of judgment; a final kind of coming to belong.

When it comes to the red steer, you're either quick or you're dead. Give it long enough, you might get to be both.

KEEPING THE FIRES IN THE VALLEY

After the fires of 1957 burned out most of the Valley the dam had not yet filled—and a fair bit of the main ridge, too, from Wentworth Falls to the Nepean River—Les Maxwell was the man the Clearys took on, to blaze firetrails down from the tablelands into the forests of the valley floor all over the upper mountains. Les was the one man the Clearys knew who'd find a way to push a blade down any escarpment. And Les was the reason the Clearys won the contract from the New South Wales Bushfire Committee.

Les was the Blue Mountains Fire Prevention Scheme—pretty much. The scheme's one big idea was to stop the fires getting out of the valleys, and it was Les who made the roads to carry water to the flames to stop them where they started in the forests. And so it was that Les spent much of the next dozen years negotiating the scarp on a D4.

LOVE AND FIRE

A young man rides to the edge of Lawson; a teenage girl drives to the last street in North Epping. Winds gust hard, and the air is parched. He tosses a lit match. She throws a towel wet with petrol into the bush behind the oval and fires it with a cigarette lighter. He rides, she drives, away. Fast. In fifteen minutes the State Emergency Service has two new firegrounds. You could see it as an angry, spiteful gesture, a lunge for power. Or you could look on it as a confused cry for belonging, for connection to the elemental world, a crudely fashioned attempt to wake the devil in the torpid suburbs, and to make the world wild again and themselves wild for a moment within it. Each of us longs for a life as stern and true as fire—though there are better ways to get one.

THE MORE THINGS CHANGE

January 4, 1814. The governor's surveyor, George Evans, was coming home across the plateau. He'd been looking at country along the Macquarie River farther west where the young colony might pasture its cattle and find room for its ambitions. He was impressed by how much the ground there looked like a park, and he realized that it looked that way because of the way the natives fired it. Back in November, when he'd crossed the mountains going west, the air had been thick with mist and light rain. But coming back east, it was different. In camp at Weatherboard (we call it Wentworth Falls today) on January 4 he wrote:

The Mountains are, as yesterday, fired in all directions: at eleven o'clock I was on the high hill: all objects east are obscured by thick smoke.

Two days later, on January 6, at Valley Heights, he was still traveling through burning forests:

The flames have been in my favour, otherwise it would have been impossible for me to measure; the flames have consumed the foliage from the highest trees.

THE MORE THEY STAY THE SAME

January 6, 2002. The fires have been burning for two weeks, and no one sees the end in sight. I wake this morning to an e-mail from a friend in Virginia who's caught wind of the fires and sends a prayer for rain.

I leave the house and drive southwest to friends at Cowra. From the road, I can see the smoke from thirty fireheads. The winds are low, but the day is warm already and the forecast is awash with northwesterly winds, with a weak southwesterly change later, and lightning.

Six o'clock that night I'm lying in the Belubula River when the rain comes. I smell it before it hits. The wind has picked up and it smells, coming off the paddocks, like hay and steaming horses, and then I feel it on my shoulders like cold stones thrown hard.

I leave the water shivering, and night settles as we drive home through the paddocks and along the gravel road, and the rain persists, and we watch a storm congeal over the dividing range to the northeast.

The window of the room I sleep in downstairs opens that way, and Katoomba lies beyond, and I fall asleep watching sheet lightning flash over the blue range and hearing rain upon the roof. Wind rushes the house and shudders the wisteria and blows the curtain over my face. I wake somewhere near dawn to find the horizon still ablaze with electricity, and the roof above me still loud with falling water.

Fifty millimeters fall in the night, and in the morning the fires in the plateau are out, quenched by rain that no one saw coming.

LIFE, DEATH, AND EVERYTHING

Two weeks later I drove north through the Mount Yengo fire-grounds to the coast. The first people believe that at Mount Yengo, Baiami, the creator spirit, left the earth for the sky again, his crafting of country, his singing and delving of it done. *This is the place, then*, I thought, as I drove through the ashen ground where creation stopped, where the magic was enskied again. Around me on every side fire had burned the woods from the ground to the canopy. Some trees still stood, and they were blackened or stark white, and all of them were stripped of leaves, and some of them had lost their crowns, and the ground had been cleared of cover and lay there as black as a coal seam. Fire had opened the earth to the sky again, and it was everywhere.

Here in this ruin, creation had started again. I stopped the car near Darkey Creek—not, for sure, the name the first people first gave to the gully. The fire had raged hard here, and the only color left standing was black. Or so I thought, until I left the car and walked into the fireground and saw the pale-green heads of bracken ferns breaking through the fired earth at my feet. And then I saw beside me that blue sessile leaves already festooned the trunks of some of the blackened eucalypts, like prayer flags.

Fire does not kill what grows here—not all of it. It feeds the forest differently, creating where it destroys. This is the work of gods. What survives—and much here does; indeed, it waits for fire, storing seed in readiness for smoke and ash—what survives, begins again in clearer air, and so the thing goes on.

I spent a week at work in a house by the ocean, and at the end of the week M. telephoned. "We've lost the baby," she said, and she cried. And I cried later, too, driving home to her. Sometime in the middle of those days of fire, our child had simply stopped; that small god had gone. For two weeks after that, it rained all over the plateau. Even late in February, the sky still had nothing to say but cloud and falling water.

CHILDREN OF FIRE

More children came to us while we lived in the plateau. Two boys came sixteen months apart, the first of them a year and a half after the fires of the summer of 2001. But fire came back before the boys arrived. It's come again since, too, for the plateau has caught a drought it can't seem to shake; I think it's caught the future.

These are two of the oldest stories the plateau knows—two ends of the one story really—the burning and the beginning again.

GETTING IN FIRST

After five dry years, dust storms traveled over us through the middle of 2002, grasses cured and blanched, and on the ridgetops younger trees, which had known nothing like this in twenty-five years, could find no water to draw up from the ground, no memory to sustain them. They browned, these scribbly gums and banksias, and surrendered. Down in Jim's valley fissures opened in brittlejacks and gray box. Three dams on Jim's place that no one had ever seen empty dried and lay there bereft, and Jim got more work than he wanted mucking out neighbors' dams on the tractor, deepening them while they lay empty, making them ready for rain if it ever chose to come back. And from May onward he was backburning with the crew.

THE CANDLE

You start a fire in September to stop one in December, and having worked at that all day, what they were doing up there in the dark just off the Mill Creek Road was trying to go home. They were near the end of a hazard reduction burn they'd been working since eleven in the morning, and they'd been there three hours longer already than they'd planned to be because of a breakout mid-afternoon at the northern end of the burn.

John Underhill and Guy Tesoriero and Jim were a team, part of the Kanimbla Valley Rural Fire Service. Guy was the captain. He and Jim had been doing this for years, and John had been doing it long enough. The idea today had been to clear a break along the buttress that rises out of the Kanimbla behind "Rumbalara." They'd been shepherding the fire up the ridge to Hornes Point, and everything had gone pretty well, and the job was done, and around nine-thirty the three of them were leaving the fireground.

Jim was walking ahead, and he had just reached the Toyota when Tesoriero and Underhill behind him came across a big stringybark leaning over the raked trail. It was listing into "Rumbalara," and it was burning from the inside. The glow was faint and high on the tree, but Tesoriero saw it and radioed Jim.

"We got a candle," he said. "Can you come and deal with it?" Jim said a few things, including "Okay," and he pulled the chainsaw from the back of his truck and came back up the trail.

You can't leave a tree burning like that at the edge of the containment line, no matter how tired you are and ready to go home. A big tree can burn for days inside, and it'll start a fresh fire when the wind gets up or the tree falls down. Best thing to do is to bring it down and put it out.

That's what Jim set about. Like he'd done plenty of times before. Tesoriero didn't have to tell him what to do. Jim put the saw down at the foot of the tree and took a good look at the way it was leaning, and at the slope of the ground, and at the weight of the canopy. Fall downhill, for sure, Jim thought, and he choked the saw and pulled its cord a couple of times till the thing barked into life. There was enough light from the moon and from the burning tree itself to work by. So he began.

Jim knew there was a pipe at the center of the tree where the fire was hiding out. The tree was hollow, much less of a thing than it seemed, and more dangerous. You don't have to cut long to bring a hollow tree down; that's why you have to be careful. Jim took a three-inch wedge from the downhill side, and he walked around the tree and cut another wedge the same. And that cut began to open up; the tree began to surrender downhill. He put the saw down, still idling, in case, and he leant into the tree. Suddenly Underhill was there, pushing too, his hands above Jim's.

"Get the fuck outa there, John," Tesoriero yelled. "Leave it to Jim."

"It's okay. I'm fine," Underhill called back.

"Get the fuck out."

The captain went on bawling at Underhill, and Jim went on pushing, figuring, well here he is, we'll push the thing together. He bent and turned off the saw and he stood and leaned again into the tree with John, and straight away Jim heard the trunk crack where he'd cut it and he felt it give and start to fall, and then he felt it stop. He and Underhill backed off and then they pushed again. Jim heard something snap high up. He saw the near wedge closing, and he felt the tree coming back at them. It was coming fast.

He took off downhill but found himself alone. He called for John and whatever John may have tried to call back was lost in the explosion of sound as the tree hit the ground. Then—when the ground had stopped shuddering and the scalded leaves of the fallen tree had stopped rattling—there was nothing but Tesoriero's cursing and Jim's heart banging in his chest. He walked uphill frightened by what he would find, and he found it.

He saw in the moonlight how the tree's trunk had broken and fallen in two parts uphill, and how they lay side by side, smoking, and how John lay beneath one of them, cruciform.

GETTING ON WITH IT

A few things might have been different. The world might have been perfect, for instance. Absolutely no one was to blame, the coroner decided. Especially not Jim Commens, who knew exactly what he was doing and did it. But it's just a bugger of a thing to have happened, whichever way you look at it. Particularly if it's your head that ends up under the tree. Or if it's your hands that held the chainsaw.

John Underhill's life came to an end around ten at night on September 21, 2002. It was the Saturday that ended the week in which I'd sat with Jim and he'd given up most of his life to my tape-recorder. It happened the day after Jim came along and heard me read from the bones of this book at the Wentworth Falls School of Arts. The burning tree and the falling man haunted me for a long time, as though I'd somehow read them up that night.

But I don't think they haunted Jim. Or not for long. I saw a fair bit of Jim around this time, and I know he felt bad for his neighbor and for his neighbor's wife and young children. I know for a while he was in shock. But he wasn't falling apart, and he wasn't feeling guilty. What occurred was a natural disaster in which his hands happened to have been employed. He knew he had no power to do anything any better than he did. He knows how to fell a tree but not how to raise the dead.

ON EARTH AS IT IS IN HEAVEN

There's a deconsecrated church just off the Oberon Road at Lowther, a pious kind of shearing shed. It stands as straight, as square-shouldered and dour, as a Presbyterian elder. The red paint is peeling from its roof and rust is blotching its tin walls, but it's a handsome, practical building, still keeping the faith. The church sits in grasses, pale this October midday, cured by years of drought and the long months of winter.

A small community of the departed still surrounds the church, a hundred weathered headstones in the grass, up and down the hill. This is the Kanimbla, and men and women from most of the valley's families stand here in the sun to bury a neighbor.

A mound of sand and a white cross painted with his name and the day of his death mark the place where John Richard Underhill lies interred. A wreath of waratahs and eucalyptus leaves lies spent beside the mound.

In the cemetery at Lowther there's a girl killed in an accident at seventeen; there are two men who drowned before they got to twenty; there are quite a few who didn't make it much past sixty; and there are some who lived on into their eighties. And now there is John Underhill, who died at fifty-two stopping a fire. How long a life is long enough?

Looking northwest on a day that prophesies fire, driving home with the plateau's walls cobalt and amber beside me and high cloud stretched like scar tissue across the sky and the afternoon asleep in the paddocks, eternity itself seems too short a time to spend on such an earth.

IT'D MAKE YOU WEEP

The summer that began with John's death was as dry as any the plateau could remember. Had there been water to spare the trees would have wept. All the storms were dry storms, loud and purple with cloud, vivid with electricity but good for nothing more than a hundred plump drops. Now and then some virga teased the canopy.

It's troubling to see trees die—trees, those gifted survivors of weather. It's as though we know who's next. Some of the younger gums and sheoaks—the small heath trees and banksias—browned and gave up their ghosts and stood there. But the bigger trees managed; they shed leaves. They withdrew into themselves. And they wept flowers. The summer after John died, the eucalypts, each for its appointed week or two, flowered in cream or crimson more prolifically than anyone had ever known.

And later that summer, notwithstanding the flowers and the work John died performing, there were fires all over the place, though none of them reached the Kanimbla, and none found the Kedumba, which still aches to burn.

HOW THE PLATEAU REALLY GOES

The truth is no one can say clearly anymore what seasons the plateau knows, or what we ought to call them. But this much is clear—there aren't four seasons here. The plateau knows nothing of summer and autumn and winter and spring. The place runs by a regime of its own, and most of us latecomers have never really stopped and listened hard enough to make that system out. May got close; Jim's got closer. But it would take a couple of lifetimes to really get the hang of it. Maybe there are even seasonal decades, as some of the original people have said, cycles measured in years.

September will be warmer and drier than November, when there will be fogs and cold days. In 1968 it snowed in Katoomba on October 25; three days later it reached ninety degrees Fahrenheit, and a bushfire got going at Blackheath. Now and again, it has snowed at Christmas. The really hot days come in January and February and on into March. They come with storms, with rain and hail and lightning. March is a month of humid air that runs to rain and thickens to fog. You'll get two or three cool nights and days, just to let you know the year's moving on. More in April, but still not many.

April is the kindest month; the air dries and the sky stills. And the days stay warm till May. Early in May, the cold comes hard from the west, sometimes bearing snow. Then the sky will ease back a bit, as though it had just been rehearsing winter.

It won't be properly cold till June. July and early August it stays cool, though the temperature rarely falls below freezing at night. These middle months are the time of frost in the valleys, of ice in the waterfalls. Sometimes, as in 1967, you get some freezing rains in July. If the winds are right and the air is cold enough, some of the rain will turn to snow.

August belongs to the wind. When it blows from the south, it feels colder than the grave. Mostly it comes from the west, carrying the smell of the flat warm inland, bringing the start of the heat. August's winds are the heaviest of the year, and they will shake the house hard and go on shaking it, until you think the house will fall, but usually it doesn't. The plateau shakes itself warm in these winds, making ready for September.

September is the driest month. Mostly the winds will fall away, and the days will grow warm. But if things are dry, and the winds hang on from August, there will be fire. September and October are the real season of fire. Some years, that season may not kick in until December; other years it will return then. Christmas in the plateau may be black or it may be white, but mostly it will be mild and clear.

Every month carries traces of every other, you see. Each year the sky shatters all its moods and tosses them in the air. Because they fall on the same ground and because the same sky throws them, conditioned by synoptic habits of a lifetime, they fall—the dry, the wet, the fog, the fire, the snow, the languor, the gale, the storm, the frost, the heat, the cold—in a pattern fairly similar from one year to the next, but never quite the same. Some days in July grow as hot as summer, and I felt the truest winters in the early days of November, and the coldest winds in early May, followed fast by Indian summer.

We need some better names for the seasons on the plateau. We need names that tell the true stories about the yearly circle of the days. Names like *the month when, in the valleys in the mornings, the grasses are brittle with frost; the month of the heavy west wind; the month when fire will come if the winter has been hard and dry; the month when the rains fall longest and the birds flock ahead of the coming of the cold. Let's ask the trees; they seem to know. Let's ask the people in the Gully.*

LOVE IN A WARMING CLIMATE

But the way things are never did stand still. And who can say how they'll go from here? For they are changing, and they seem to be changing fast. Across the globe, the wet are getting wetter, and the dry are getting drier. And it's not going to stay as orderly as that.

Here in the plateau, warmer is what all the seasons have become, and drier. So much, then, for winter. In the seasons ahead, what will become of the forests and the swamps, the streams and the rainforests? They'll change, I suppose, like the weather, and some of them will pass away forever.

You could start feeling philosophical about that—change being the nature of nature—if it weren't for the fact that the way you'd lived your very own life, the oil you'd burned, the coal they'd dug for you, had reconfigured every season into a mongrel kind of summer. You could resign yourself to these eventualities if it weren't for the children, who have lives ahead of them to attempt under this harsh new sky.

VII

HOME

HIS FATHER'S ONLY HOPE, HIS MOTHER'S ONLY JOY

When Billy Maxwell was a young man, bushrangers called for tea. When a journalist from a Sydney paper came by in 1927 and asked him about it, Billy said he remembered one by the name of Walters, who'd come in and asked for dinner, and his mum had made it for him. Killed a chook they'd rather have kept, and plucked it and boiled it into a stew while the man lay back and slept with his hat over his face on the porch. Billy recalled other renegades from those days, when the Kedumba was the part of the ends of the earth you could reach most easily from the city. Wood, Russell, and Sullivan. These were men his father must have known. Perhaps well.

If you wanted to get lost, from the law or anyone else, this would have been the place to do it. But by 1927, those days were already over, at least as far as the law was concerned. There was a new century in full swing. By the twenties, the Blue Mountains was the place the well-to-do from Sydney drove to for the weekend. There was no place anymore for bushrangers, not even down in the Kedumba. The tourists could look down on the Maxwell farm from the lookouts in

Katoomba. Bushranging had reduced itself to ballad, and left the valley alone.

But on the parish map of 1927, the steep way out of the valley up the Kedumba Walls is still called *Bushrangers, or the Goat Track.*

And here's Les that same year, a boy of eleven, at his lessons. It's late January, and the day is hot. The weather is brilliant, and Les's mind is not on syntax or prosody or meter. It's out mustering in the far gullies of the plateau; it's stealing from the rich with dignity and nerve; it's defending freedom from the back of a horse. The boy himself, though, sits at the desk in the dark swelter of midday in the primitive two-room hut his father Billy had built himself seven years before the end of the last century, when he moved across the creek from his father to take up this new allotment. When, in 1924, having got himself a family, Billy put up the six-room slab hut, he left his first cabin standing beside it—for storage and he didn't know what else, but he knew it'd find a use. Sometimes they send the boys there to sit and practice remorse in the dark. Les sits there now. He copies into a Monster letter pad a poem and then another from the Blackfriars lesson book for this week. He's trying to write the verses neatly; he's caught up in their heroic narratives, and he's dying to get outside. His mother has made him stay here until he's formed up all the letters right, until he's got his spelling straight, until he's made the punctuation perfect. He's practicing calligraphy for a career at a desk he knows he'll never sit at; he's dreaming his own life to the doleful, noble metrics of the day.

He's plotting his escape in pencil and in someone else's rhyme:

It all very well to write riviews
carry umbrellas and keep dry shoes

say what every one else must say
wear what everyone else must wear
but to night I am sick of the whole affair
I sigh for the canter after the cattle
the crack of whips like shots in battle
the melo of horns and hoofs and head
that rings and wrangles and scatters and spreads
first to get the feel of the new nib

And now he's committing his life to freedom in his mother's
new red ink:

Tis of a Wild Colonial Boy Jack Doolan was his name
Of poor but honest parents he was born in castle-maine
He was his farthers only hope, his Mothers only joy,
And dearly did his parent, love the Wild Colonial Boy
Come all my hearties we'll roam the mountains high
Together we will plunder, together we will die.
We'll wander over valleys, and gallop over plains,
For we'll scorn to live in slavery, bound down with iron chains.
He was scarcely sixteen years of age when he left his fathers home,
And through Australian's sunny cline a bushranger did roam.
He robbed those wealthy squatters, their stock he did destroy
And a terror to Australia was the Wild Colonial Boy . . .

Cicadas drum. He hears the lazy lowing of the cows and his
mother's footsteps coming from the house. She'll find out all
his errors and make him come to lunch and set him back to
work again afterward, but it won't be long, he knows, before
he leaves his father's valley and breaks his mother's heart and
scorns forever after to work for wealthy squatters. He knows
that soon he'll leave his home and roam the mountains and

ride forever the plains, and he knows he'll bow to no one and wear nobody's chains. He's sure of it. And bugger the way it's spelled.

WHO'S BOSS

Les would be about sixty when this happens.

Down in his valley, Bill Cleary has a favorite bull. He bought it at some auction and brought it down the valley to breed from, God knows why. The animal's a giant black Angus that Cleary calls Ferdinand, and it knows how to do everything—like gore the hell out of any horse or man that gets too close—except service the heifers. It's one of those bulls that's just plain bad. It has murder in its eyes. Cleary won't hear a word against the bastard. But he's not the one who has to handle it. That would be Les.

So this one Saturday in July, Les has been fixing a fence the heifers got through into Dawson's paddock, and now, that done, he's bouncing home in the Ferguson across the paddock they got out of. Les stops the tractor and climbs down. He looks back to where he's mended the fence and up to where the walls are growing livid with the coming evening. He pans across to Dawson's Wold and thinks he should have another go at the road up there, before Bill bawls him out about it.

He turns back west to consider Solitary. He takes a few steps away from the tractor without realizing he's doing it, wondering which fold of shadow holds the three steers that bolted last week when he was mustering on the bike. He sees the furled bale of wire that fell off the tractor earlier and goes to fetch it, and it's about then that he hears the ground quaking behind him and remembers the bull. He forgets the wire and turns back for the tractor. Bloody Ferdinand is going for him like the hound of hell. He's lined the man up and waited till he thinks he's got him out in the open, and now he's coming at Les, head down, faster than he's ever moved in his life.

It's years since Les could make his back and legs do anything resembling a run. It's hard to say what his limping, skipping, loping haste resembles, and it doesn't look like it's going to get him out of trouble until he takes the last few meters at a dive and ends up under the Fergie, just before the bull reaches it, horns and head first, and nearly shunts the little tractor over. The bull is stunned at first. Then he's baffled. And then he's just pissed off. He lowers his head and blows dirt and fury under the tractor at Les, who's lying there hoping the little tractor's not been buggered, worried that the bull might yet lift it and find him lying here, breathless. The bull stamps and raises hell and tries from each side to shift the tractor.

Finally he nearly knocks himself out and decides he's had enough and backs off. Les crawls out from underneath, on the offside of the machine, and he pulls himself into the seat and tries the starter. The engine chugs; the bull turns and looks; the motor turns over; Les lets the clutch out and fair races the thing down through the brown grasses to the gate. He's halfway there when Ferdinand decides to have another shot at them, but he's lumbering now, half-hearted, over it. Which means Les has just enough time to open the gate, slip through it, latch the gate again and leave the Fergie to look after itself.

He walks home then along the darkening road. Norm is at the house. May is drinking tea with him in the kitchen. Les takes the shotgun from the porch. He tells them what's gone on.

"I'm going to teach that bastard a lesson he might remember for a while," he says and leaves. Norm goes after him, curious. Les says nothing. What Norm's curious about is what Les is going to do with the gun. The one thing he can't afford to do is kill the bull. Bill would sack him outright.

In the paddock, Les walks as close to the grazing bull as he dares—which is about twenty feet. He's got the gun; it encourages more intimacy than he'd feel like otherwise. Norm is standing at the gate, still curious. The animal lifts his great stupid head and looks at the man, whom now he doesn't seem to remember. Les raises the rifle and seems to fire right at Ferdinand, but he's shooting across his bows. He's shooting close enough to pepper his rump with shot, close enough to graze him, to cause him pain, but not close enough to kill him. It's a fine line, particularly in the gloom, but Les is still so mad he's almost past caring too badly if he finds it. The shot draws blood. Norm hears the animal bellow. He sees pieces of the bull's back fly; he sees blood stream out of his hindquarters; he watches the bull run in circles trying to bite his wounds or kill what's wounded him or both at once.

"That should teach you who's in charge here, you mongrel," Les booms slowly.

Walking back, Les says, "Bastard'll live, which is more than he deserves. And he'll remember who did that to him. Won't remember why, but he will remember who."

Next time Bill comes down, he asks Les what had happened to Ferdinand's back. "Must've had a fight with a fence," Les says. Bill doesn't believe him, but he doesn't know what to accuse Les of, except neglect, his usual charge. "You'd better take care of him, Maxwell. He's worth a whole lot more to me than you are."

Les nods. Thinking, . . . *these wealthy squatters, their stock he did destroy . . .*

WHAT YOU'VE GOT TILL IT'S GONE

Les was the valley's prodigal son. He was the one she loved best, the son who left for the world and who returned.

Jimmy was the brother who felt he'd been robbed. The son who stayed and felt he'd lost.

Jimmy, you suspect, coveted the place more than Les did and loved it less. His was a more grasping and anxious, a more calculated love than Les's, whose love was nonchalant.

Les was not, like his father, a man with a calling for staying put and building the future. He was not, like his brother, a man with an eye for the main chance. He was a man—like the valley, like the whole plateau—who surrendered. So, when he left, and again when Jimmy sold it to the Clearys, Les let the valley go, and he got on with being wherever he was, doing whatever he was doing, which was mostly digging holes and making roads and drinking at night with May, or drinking at night by himself.

While Jimmy, who'd wanted the valley and gotten the valley and given the valley away, spent the next ten years realizing every day how much he'd lost and how much he wanted it back.

When the boys' mother died in January 1964, Jimmy picked a fight with Les. Within days, Jimmy, who was living back in Camden at the time, sold all his mother's furniture, everything he could get a dollar for and pocketed the proceeds. Les paid for the funeral, and when he suggested they put up a headstone for Olive in the Camden Cemetery, Jimmy said Les could bloody well pay for it since Les hadn't helped sort out the furniture. Jimmy never quite got around to offering Les anything for the funeral, and later he accused Les of not wanting any kind of memorial for their mother at all. It's the way these things sometimes play in families; grief can bring out the worst in us, for a while.

In his whole life, Les wrote just five times in a diary—each time it was May's. Four of those times happened in early 1964. Les's handwriting is like a child's. A man grown unused to a pen.

Monday 13. MUM Died.

Tuesday 14. Mum buried.
Tuesday 21. May operated on.
Friday 24. Jim sold furniture.

A tough couple of weeks. And Les got about as mad as he ever got over this business with Jim and the funeral and the furniture.

One day soon after, wrote May in her diary, Les bumped into his brother in Orange, and Jim just grunted at him. Les phoned his brother later and tried to reason with him. They fought, and Les hung up. He didn't say anything harsher than "mean old bugger," and "miserable bastard," because he usually didn't like to curse with May about. And she was about, fresh back from the city where she'd had some cancer scraped out of her stomach.

For a year, lawyers' stilted letters changed hands, and the men stopped talking with each other at all.

And then Jimmy's solicitors write to Les's one last time, making the same tired allegations on Jimmy's behalf, and a concession. Notwithstanding, the lawyers write, that Les had walked off with half his mother's estate, "our client is not prepared to bandy about the good name of his Mother in Court proceedings over her funeral costs and, for this reason, is prepared to withdraw his action and to bear the costs of the funeral and headstone himself."

It's May 21, 1965. Les and May have just moved to the Kedumba for keeps.

May writes in her diary: JIM CALLED CASE OFF. V DAY.

LEGENDS OF THE FALL

There's a bird on the Kedumba Walls.

Les had been considering that bird all his life. He could not look up there without his eyes making out the dark form of that emu splayed across the rock. He knew a story or two about the emu, and he had stories, too, for the other shapes he could read across the scarp. A bull and a heifer mating, was one. A wombat rooting. He pointed them out to Jim Commens late some afternoons after mustering, when the light was best, low from out of the west, when all Jim could think of was getting cleaned up and downing a beer. And Jim couldn't make out any of them, or care much less. But he could see the emu. You can still see it if you know what to look for, from the lookouts along the Prince Henry Track. It's not the bird it once was. But there it stays, a dark and shabby ghost petrified.

By the time Les was showing it to Jim in the early eighties it had lost a big piece of its neck.

Les remembered the night it fell. It woke him from his sleep in the valley, a crack like a stockwhip, then a muffled avalanche and a snapping of trees. This was the late sixties. I don't know if Les ever thought about it along these lines, but think of the symbolism of that fallen neck. What an image of how things fail, in the end—the escarpment, in particular. How the past can fall silent. Think of being there to hear a story as old as the dreamtime and a rock form old enough to have given birth to that dreaming, stop. Without a neck, how can a bird breathe and feed and carry on? How can it sing?

The story of the emu Les recalled was the same one the settlers knew from the Gundungurra men who were still about the Valley, whom they had harried from their homes in the first generation of white settlement. Les got the story from his own father, who had it from his father William, who had it from the black men he worked, mustering and droving cattle and sheep in the Burragorang. It's a story one of those Gundungurra men, old man Shepherd, told a journalist in the fifties.

Back in the plateau's dreaming, the spirits, good and evil,

took a close interest in the places of the earth and the people who lived in them. Migge, the Great Spirit, had gone into semi-retirement among the clouds; and the Dark Ones, evil spirits determined to embarrass, even defeat, the Great Spirit, hung out in certain pools. As part of an endless war with Migge, the Dark Ones, goaded by their medicine man Warrawee, hit upon the idea of conjuring a giant emu from clay, from the oil of lizard, the hair of wallaby, and the wax of the native bee. They made it big enough to fill the Kanimbla Valley from top to bottom. That's a big bird. It was meant as a gesture of the Dark Ones' power. It was meant to humiliate Migge right here in this valley he loved best.

At first their emu lay flat on the ground. But the Dark Ones coaxed their Frankenstein to life with the scent of local flowers like the boronia, with the fruits of others, like the native cherry and the lillypilly, and with the roots of the bracken ferns. And then, at the rise of the new moon, the Dark Ones turned their emu around and had him drink the light of that crescent moon. And with that, it stood and ran, and for weeks it laid the Kanimbla low. It felled the forests beneath its clawed feet. It took the life of one of the young women of the Kanimbla tribe and got a taste for blood. It savaged the locals. With its bill it carved new gullies and canyons in the plateau. It cried so loudly that it shook great slabs of the escarpment loose and sent them crashing into the valleys.

The Kanimblans tried to fight the bird, but it crashed their barriers and swatted their spears. Their distress was so great in the end it reached the ears of Migge, and he came and confronted the bird. It rushed him, but he took its beak in his hands, and he lifted the bird and he swung it over his head, and it flew, high enough to part the clouds, over Narrowneck, over Solitary, over the Kedumba Creek and hard against the

Kedumba Walls. Its landing shook the plateau. It reduced the bird to two dimensions; it spread the bird against the orange and purple stone, a darker shadow of its former self. In this way, the shaping of two valleys was advanced; a round of the endless fight between creation and destruction was won by the good guys, but not before the plateau was a little further collapsed; and a lesson was written upon the scarp.

One September I was down in the Kedumba with Jim Commens, and he showed me the emu. Standing in the paddock south of Waterfall Creek, looking east to the walls in the orange light, I could see how this wounded, once malevolent, shadowy thing is the valley's only ornament. It may also be its god, its disgruntled, failed demon. Its angel.

What the emu says, though its neck is broken, is that things fall apart, and that's why the face of the earth, like the face of your child or the woman you love, or the late sun on the Kedumba Walls, is beautiful. It is ephemeral—like the sunset, like the baby's skin, like the woman's breast, like the look in her eye. All this will pass; and we know it, and still we love it. It is part—the sad and unfailing part—of why we love. A full half of our love is grief.

ANTIPODES

The sky had fallen—pieces of it. It was early morning, and down below the escarpment, cloud sat like snowdrift, and it had the whole valley covered.

On cold, clear nights like the one that had just ended, the valley surrenders its warmth fast, and the air inside the valley cools more rapidly than the air above it, and it finds itself stuck. Moisture—the perspiration of the soil, the transpiration of grasses, the breathing of the streams—saturates the cold incarcerated air and gives it form and turns it white. And so in the morning, the valley has pulled down the sky and trapped it and transfigured it as cloud.

Down where the Kedumba should have been, five white cockatoos flew up out of the cloud and perched in the crown of a eucalypt on the scarp. The birds stayed uncommonly silent; cloud insists on silence. They sat above the cloud, three hundred meters below me, and they waited for the sky to work out which way was up. The world was upside down.

But it wasn't the sky that had fallen; it was the valley trying to leave. And the sky was having none of it. High above, a sheet of altocumulus flowed in from the south. It too would pass, and the day would slowly warm, and by midday the night prayers of the Kedumba would have dissolved the sky's resistance; they would have been accepted and forgotten. The valley would be the valley again, and the air would all be blue from top to bottom.

A STRING OF PEARLS

The morning was cool, and mist drowned the valley. It was a Friday in early November. May was in the house smoking a cigarette at the kitchen table. She smoked through a filter, and it gave her a demimonde air. It wasn't the look you'd have expected this practical woman to affect, her hair pulled back roughly, a red cardigan buttoned over her round breast and glasses on her nose. But May had her aspirations. And one of them was staying alive; she had convinced herself the filter would keep her lungs from harm.

Nearing one o'clock, she sat knitting Les a pullover and thinking about fixing some lunch, and she had the radio on. 2KA. She was listening harder than usual because they were running a competition, sponsored by the local jewelers, and the prize was a string of pearls. Neither of her husbands had ever given her pearls, and she fancied some. Sometime this hour, the announcer had said at noon, they'd be playing the song of the day. And when they'd played it, there'd be a question. The first caller to ring in with the correct answer got the pearls.

She knows she doesn't have much chance, but she's nothing better to do, no place other than this she can be, so she's been listening to all the songs this hour, noting them down just in case. This one's by Doris Day. May sings a bar here and another there. She mumbles some approximation of the words. Her voice is a high harsh grating, and she doesn't come near the tune, not that she knows it. When the song ends, there's an ad for the jewelers, which she hardly notices. Then the announcer says that if listeners had been tuned in just before the advertisement they would have heard the song of the day. "What we want to know is who was singing it. Dial in now. First correct caller wins the pearls."

May staunches her smoke in the ashtray on the kitchen table and bounces to the phone in the hall and dials the number.

"I'm ringing about the song of the day," she tells the woman who answers. It's the producer or someone.

"So who do you think that was singing 'By the Light of the Silvery Moon'?"

"Doris Day," says May.

The pearls came a week later. She wore them every time she dressed up. It was the one thing she ever won, she'd tell anyone who noticed them. "Pays to listen," she would say.

FIRE AND RAIN

1969 in the valley was a cantillation of rain and fire, of flood and burning. Not the kind of fire that almost burned the plateau to the ground in 1968; 1969 was burned by hand, set on fire in pieces by Les and the Waterboard men, whenever the rain let up.

They torched the fringes of the valley and all along the Kedumba to the dam, much as the people they had displaced used to torch it—fires lit to keep fires out.

The rain in 1969 was the plateau's idea of a joke, an overcompensation for fires that savaged the forests and the people of the sandstone country the year before. There were floods in February and August and November and December. Each time, the creeks in the valley rose and rose and cruelled their banks. Each time, the crossings over the Kedumba and the Waterfall washed out and Les had to make them good again. And each time, another part of the road slipped off the mountain, and Les took the machines up there to put it back again. The road was a horse that was never quite tame. The scarp kept trying to efface Les's work, but he wouldn't be effaced.

In August, Les nearly lost the 'dozer in a dam he was digging west of Kedumba Creek. The D4 slipped in the mud the last week's rains had made of the week before's work. And three days before Christmas, after a humid day that reached 93 degrees, 100 points of rain fell in three-quarters of an hour in the afternoon, and Kedumba Creek was torn from its bed, and the road came down the mountain again. Les spent December 23 and 24 putting the river and the mountain back together again, and on Christmas Day, in the sun and silence—for the boys were with their families and weren't coming down till New Year—they sat and ate May's cake and got drunk.

They had something to celebrate. May had lasted another year. Back in June, she was in hospital in the city. She arrived in terrible storms. Her first night a woman died in the ward, and two nights later a baby was stillborn. All day and night the noise of traffic came up from Missenden Road, and May couldn't sleep. She put these events in her diary like omens. Les and Norm called to see her on the Saturday. On the Tuesday following, the doctors took out a piece of her liver and some marrow from her breastbone. It hurt like hell, she wrote. And it was raining again, in the city and all over the plateau.

Back in the valley in July, there were gales, fogs that lasted till afternoon, big frosts, and more rain. May learned to eat again. Her bowel was better, but now the gout was bad. Sometimes she got the fidgets in her legs. The sun came and went. And there were enough clear dry days for Les to burn the edges of the valley.

Sunday, August 3, for instance, Les burned the hill, that breast, west of Kedumba Creek, and he barely got the burn reined in before a gale ripped down off the scarp late in the day. Friday, August 8, he was burning again, this time among the trees on the valley's eastern selvage, burning the trees up to the Kedumba Walls. This time the wind came early and fanned his tidy burn into a conflagration and blackened the forest and the face of the scarp right at the emu's feet.

On August 15, five inches of snow fell on the plateau. On August 16, Les was at the chiropractor in Kedumba. Not one thing—not fire, not flood, not snow, not heavy morning frost, not broken drive arms, not a half-broken back—stopped the man husbanding the valley.

Around ten on Saturday, August 30, May heard showers fall again on the metal roof at the end of a warm day. Listening to the night, she let her left hand and the cigarette it held drop to the table where she had been writing in a small green diary, and she burned a neat crescent in the trim-edge of the page. It looks like the kind of burn a child makes on a map she's drawn, trying to age it fast, as though pirates had drawn it a hundred years ago. And it runs, this fired edge, this cancer, this sudden aging, through two weeks of wind and showers and a late fall of snow. Then the year gets back to business. One weekend Norm shoots a dingo and Les shoots a wild dog at the crossing. Then Cleary is hauling white gums out. Les is fencing and cutting lucerne and firing the bush till smoke fills the valley, and he's sinking dams and robbing the bees' hives.

SNAKE OIL

Snake sticks and rifles were how you dealt with snakes in the valley. You kept your distance; you blasted the hell out of any that came too close. You practiced respect and you practiced your aim. Too little of either, and you might easily die. May took out as many snakes as anyone else. Along with the crows, they were at the top of her list. And she didn't often miss.

I notice, though, that Les and May and Norm and the rest of them were just as happy to shoot the red-belly blacks as the browns. Now, the brown snake could kill you many times over with a single bite. And it will go after you if you give it half an excuse.

A red-belly black can kill you, too. But it won't come looking for you, and when it runs, if snakes can be said to run, it'll be the other way. And here's a thing Les didn't seem to know, a thing I've heard snake people say: the red-bellies feed on the browns. They eat their young; they even eat the grown ones sometimes, when there's nothing much else to eat. Part of the valley's poetic justice—lost on the men and women with the guns, whose justice was rougher and faster and more prosaic—was this: The meeker snake preys, sometimes, upon the meaner. Les and May should have been cultivating the red-bellies, not blowing them away. Killing red-bellies, they cultivated the browns.

An ecologist I know tells me that the idea that the black snakes predate the browns is pretty much a new-age old wives' tale. The red-bellies eat the odd brown, apparently, but they don't make a habit of it, and they don't take enough to make a difference. Probably that's what Les would've reckoned as well. And he wasn't going to get close enough to run any kind of experiment. The best snake was a dead snake, black or brown.

Black or brown, the valley's theirs again now. And all the men with sticks and guns have gone.

ONE MORNING

There was a heavy wind last night. I don't believe night ever pressed down harder on the plateau.

When the west wind swarms like this, which it does quite often through the middle of the year, saving always its worst violence for the darkness, I'm reminded that the ridge belongs, really, to heathplants and low rangy gums, those shepherds of the wind. The ridge belongs to the sky, which floods it tonight. The ridge can't ever belong to us; we can't hope to stay.

Older people, wiser than me, took, in the cold months, to the valleys. That'll work for you if your house is not a weatherboard cottage, set upon brick footings concreted into sandstone stained with the blood of old iron. So you stay, for now. You hold on tight and try to dream. And all night long the wind tells you to go.

But in the morning we're still here, and it's the wind that's gone. Turning from Merriwa onto Cliff Drive, coming back from town, I see that the valley is still here, too. There's a rainbow bridging Solitary and dying in the Kedumba, like a dream of water too beautiful to last. It ends in the old Maxwell place, the only bit of pasture in that wilderness of trees. There's a cold sunlight upon the Kedumba Walls, and the valley is steeping itself in an amber light that is half the work of the morning and half the work of the stone. So there's sunshine below, the color of memory, and there's a rainbow broken in it, rehearsing in its pieces all the colors the universe knows.

Up here, though, I'm driving home in straight blue, under the shadow of coming cloud.

A fine sleet is swimming up from the south in cold slow currents of air. Already the sky has swallowed half the mountain. Now it's taking its rainbow back. As if to say, there's no way out. I can feel the temperature dropping and the wind pulling itself together again. Later in the day, there will be snow at Blackheath and a fire in the grate here at Katoomba.

It's hard to hold on to the plateau. For Les Maxwell hanging on was a calling; I'm just here to witness. Les had to fashion a life out of all this wind, out of all this rock, out of all this vivid and miserable soil, out of all this light and relentless beauty. But a morning like this—this is why and this is how you stay. For as long as it takes. For as long as it lets you. You stay like this morning stays, in many minds at once.

A CAREER IN SMOKE

Jim never saw Les smoking. Not like his own dad, who never didn't have a cigarette hanging off his bottom lip, as he swung an axe or sat a horse or yelled at the boys to behave. "Musta made everythin' a whole lot more difficult, you'da thought," Jim says, "but it never seemed ta bother Dad." No one ever thought about not smoking in those days. May smoked her whole life, cigarettes in a filter. In the end it's about all she did. And Les smoked, too. Most of his life he never had a pipe out of his mouth. And he carried on after May died.

But by the time Jim met Les, the old man wasn't smoking anymore. When I showed Jim a photograph of Les as a younger man, a smoke hanging off his lip, sitting the mail horse, Jim saw a man he'd never known.

Down in the crook of the arm of the Waterfall that night in 2003, Norm told us what happened.

"One morning, Les starts coughing and hacking, and he carried on until I thought he'd bring up pieces of his lungs. He could hardly breathe. We were leaning over the veranda, looking through Mum's climbing roses. Great circle of red ones that lived on long after she'd gone, not that Les ever did anything to help them along. So I stood and watched him, coughing his life out. Finally he stops, gets his breath back, and starts to fill his pipe again. Dutch Amphora sweet tobacco.

"So I say to him, 'You enjoy that, Les?'

"'What do you mean, boy?'

"'Smoking that stuff. Looks like fun. I thought we'd lost you that time.'

"'Scared the shit out a me, too, boy.'

"'So why don't you stop?'

"Then he looks at me straight for a bit, and he says, 'All right, boy. I will.'

"And he took his pipe and the bag of tobacco, walked inside and dropped them in the kitchen bin. Never smoked again."

Actually, Les had tried to give up the smokes at least once before, in 1967. May noted it in her diary: Sunday, September 3. He was crook for a week after that. She noted that, too. And by October, he was back on the smokes, back to health and back to work.

But he did make the second retirement stick. It's easier when you don't have to sit there, not smoking, and watch your dear one smoke. So a man smokes all of his life, and one day in his late sixties he stops, to dedicate himself to drinking and watching the valley erode.

WHAT LOVE LEAVES BEHIND

I suppose Les loved the Kedumba the way a man loves his wife, the way a blackfish loves its river. He loved it, but he didn't spend too much time liking it. Les was in the valley the same way the weather was. He was never in love with it; he was just in it. The way the light is in the air. And then it's not.

He loved it, I'd guess, as he loved May—without a lot of effort. He made her miserable by leaving her too much alone; he wore her out, not that he really meant to. In the valley he shot more snakes and dogs, more parrots and wallabies and wild horses, he dug more dams and made more roads and cut more timber and blew up more old huts than was strictly necessary. He reshaped the ground and altered the grasses and put out more superphosphate than the valley would have liked. He diminished the valley he loved. He weathered it, and he weathered May, and he weathered himself in the process.

Don't we hurt most those we love best? Isn't it those with whom we live who are most touched by us—aged and damaged, improved and transformed by us? Each of us erodes and is eroded by what we love. We are made into what we become by what we lose of ourselves in intimacy.

Who we are in the end is what love leaves behind.

THE END OF MAY AND INTO JUNE

All her life May was plump. She knew how to cook and she knew how to eat. She was only a bit over five feet tall, bosomy and round.

But ill-health thinned her in the final couple of years. She gave up. The pale joy of life abandoned her and left her small. She got tired of never getting better; she got tired of getting tired. She'd known for a long time that happiness was not all it was said to be; now she just gave up on it completely. There was too much room for sadness in what she had thought of as a happy life; there was too much struggle; there was too much memory. And in that valley there was too much time and space altogether.

The problem was that the valley needed her for nothing. It went on and on without her. And she was a woman who needed to be needed, even if she couldn't be happy. Especially if she couldn't be happy. It's hard for anyone, and it was plain impossible for May, to cope with being so exquisitely unnecessary.

For years, but with gathering speed through the 1970s, illness ate away at her faster than she could replenish herself from her usual sources—Les, the bottle, the garden, her children, her pets, her cigarettes, her keeping note of things. She got every complaint it was possible to get and still go on breathing.

In the end she just stopped eating. She fed Les, and the others when they called, as heartily as ever. But all she had, herself, were cigarettes and sherry. It wasn't enough. She hollowed out; she collapsed in on herself.

1977. The year goes on as ever in her diary. It begins with heat and a train wreck in Granville—she records the carnage as though it were rainfall: 82 bodies, so far, January 19. Les is watering corn all January. Then it's raining all February, and Les is grading and carting gravel. He's cutting and baling and hauling lucerne in the rain; he's mustering steers. In early March, May falls answering the phone. It was Bill, she notes, as if to say, "who caused it." She spends two weeks in hospital, during which her diary has nothing to add. She comes home, but her writing is never the same. It peters. And May keeps falling. In the end she doesn't know how to get up again.

Her entries become a scribbled and discontinuous testament.

Sunday, April 17. Very cold / morning, nice & sunny / later. Les
    broght stears / in for Rege Bond.
Friday, April 22. We went / out

Sunday, May 1. Norm & family / came down. / Bondie had
    accident / with stears on Mtn.
Friday, May 6. I went to / Dr Day.
Monday, May 9. I fell down / back stairs.
Tuesday, May 10. My back / very sore.
Friday, May 13. We went / out nice day.
Saturday, May 14. Rain all / day & night /, back still crook.
Wednesday, May 18. Rain
Thursday, May 19. 1160 pts. Fine in / the morning.
Saturday, May 21. I went Dr.
Sunday, May 22. Nice day. / Cold night.
Monday, May 30. Les slashing / May bush.
Tuesday, May 31. Les carted / rubble from W Falls Crk to fix
    causeway.
Wednesday, June 1. Slashing
Saturday, June 4. Cold. Les / put fence across Kedumba / Creek. I
    had bad / fall at night.
Sunday, June 5. Cold night. Cloudy.
Monday, June 6. Bad fall in Hall.
Tuesday, June 7. 75 pts, fog.
Wednesday, June 8. Very cold. / I still can't walk.
Thursday, June 9. Still very / cold. Still can't walk.

After that, the days turn white. May goes to hospital at
Katoomba. *Anemia*, they write on the certificate. But that's just
to give a medical name to starvation and surrender.
On Thursday June 30 there's another entry in May's diary:

May passed / away. 1977.

Les writes that. The letters are large and ruinous. They
stagger like drunks, and Les pushes the ballpoint so hard into

the page May is still passing in the middle of August.

THE REAL WORLD

The night of the day May dies, after he shuts her diary, Les picks up the phone and calls Norm. It's four hours since he watched May stop breathing. He's left her body for the nurses and the undertakers to think about, and driven home to the valley. And he's done nothing since but sit here on the veranda trying to work out who he is now and how the valley and his life within it can go on now. By the time the light has left the Kedumba Walls and the house has fallen dark behind him, he's drunk a flagon of sherry. It's helped him see that life can't continue, that the sun will never rise again. But he's still having trouble getting used to the idea. So he calls Norm. It's nearly midnight. He should have called him long before.

"Your mother's gone," he says, his voice a ruin. "She's gone, and I think I'd better go too."

"Hang on there, Les," says Norm, waking up now. "Just stay right there and wait for me. I'm coming up."

His mother's dead. It registers. But she's been gone—and Norm's been saying goodbye to her—for weeks already. He gathers a few supplies from the fridge—fresh meat, fruit, bread—and he goes out the backdoor to the Rover. He can get on with missing her tomorrow.

It's an hour's drive from Blacktown to Wentworth Falls, and another half-hour down the Kedumba Drive to Les's. Norm makes the whole trip in an hour. He knows the corners pretty well, but he's driving too fast, and he knows that too. He makes it, though, and the house is dark when he pulls in. Les hasn't lit the lamp. He hasn't made a fire in the stove.

"Ya all right, Les?" Norm calls out, and he steps down onto

the gravel, into the cold night and the dead quiet. "Ya there, Les? It's Norm." His words become smoke in the night. Then they become silence. He feels his way up the steps. Les isn't sitting on the balcony. Norm opens the door and goes in. The boards creak under him. In the hall, he feels the rifles where they always stand. He makes out in the blackness the blacker shape of Les slumped on the kitchen table. "Les?" he says.

"I'm still 'ere, boy," comes Les's muffled voice from the table. "Decided ta wait." He lifts his head. He shifts the arm on which he's been cradling it, trying to forget, trying to sleep but not to dream, and he knocks his glass to the floor. He reaches for it and nearly falls, and Norm holds him steady by the shoulder and says, "I'll get it, Les. And I'll get ya to bed."

"She's gone, boy," says Les, trying to sit up in the chair.

"I know. But it's as cold as buggery in here, Les. Let's get ya to bed."

"Think I'll follow her, boy," says Les.

"Bed's about as far as you're gonna manage, tonight."

Norm gets Les into the bedroom and onto the bed. He pulls the blankets over his stepfather and leaves him.

He clears a space in the fridge among the leftovers, and sets his supplies there. He screws the lid on the sherry flagon and puts it on a shelf. He washes Les's glass and sets that in the basket to drain. He puts himself to bed on the couch in the front room. And he lies there for hours, waiting for the rest of him to arrive down the mountain, trying to remember his mother in better days, planning the funeral already, worrying about how Les will get on now. Around two-thirty, he hears Les snoring. Only then does Norm fall asleep.

Next thing, he hears his mother's voice in the bedroom. His heart thumps in his chest, but he finds he can't move. His mother is in the next room talking to Les. He can't make out what she's saying, but it's her voice, and she's upset. She's not going quietly.

Norm hears Les mumbling in reply. His mother speaks again. Then he hears Les say something, firmer now and louder: "It's time to go now, love . . . We'll be right . . . You have to leave us now . . . Go on, now, love . . ."

May says something meekly. There's silence. Then Norm hears the sound of feet in slippers shuffling, as May shuffled, out of the bedroom and into the kitchen. Her steps slow and stop, and then he hears the sound of glass on glass. Silence. And then the sound of glass on metal. Still he can't move. This is not happening. This is not something that can. But he turns his head then and sees a form like a tightly wound spider's web, dully lit, making its way toward the door and away. He hears and sees nothing after that. Before long, he hears Les snoring again.

Norm doesn't sleep again. Well before dawn Les gets up and goes out. Norm is up and sitting in the kitchen when Les returns. The Vegemite jar his mother used to drink from is sitting in the sink, where it had not been last night.

"Did I hear you talking in the night, Les?" he asks.

"Your mother come back, boy. She didn't want ta go. She's worried about me, and about you, boy. But I told her she had ta go on to the other place now. This is not the place for her anymore."

Norm is silent. Les says all this as though he's explaining how the heifers got out a busted gate in the night and how he's just been and put them back.

It strikes Norm then that Les's world contains mysteries Norm will never plumb. It strikes him suddenly that his own ideas of how the real world works—the laws of physics, the principles of engineering, the rules of business and reason—have left out a whole order of knowledge, a whole other world, that Les knows as well as his own name. It strikes Norm that the natural history of this man and his valley includes, for instance, ghosts. Last night proves to Norm what he has often suspected—the valley plays at many frequencies, and most of them are lost on him.

The whole place is an endless improvisation upon a complex chord, whose structure only the locals can play. They are its various notes; they know their parts, and off they go. Among the voices, apparently, are the newly dead. But it's not for them to linger. Les knows that; he knows the score. His part was to help May go; hers was to help him stay.

Norm says "So, what about you, Les? What are you goin' to do now?"

"She told me she'd wait till me time comes."

"That'll be a while yet," says Norm.

"We'll just have to see, boy. We'll just have to see. But when the time comes, bury me with your mother. Promise me."

"We'll have to get her buried first, Les. But I'll put you with her if you like. Later, I mean."

Les nods and goes outside to get about another day. Norm uses the phone to let them know at work that he won't be coming in. It's a Friday.

That night Norm cooks them some steak he's brought and some potato. He trims the wick on the oil lamp and lights it. He makes a fire in the stove. Over dinner, Les says, "We'll be hearing the stone-curlews tonight."

"There haven't been stone-curlews here in ages, Les."

"It's ages since someone died."

And that night, as Norm lies and tries to sleep, he hears the keening of these big, sad, brown-striped, ground-dwelling, doe-eyed birds come across the paddocks from some other world. And after they stop, the night changes key, and he sleeps.

TAKING CARE

Once May was gone, it was Norm who took care of Les. Every couple of months, for instance, he'd cut his stepfather's hair the best he could. Now and then, Les would hack at it himself with some of May's old scissors. Once Les took a piece out of his ear, though he didn't seem to have noticed.

Les was going to seed.

Weekends, anyway, and probably most weekdays, he'd start drinking sweet sherry out of a tall glass about nine in the morning, after he'd done a few hours' work on whatever it was that was broken or needed doing, or just walking around. He took water with the liquor to make it a long drink. And he drank until the day ended, sitting on the veranda or at the kitchen table. Sometimes he lit the lamp; mostly he just let it grow dark. In winter, he'd have a fire burning in the stove. He kept its door ajar to make the feeding easier, and the light it threw was all that lit his journeys from table to kettle to sink, down the steps to take a piss, if he remembered to get up for that at all, and finally to sleep.

DANCES WITH BARBED WIRE

One time, late morning, sometime in September, and the sun mild on everything, Terry from the Catchment Authority is driving the Toyota up the valley. This would be late in the eighties. It won't be long before the Authority wants Les and all the cattle out and the gate locked. But the guys on the ground know Les and worry about him. Whoever's driving past, back from the Big Water, looks in on Les. This day it's Terry. He turns off Kedumba Valley Drive at William Maxwell's grave and drives down to the caretaker's house. He pulls up, cuts the motor, sees Les nowhere, takes the three steps to the door, and knocks. There's nothing. He knocks again and calls out. Then he hears something from the back of the house. He hears something moaning, softly. He calls out that it's him and is everything all right. He lets himself in and walks through the kitchen to the back bedroom, where Les is lying on the bed; he's been bleeding from wounds about his shins and arms and hands. The blood is dark. His clothes are torn. Les is barely conscious.

But he wakes when Terry comes in. He says he'll be all right in a bit. Terry finds some disinfectant and things in the bathroom. He boils some water and tidies Les up a bit.

Then Les tells Terry he got into a bit of a row with some barbed wire down by the shed, but he doesn't say he went out to take a piss at night and he lost his bearings and ended up in the rolls of fencing wire down near the sheds, and couldn't get out. He must have passed out and lain there for hours. It was light when he came to, and mid-morning when he managed to get himself free. And thinking about it now, that must have been yesterday. He was buggered when he made it to the house. All he could manage was to find the bed and drop himself into it.

Terry gets him a cup of tea and leaves him. When the man is gone, Les pours himself a long sherry and water. What he really needs.

BONES

At the top of Bodington Hill there's a cemetery. Some places on the ridge, where the heath has been cleared but you can't see the valleys, feel unbearably bleak, and the cemetery is one of them. Here you'll find the grave where whatever remains of May and Les Maxwell lies. Here they are eroding together, bones becoming fragments becoming plateau again.

It's not much of a grave; it's not much of a cemetery. It's not in the valley, where they belong—where Les belongs, anyway. But here they are, together. And down below, the valley is returning slowly to forest. It is getting on with forgetting all about this man, in whom it lived for eighty-odd years, and this woman who was for a time its grudging witness.

THE IDEA OF GREEN

Sheoaks make love with the wind. They have their reasons. It's the wind that carries their pollens. Without the wind, the trees'd be barren. You might love the wind, too, if it helped you make your children.

The sheoaks are male and female. A few of them even manage to be both. Come when the males—which should be "heoaks," I guess—are in their rut, and you'll know which ones are which. The males will look rusted at the tips of what they like to think of as their leaves. Come when the wind is high and you may see one half of the love it makes with these trees. The other half is the song the females sing to call the pollens down out of the lusty air.

Up on the ridges, I lived among the black sheoaks. Plenty of wind to work with here. There's a bird, the glossy black cockatoo, that eats nothing but the seeds of these trees. In the heathland, you'll find the dwarf sheoak nana, which has learned two tricks that work in the dry exposed ridges; these sheoaks lie low, and they know how to regenerate after fire. And down in the valleys are the riveroaks, the grandest of all the fifty-six casuarinas.

Sheoaks colonize broken ground; they get started early after fire or flood or blowdown. But in the succession planning of the forests, they are not meant to last. Maybe that's why they give themselves so freely to the wind. The riveroaks make it last, though—eighty years or more down by the river, standing by her when she's low, letting her run when she needs to run. Holding the course.

Here's a tree whose idea of a leaf is hardly a leaf at all; here's a tree whose idea of green is hardly green at all.

This is the foliage, these slender bunched slate-green branchlets, the wind runs its fingers through. This is the hair the trees toss about, like girls on a balcony, like mothers unhinged by grief.

So, if they're holding a ballot for the world's loveliest tree, I'm voting for the sheoak. And if I had to pick one of them, I'd choose the riveroak. It's honed everything it does—from sex to photosynthesis—down to the least thing it can be and still work. It's sculpted itself until nothing is left but what is essential. It is the wind incarnate.

THE TREES AND TIME

But did you ever see what the sheoaks do to the light? They take a morning or an afternoon, particularly an afternoon, and they extract its cyan and its cobalt, they strain those tones out of the daylight and take them for themselves. They fraction the light among their slender fingers, and when they give it back, it's not the same thing it was at all. For they've painted the pieces of the light, tainted them with pollen and their shady blue exhalations. They've disassembled the morning, if it's morning, and put it back together, changed. What was shadow is now light, and what was light is shadow. So that all about the trees, the air now belongs to some other time, to some other place, to all times and places.

And that's roughly what the sheoaks were doing along Waterfall Creek that day in 1856 when William Maxwell led his horse to water there the first time. That's what they were doing this heat-blasted afternoon at the start of 2003, when I walked the shallow amber trickle of the Kedumba, and the hawks cried out. That's what they're pretty much always doing if there's any sun to do it with. When there's not, they busy themselves muting the gloom and catching what they can of the rain or the mist upon those same time-altering fingers.

But they're doing none of this, those sheoaks along Waterfall Creek, one afternoon in March 1932. That dull afternoon, Les sits on a dapple gray, leaning his weight back on his left arm, which rests on the animal's pretty rump. The horse is looking where Les has just turned from looking: clear across the creek and on past the house and up to the bluff beyond. Les and his brother are easing back on their stockhorses in the paddock that was the first allotment their father and their grandfather cleared. And it's still clear. So is the horse paddock around the slab hut, across the stream. You can see that, from here, because the sheoaks along Waterfall Creek are gone.

Les probably knows what became of the trees. So does his horse, by the look of it. But I may never know. The boy on the horse is now a man in the ground, and he'd been buried there five years before I saw this photograph.

But the trees have returned since Les sat his horse there in 1932. They are back and tall again by the seventies, when Les could barely see over them from the caretaker's cottage.

His father had felled the sheoaks, most probably, for timber to burn or build from or sell, or just to open up the river bottom for planting. Or else flood had taken them, or fire. Only Les then knew, and later he was happy enough to have them back and to watch them, season by season, do to his childhood what they do to the light. He was glad enough to lose that view of where he began, from where, even in 1932, he had started to turn away on a horse.

WHEN THE WATER RUNS OUT

"So me horse jumps about ten feet sideways," Jim says, turning in his saddle, "an' I hear this thump on the ground behind 'is back legs, an' I turn ta see the snake gettin' up ta have another go. Bloody great brown. Missed again, thank Christ, an' Bully gets us the hell outa there."

It's the week before Christmas 2004. I'm riding with Jim through lean brittlejacks toward the creek. The creek is dry when we get there, and the sky is blue as all eternity.

Summer in the grasslands is the season of the brown snake, and I wonder if it knows it's the second most poisonous snake in the world. They're good at finding Jim, and he's been good so far at losing them, mostly thanks to horses. But his time may come, though he's not losing sleep wondering when. He's just telling me one of the stories that make this valley and his life in it what they are.

Two weeks ago down at the mouth of Butchers Creek, where the snake missed him twice, where Jim and Dave should not really have been riding, but were, Lake Burragorang had fallen so far that the men discovered an army tank, listing in the silt. It should have been twenty feet under water, where it's been for fifty years. But the drought all over the plateau has taken back half the Big Water and uncovered some of its secrets.

The tank's a relic from the War. They'd have used it, Jim tells me, to snig the timber they felled from the shoulders of the valley floor before they dammed it in the fifties. And then they'd have left the tank to drown.

But the dam's fallen south of forty percent now, where it's never been before. And no one in the city that drinks it is as worried as they should be. "I don't know what they think they're gonna drink when the water runs out," says Jim.

The future has abandoned us. The Burragorang is rising again. The plateau runs on empty, and the city slips, like some blind inebriate, into the sea.

LESS IS MORE

There's a path that'll take you up, if you can find it, from the Three Sisters to the road at Katoomba. It's as thin and pale as a scribbly gum, this track, and it traces one of the ribs of the plateau—the one from which the three sisters, or the seven (depending on which version of the story, the old one or the really old one, you've been listening to) were born—the ridge at the end of which the women were turned to stone and still stand, three of them. Take this path around seven at night on the second day of January, say, when the scarps are dying embers, and you'll find, as I did one year, the inner life of the plateau lying all about you.

For this track is nothing more than it needs to be, and there is nothing lush or plump along it. The texture of everything here—rock, sand, leaf, limb, flower—is coarse, is unvarnished. Its attitude is tough-minded. Every form is angular, gaunt and elegant. Every plant is composed of more sky than plant. Every leaf is thin. Every point is sharp. Nothing is replete. No pastorals play. And you can forget about nymphs.

To walk here among pale scribbly gums, petrophiles, iso-pogons, geebungs, dwarf casuarinas, red mountain devils, tea-trees, boronias, grasstrees, and a thousand or so others whose names I have not learned; to walk here where nothing is tall, for the winds howl; to walk where everything, except the merest scratch of red and yellow, is decked out in gray or gray-green or black or off-white—to walk here is to join a lyric essay in restraint. It is to know the loveliness of sclerophyll forms—the beauty of what is leathery, tough, thin, and spare. Here's where you can learn how less gives rise to more.

Nothing speaks of water here. What lives here survives on what it can scrape from the clouds. What is beautiful, almost heartbreaking to me, is that it takes such elegance to survive in and draw nourishment from this exacting terrain. Nothing here is easy. Nothing in the whole plateau.

THE WOLD

He'll be fifty-two tomorrow, and all day Les has been trying to make a road up the ridge to Dawson's Wold. Cleary wants to put a shack up there, and Les is pretty sure the Wold doesn't want a road or a shack, and he's almost certain he'll never get a road to stick to that slender buttress. He has a strong feeling he'll never reach, in his 'dozer, the heaven his father never paid off and that Dan will never get to put his dream home where Les's father never got to put his dream. But Les won't be telling Dan. He'll work on for a bit until the valley proves him right, and then he'll get back to the care of the perennial mountain road and the pastures and the creek. He'll let Dan find out later the Wold is beyond his grasp.

The day has been hot, and Les has been pushing trees over since early morning. There was a storm at lunchtime, but then it eased, though the heat didn't, and Les kept on, and the rain came back at three or four, but Les kept on. At seven, the day gathered itself up and became a late storm, and Les graded on; he wanted tomorrow morning off, and there was plenty of light yet. But by seven-thirty, it was pissing down, and Les, on the 'dozer, felt like the boy with his finger in the dyke. He cut the engine and left the 'dozer on the slope. It'd probably be there tomorrow.

It's summer, so there's still some light to see by. But there's this cloud and all this rain. The scarps are gone. The clouds have them, and the rain has everything else.

Les hasn't got a coat. He pulls the torch from under the seat in the cab and walks in the rain down the rough track he's cut, and he walks in the last of the light until he's halfway across

Dawson's paddock, and it's truly dark and he switches on the torch and points it down the road ahead of him. By then he's getting what you might call wet. He's not thinking anymore. He's just rain from the outside in. He's a river, top to bottom, going home.

May at the kitchen window sees a wedge of light come up over the rise, and she guesses it's trailing Les. It's a comet coming tail first, and she watches Les take shape, an angel treading water, becoming a man walking home like an idiot in the rain and the dark on the muddy road, and she thinks she sees him lift his arm to wave, but probably he's just sweeping the water from his brow. She draws on her cigarette. She shakes her head. She breathes out smoke, and the rain carries on drumming the roof, and she empties the glass of sherry and pours another one, and she pours one for Les and sets it on the table. She thinks, that man will not live to see his birthday, dawdling home in the rain like a fool, and she goes to the bathroom and gets a bath running for him, and she shuffles back along the hall and puts the dinner she had ready for him an hour ago into the oven. She stands at the window again and watches him come.

Les sees the amber light of the lamp falling from the kitchen window, pooling by the house in the rain. He hears the cattle bawl faintly through the rain that pounds upon the clay and rubble of the road, upon his head and shoulders, and even in the rain the road and the paddocks steam. He hears a lapwing call and he turns the flashlight on it and watches it fly from its nest in the grass. He hears bullfrogs groan in Reedy Creek. The house is coming closer, and what he sees of it is mostly the same light the same damned lamp has been making slenderly for more than a hundred years. Hundred and fifty nearly. The lamp that came into the valley with his grandfather. It goes as well, he thinks, as it ever did and probably always will, till someone breaks the glass, and it's a miracle no one has all this time. Probably it'll still be burning when he's dead and dry as bone and gone to buggery in the ground.

He turns off the torch, and May loses him then.

EPILOGUE

HERE I AM

Let's just say that a place is all the interconnected stories, relationships, energies, and forms of life at play in it, including one's own being there, the memories, dreams, and desires one has known there; let's just say, as a philosopher has reasoned, that it is these complex structures of place that make an experience of self possible at all—then to witness one's place, or even just to do one's work under the influence of that place, is to draw a picture of one's soul. And to lose sight of one's place is to lose sight of one's self.

So a man might write you a memoir by telling you where he lives. But what happens if he leaves? Who is he then?

ORIGINAL COUNTRY

I lived for seven years where you could lie down with the moon.

When she was full she'd slouch across the northern sky and loiter around midnight in my bedroom window. When I turned off the light she fell on me. For three or four nights at a stretch each month that is how sleep would come. Out of a crow-black sky.

I dreamed well in the plateau. I made some poems. I made some books. I made this one. We made, M. and I, a marriage, and a couple of children. I tried to let a plateau dawn on me. But when the children came another kind of reality dawned, the kind in which they had to be fed and schooled and I had to make my work pay for what my love and I had made. Not long after the children arrived, though we didn't know it then, we began to make ready to leave.

At night in Katoomba you can look out across a world of gesturing eucalypts and see the city attenuated and brilliant and diminished in the dark, like light leaking under your bedroom door. I remember how, on our first night in the cottage, we lay down and the silence rang and an utter dark pulled itself about us, as though I'd turned off the known world at the switch on the wall. And it was the night that brought me in those years in that place closer to heaven than I'm likely to come again soon.

Many nights I walked out late and looked up, especially in winter. Across the taut black canopy of the sky the Milky Way, desire path of so many gods of so many cultures, splayed like a stream, near enough, it seemed, to touch. For seven years under that sky, strewn as it was at night with fragments of original time, with pieces of the true creation story sown wildly across its black field by some mad and profligate original god—I felt nearly part of a dreaming world, part of a plateau fallen just that very moment from the selfsame infinite and haunted sky. Like a gift I didn't deserve. And I came inside, and often I dreamed. I dreamed well in the plateau. I dreamed we'd never leave.

But I've come back down to the city now, and the night has faded, and the moon has paled, and the dreams have stopped coming down as often or as deep.

THE BALCONY

The night is our original country. It knows things about us we do not know ourselves. In the city, night is lost to us, and one is much less oneself.

By day from the balcony of this thin old house, which is my new home, I can see west as far as the dark contour of the plateau. Where I used to be makes my horizon now. By night I look out across old suburbs at the city's edge, and I cannot see the plateau; it casts no light. I look out through the low-voltage glare of stevedoring yards and the spotlit gigantic bridge above them to the streetlights of Rozelle and Lilyfield and Annandale, and I see traffic lights and factory lights and the headlamps of moving cars, and I can see desklamps in bedroom windows and garden lights and floodlights where roadworks and rail repairs are run in the dark downtime, and I can see floodlights in parks where men and women play touch football and night cricket and schoolchildren train for athletics and soccer and basketball and parents like me walk their toddlers to sleep; and I look through the incandescent aura of the city, which lies across a narrow inlet of the harbor just here and whose office-blocks stay lit all night, to where I cannot see the plateau. I look up at the anemic sky from which most of the angels have fallen.

Cities put out the sky; they untell our stories; they consume the earth to illuminate the present; they forestall the inevitable.

And I am living in the city again because I feel I must. I am here because work is here, and schools and libraries and all the things we say we need. I am here, along with these four million others, because of the city's centrifugal pull. The city is a white hole, which swallows whole galaxies and lives and legends and histories and out of them makes the superabundant present tense that we all feel compelled to live. And I miss the night; I miss the plateau that slept so well in it. Life goes by in the city like a television drama; it is linear and episodic. A succession of days, and then the repeats. It does not go as the plateau did in circles; it does not have the amplitude of life in a place over which the sky still arcs so big and clear.

And yet, much as I hunger for landscape and the stars, I sit here at night in the city and I know I am an animal at ease in this habitat. It's just that ease isn't quite enough.

PLATEAUING

We left the plateau at Easter 2005, and by then I had come to love her less than I thought I would.

It was not the landscape, itself, that I fell out with, not those two valleys, and my home ridge and Henryk's ridge and the river, which is the author of us all; no, but the towns and suburbs, which sit upon that parlous ridge with so little grace, aghast at what surrounds them. Les said in his old age that Katoomba had become nothing but a tourist attraction. And I think he's close to right. The place is a tawdry theme park, perched in an astonishing terrain. Some find beauty in the dissonance, but it palled on me. The thing is, one lives mostly in the town, and there are better towns.

If I could have stayed, I might have moved to one of the valleys. But I couldn't stay, and I can't afford much valley yet.

I must not blame the place, though, for my leaving—not even the town. I was always like this: I plateau. And I plateaued even there. I'm not much good at perpetuity; I love and I leave.

So be it. I do not have the gift I thought I had for staying put. I am a migrant. I am a faster kind of sandstone, deposited, compressed, uplifted, and carried away all in a matter of years. But I wonder if this place or any place needs us all to stay and stay. Maybe it's how one stays that matters, not how long.

HOME IS A VERB

Leaving, the plateau told me, is part of what belonging, and for that matter becoming, entails. Passing away is what the plateau does. That is its calling. Non-attachment is what the place practices and what it quietly preaches. Eternal impermanence.

The plateau is a verb, and I am, too. For a while there I thought we were the same one. And perhaps for a while we were.

Home, too, is a verb—a word that dwells infinitely between those who say it often enough together. Home is the sayer and the said and above all it is the saying. Home is the conversation we make with what, and whom, we say we love; and what it's about is who we are and always were. Home is a word—sometimes it is a whole sentence—for the ecology of belonging, and it includes deposition and erosion, the wet and the dry and the cold and the wind; it includes the making and the unmaking, the coming and the going, and it isn't always happy. Sometimes it rains, and sometimes it burns, and sometimes it falls and you fall with it.

But home runs deep, and it runs hard, and sometimes it runs dry, and once it starts, it never seems to end. Home happens in fire and falling water, in snow and flood, and in the shimmer on eucalypt leaves; it happens in west wind and cold night and embers in a hearth; it happens in massed stars—heaven shattered—in winter dark sky; it happens in erosion and drought; it happens in the cry of black cockatoo returning and in the cry of a new child waking; it happens in staying and in leaving for good.

For seven years, home happened to me in the Blue Plateau, and although I thought I'd left, home doesn't want to stop.

THE GRAMMAR OF RETURN

All endings are contingent, someone said to me once. Who can write the end of love? Who can say when a thing is over, or if it's even really begun?

Some things last. Some original things. Sorrow, for instance, and its rhythms. Love, sometimes. Belonging. And home—where, as Frost said, they take you in. No matter what. Some people—or their people, or theirs—get, sometimes, to return to a place they were pushed out of.

"Where are the Indians?" another poet, an Acoma man from America's southwest, liked to ask wherever he went—and he came to Australia and he asked it here too. Where are the Indians? I spent too little time on the plateau in the company of the first peoples. Right at the end, as I packed to leave, I met some of the elders who had worked for years to have the Gully declared an "Aboriginal Place." An Aboriginal Place—a place from the very beginning. A human place, though not merely human; a place for desire and commerce, for dance and rage and prayer and folly and, above all, story. A place where the soul of the plateau and its people was dreamed and made flesh.

More than likely, the Gully was such a place and there were some locals in it, hanging out in time-honored ways, doing what you do in a place of that sort in the early summer, checking out the boys, disobeying your parents, fooling with fire, remembering occasionally your customs, when the white men whom the plateau had been waiting for, apparently, all these long millennia of aboriginal history, discovered the selfsame plateau and the way across it, in 1815, following and losing and finding again trails the first people had been finding and following in their sleep since the very start.

And the Indians were still there till they shut the Gully down in the nineteen-fifties, and then they lost their place—or the center of it—for fifty years, but they never weren't in the plateau. They were just here and there, waiting or giving up hope, depending; remembering or forgetting, depending. Mostly it was the women who remembered. And then in 2002,

Katoomba apologized and gave the Gully back. It doesn't look like it most days, when it's the same old recovering swamp it's been since it stopped being a speedway, but the Gully is the largest Aboriginal Place in the State. It never really stopped, of course, being a place. Home doesn't stop. But for a while there we stopped seeing it. Stopped seeing it as one of the homes of the original soul-makers of the plateau, of the water people of the Burragorang. The headwaters of their being. And ours, here, for that matter.

I never knew when I was young in the suburbs of Sydney that the water I drank, which came down the pipes from the dam in the plateau, was laced with trace elements of dreaming—of misery and mystery, of sex and gods and death and beauty. I was tasting the sediment of an Aboriginal Place; I was swallowing myth and profanity with my fluoride.

Where are the Indians? Where they've always been. Home. A verb that I left but which won't leave me. The stories are being told again at night; they're leaching into the plateau. And they probably won't stop till the water stops. Or the plateau.

THE WORD

Late that Easter Sunday, two months before he turned two, two days before we left, the boy touched the browning leaves of the young maple above the house, and, for the first time, he said the word. Tree. Tre. First syllable of his last name, a sound that means place. He turned to me, and his face was painted amber by the falling sun, and his hair was the end of summer, and his eyes were where the morning had gone. He smiled, as though he knew what he'd done. He'd named the thing that was staying here. He'd named the start of himself; he'd said the place in his name; he'd said here. Where we have lived. Where I was in the beginning. Word without end.

THE PAST

When the men had been and gone, when they had emptied the house of the boxes we had emptied the house into, we stood in the front room, which had long ago been a veranda where the plateau came inside and sat, and it was as though everything we had lived here, dreamed and made, broken and mended, everything the place had made of us, was yet to be. And it felt to me like I'd never see any of it come to anything now.

THE WORLD IS A BOOK OF SORROWS

So I've told some stories here. Some pieces of the past and present lives of the plateau. Most of the stories, of course, eluded me. Which is as it should be. A place, like a person, must keep most of her secrets. You'll never fit a beloved in a sonnet; you'll never fit a plateau in a book.

To be born to a settler culture and come, late in the day speaking English, to country such as this, held sacred in languages much closer to the dialect of the place itself for as long as human beings have been capable of reverence, is to inherit a gift one will never live long or deep enough to learn how to return. But I knew I had come to a sacred geography. Sacred, like every place on this continent, but holiness here is locally inflected, and that inflection—scarp and canyon, persistent plangent stream and hanging swamp—spoke to me in a voice I seemed to know. Speaking of itself and who I might be if I stopped trying so hard.

To come to such country as I did is also to know the shame of the survivor of history, the guilt of the inheritor of unearned wealth. It is to be complicit in a crime one did not enact but from which one has profited with one's life. Anyone from a settler culture who opens themselves to the landscape where they find themselves and the history they inherit must carry indigenous presence, past and present, in mind. All settlers belonging in Australia must feel subjunctive.

In each of us, in our deepest humanity, there's a place where we can know each other. There's country. We share it; we have all lost it; we ache to know it and return ourselves to it. To our larger selves; to the given world. Our common inheritance. I felt that longing here in the plateau, but my longing is not merely my own. I think it's human; I think it is the divine comedy we all live out. For we are nature's anchorites. We get back to the world through song. In poetry we make our souls and we put them back, sometimes, in the body of the world.

To tell the life of the plateau then is also to tell the story of the people who have belonged to the plateau. If you would know me, know the country and the people that I loved there; if you would know the people who belonged to the plateau first and claimed it with their lives and their minds and voices, know the plateau first. The Gundungurra and their brothers and sisters knew this, and know it still. The plateau knows it. And the rest of us are only just remembering. A thing—hopelessly, helplessly—I set about here. In case it's not too late.

But each of us needs to do the work alone and for ourselves. The work, I mean, of forgetting ourselves and recalling the world and giving ourselves back to it. I have liked to think—and perhaps I've been fooling myself—that taking the path beyond myself and into a plateau, back to the world in itself (and me within it), I may have come as close as I'm going to get, not only to a plateau, but to understanding the belonging of all of the people who came here and sometimes forgot themselves for long enough to make some stories and to make the plateau human and themselves holy within it. Who sang its sacred geography.

The plateau came in the river. It fell; it rose; it falls again. The sky came, and it fell down into the valleys the plateau keeps abandoning, and it makes the whole thing blue. Or white. Depending. Something's going on here, and it never will be finished. We call it the Blue Plateau. And most of it is made of loss.

AFTERWORD

This is not a novel, but you can read it that way if you like. *The Blue Plateau* is a true story. Nothing in it is invented, but its logic is poetic. I tell no lies, but I take one or two imaginative leaps inside events I didn't myself experience. If there is a literature of fact, this may be an instance of it.

Which is to say: I've got the facts as straight as I can get them, but not all facts run straight, and nothing much is certain. The point is how truthfully one tries to set things down. But this book is an artistic—not a journalistic, scientific, or academic—endeavor; the witness it bears to some people and their places must be more than merely accurate if it's going to do anyone any good. It should—at least this is what I've attempted—give a reader a partial and personal but truthful impression, in the vernacular music of prose, of what the lives and country of these people may have actually felt like.

Two things are sure, though: I will have erred, and others will remember things differently. All the same, everything in this book really happened, and it happened, as far as I can tell, in something like the order and at the time and in the place and in the way I have laid it out. Not that my book runs straight, itself. For whose life does? A good deal of what I write about didn't happen to me, and, where that's the case, I relied on others' memories, their books and photographs and my own storyteller's intuition for how things probably played out and how they felt and tasted. I've altered the odd name or left it out, for ethical and personal reasons, but the only thing I made up was the way I put the book together.

Somebody described creative nonfiction as the musical arrangement of passionate facts, and that'll almost do to characterize this book. *The Blue Plateau* isn't a guidebook to the upper Blue Mountains. It is not a social or natural history of the place. It's a kind of divination, an experiment in seeing and listening. It's also a love story—many love stories, in fact. Some of them for people, some of them for places. And it's a memoir—partial and personal and fragmentary. This is a place as it suggested itself to one man; this is him as he was in that place, and this is who he became because of it; this is what he learned about that place and about many other things, only one of them himself; this is an accretion of fragments of true stories that seemed to want to come together. If I were a painter, you'd call what you're holding a landscape painting. But I'm not, so what you've got is this book.

How places go—especially how they went before any of us were around to notice—is a thing it's hard to be sure about. Places are a mystery as profound as we are to ourselves, let alone to each other. We try to fathom a place—its nature, its former lives, its people—with ecology, geology, geography, history, anthropology, myth, paint, dance, story, and song. I've relied on those literatures and others besides. But I'm still guessing. This book is an act of wondering about the life of a piece of country; it's not an expression of certainty.

NOTES

Writing *The Blue Plateau*, I drew on my own experiences and
encounters; I walked a lot and rode a lot and listened to the place.
But I also plundered people's memories; I read books and archives
and weather charts and bird guides; I consulted botanists and
geologists; I studied maps and photographs. But let me be specific.

For the life of the Maxwells in the Kedumba, I relied on a
conservation plan for the slab hut in the Kedumba, prepared by
Graham Edds & Associates (May 2001) and Ian Jack's history of
the Kedumba Valley, written as part of the conservation plan; on a
conversation with Ian Jack; on parish maps and other documents
in the Land Title's Office (New South Wales); on notes taken by
photographer Max Hill from a conversation with Les Maxwell in
October 1990; on old photographs kept by Max and others taken
by him of Les and the various Maxwell huts in the Kedumba; on
wills, photographs, letters, cards, affidavits, licenses, some of
Les's school notebooks, newspaper clippings, and other things
(including the letter from A. L. Bennett to Billy Maxwell) I found
in the box that Les kept and left to his stepson Norm; on a will I
found in the National Archive in western Sydney; on Owen Pearce's
book *Rabbit Hot, Rabbit Cold*; on conversations with historian and
folklorist Jim Smith and one or two documents he shared with me;
on photographs shared with me by Norm; on an interview with Les
recorded by historian Martin Thomas for ABC Radio's social history
unit; and, above all, on the diaries of May Maxwell. Many of the
stories I tell of Les I've dramatized from memories shared with me
by National Parks Rangers (Terry especially), Jim Commens, Norm,
and Norm's son Ross, over a number of years.

The three photographs I describe in the first part of the book
come from the collection of Max Hill. One of them appears on the
cover, with his permission.

The two poems I have Les copying in "His father's only hope, his mother's only joy," I found handwritten in a Monster letter pad among the pieces Les left to Norm. I apologize to the authors and publishers of the poems he copied—the errant spellings are Les's.

I am deeply grateful to Norm, in particular. He shared—with pleasure, I think—so much time and so many documents and memories and places. His mother's diaries were a great gift to give to a writer wanting to enter into the life of the Kedumba. If I've gotten anything wrong, it's my fault, not his.

Jim Smith shared with me the Gundungurra name for the Bentham's Gum (you can find it in William Russell's memoir *Werriberrie*) and helped me discover the date and place of Les Maxwell's birth. I've also drawn on Jim Smith's work, *Legends of the Blue Mountains Valleys* (2003) for my retelling of the legend of the emu on the Kedumba Walls. My recounting of the natural history Les would have entered into coming home to the Kedumba at six weeks of age also relies heavily on Jim Smith's calendar of the bird and animal life of the mountains. I am indebted to him, as many of us are who've written about and lived in the plateau, and all of us should be, for his indefatigable and respectful research into the natural and cultural histories of the Blue Mountains. I refer readers to his many books and papers.

Griffith Taylor refers to the Blue Mountains as "the Blue Plateau" in his book *Australia: A Geography Reader* (1931). He calls it "the Blue Mountains Plateau" in *Sydneyside Scenery* (1958).

For the geology of the plateau I read many books, including Griffith Taylor's. The booklet *Layers of Time: The Blue Mountains and Their Geology*, published by New South Wales National Parks, the Geological Society of New South Wales, and the University of Sydney was a helpful way in. Over lunch one day in Glebe, University of Sydney geologist David Branagan took me much deeper; his essay in Peter Stanbury's *The Blue Mountains: Grand Adventure for All*, his *Field Geology of New South Wales, An Outline of the Geology and Geomorphology of the Sydney Basin* and his other essays and writings helped me get the rocks in my head. I am especially grateful to Branagan, whom a mutual friend, the late George Seddon, recommended to me as "a literate geologist," and who proved to be. Geoff Mosley's *Blue Mountains for World Heritage* also offers a terrific summary of the geology of the plateau.

My passage "What the plateau belongs to" contracts and abstracts details from *Native Plants of the Upper Blue Mountains* by Margaret Baker, Robin Corringham, and Jill Dark, with thanks.

The bird book from which I quote the voice of the friarbird is Graham Pizzey and Frank Knight's *The Field Guide to the Birds of Australia*.

"'The real world'": I sample the opening phrase of James Galvin's book *The Meadow*.

"Nothing is pure," in "The Gully," I borrow from a song by Bruce Cockburn, "Isn't That What Friends Are For?" But it's a wise thought, often expressed in smart writing, and it belongs to all of us; I'm conscious that one or two of my favorite poets have expressed it, and I thank them for the loan.

The philosopher in "Here I Am" is Jeff Malpas; his book is *Place and Experience: A Philosophical Topography*.

The poet I refer to in "A short history of belonging V" is W. H. Auden; the poem, "Leap Before You Look."

"Sorrow, for instance, and its rhythms" in "The grammar of return" echoes Charles Wright's words—"Only pain endures. And the rhythm of pain"—in his introduction to *The Best American Poetry 2008*.

I met Ian Brooker in 2003 or so, when he came to one of my nonfiction writing workshops in Canberra. We've talked a lot about eucalypts and grammar and country and opera since. "The lay of the cliff mallee ash" describes a walk we took along the Prince Henry Track when he stayed at my house in Katoomba one year. My descriptions of the tree come from his book *Field Guide to Eucalypts, Volume 1, South-Eastern Australia*.

My retelling of the story of Oonagh Kennedy and her friends lost on the river relies on the memories of Jim Commens and the excellent self-published book *Megalong Tragedy* by Michael Baker. I am indebted to Mr. Baker for his permission to retell the story again, in my words, in this book. He also helped me with my account of the death of David I., though I drew mostly on newspaper accounts and weather maps for that story.

John Lowe and John Merriman helped me find out some more about David C.'s disappearance, an incident I became aware of through May Maxwell's diaries. The death of Ken Cleary I've depicted from Jim Commens's account of Les Maxwell's recollection of the event. I hope my tellings of these tragedies seem fair and truthful and gentle to the families of these young people whose lives the plateau has taken.

The passages on the Gully and the lives of the Indigenous people of the upper mountains rely on newspaper stories, conversations with some locals and, above all, Diane Johnson's grand book *Sacred Waters*. That book was preceded by a wonderfully detailed study (*Upper Kedumba Valley, Katoomba: Report on the cultural significance of Upper Kedumba Valley*) Di Johnson conducted, with Dawn Colless, an Indigenous leader, for the New South Wales National Parks and Wildlife Service. That report was instrumental in the declaration in 2002 of the Gully as an Aboriginal Place. I've also learned a lot about the history, ecology, languages, culture, and contemporary society of the Indigenous peoples of the upper mountains from reading and talking with Eugene Stockton. His *Blue Mountains Dreaming* is essential reading in this area.

The American friend I refer to, when I'm riding with Jim Commens in "Watercourse 101," is Barry Lopez. The book of definitions of American landscapes, landforms, and places is *Home Ground: Language for an American Landscape*. Edited by Barry Lopez and Debra Gwartney, authored by nearly fifty fine writers, it was published in 2006 by Trinity University Press.

Many books on the plateau talk about its fire history, and I read a lot of them while watching the fires surround us at Christmas 2001. (Fire is a personality trait of the plateau, and so it is touched on in most of the books I list below.) The bulk of the pieces on that particular summer and the one that followed I wrote from my own experience, from listening to news bulletins, and from reading newspaper accounts. There is now prodigious literature on fire, fire ecology, and fire-stick farming in Australia, spawned by Stephen J. Pyne's *Burning Bush*. We're only beginning to understand the complex, codependent relationship between sclerophyll forest and fire, how Aboriginal firing practices altered things, and to what extent colonial firefighting and clearing are altering the fire ecologies of the plateau and other areas. It wasn't my purpose to enter far into the fire grounds—simply to watch fire in the plateau and think about it from several points of view, including the plateau's own.

Most of Jim Commens's story, including the many portions told in his own vernacular, I have taken from conversations had with him—sometimes on horseback, sometimes on the phone, sometimes over a cup of tea in his shed—over many years. I have also written from some family photos he shared with me. Small pieces of his family's story (and Les's) are told in Owen Pearce's *Rabbit Hot, Rabbit Cold*; the book in which his grandfather's tale is told is Bernard O'Reilly's *Cullenbenbong*.

I wrote "The candle" and the ensuing passages from what Jim told me about that night, and from reading the transcript of the report of the inquest into the death of the man I have called "John Underhill." My life in the plateau was blessed by Jim's company and friendship, and by his wife, Judith's; this book wouldn't have happened without them. So, thanks. I hope I have done you, and your country, justice.

Thanks to Henryk Topolnicki and Philippa Johnson; the same is true of you. As with Jim, the passages in Henryk's voice are written from taped conversations, which I've edited, cut, pasted, and adapted to capture his distinctive vernacular. Other pieces of Henryk's story I've told from my memory of conversations.

Philippa tells me the incident described in "The Bells" didn't go quite the way I've described it, and maybe I didn't even write it the way Henryk described it to me, but she has been gracious enough to let it stand.

Jim Barrett has walked in and loved and written about the plateau country most of his life. I've read many of the small books he's written about the place, and, for my understanding of the Burragorang before it went under, I've relied on his *Life in the Burragorang*.

Other books that helped me find the plateau:

Audrey Armitage, *The Katoomba–Leura Story*
Croft & Associates (with Meredith Walker), *Blue Mountains Heritage Study: Final Report*
Chris Cunningham, *The Blue Mountains Rediscovered*
Michael Duffy, *Crossing the Blue Mountains*
Brian Fox, *Upper Blue Mountains Geographical Encyclopaedia*
James Kohen, *The Darug and Their Neighbours*
John Low, *Blue Mountains: Pictorial Memories*
Andy Macqueen, *Back From the Brink*
Peter Meredith and Don Fuchs, *The Australian Geographic Book of the Blue Mountains*
Keith Painter, *Prince Henry cliff walk*
Les Robinson, *Field Guide to the Native Plants of Sydney*
Jim Smith, *How to See the Blue Mountains*
Christopher Woods, *Skylines of the Blue Mountains*

ACKNOWLEDGMENTS

Small pieces of this book have appeared, in similar form, in journals—*Connotations, Island, Isotope, Kunapipi, Meanjin, PAN, World Literature Today*—and books—*A Place on Earth* (Mark Tredinnick, ed.) and *Let There be Night* (Paul Bogard, ed.). I thank the editors of those journals and books for running those pieces and for letting me use them again here.

As well as those I've thanked already, I express gratitude to:

John Cameron, who supervised a thesis that became my book *The Land's Wild Music*, and who oversaw the beginnings of *The Blue Plateau* and never stopped encouraging me.

Jim Galvin for reading this in an early form and helping me, through what he said and how he writes, to see how to erode it into something more like itself.

Roland Hemmert, painter, friend, reader, for doing on canvas what I try to do on paper and for walking nearly every step of the Blue Plateau with me.

Laurie Kutchins for reading it and inspiring me and standing by.

Barry Lopez for the example of his life and work and for encouraging me.

Barbara Ras for telling me to cut it in half.

Kate Rigby and my colleagues at the Association for the Study of Literature and the Environment–Australia and New Zealand.

Carolyn Servid and Dorik Mechau at the Island Institute for a residency among whales in Sitka, Alaska.

Scott Slovic for his friendship, his support for this book, and for his work in literature and ecology.

Frank Stewart at the University of Hawaii and Takiora Ingram at the Pacific Writers Connection for having me read from this book and teach in wonderful company in Hawaii a couple of years back; particular thanks to Frank for his poetry and for his scholarship on nature writing, and above all for his friendship while this book happened.

The University of Wollongong for a visiting fellowship during which I finished this book.

Macquarie University, where I now have a post, for cutting me some slack while I worked on the final edit and the proofs.

The Hunter Writers' Centre, the Historic Houses Trust, and the John Paynter Gallery, sponsors of the Lock-up Artist in Residence in Newcastle, where I worked on the final proofs.

Elaine van Kempen and the board of the Camden Head Pilot Station, New South Wales, for residencies that got me started and for founding the Watermark Nature Writers' Muster, at which I've read from this book more than once. (And of course to Eric Rolls for showing us all how this literature could be made and why it mattered.)

Geoff Whyte, who read and edited the manuscript at a critical stage and convinced me it amounted to something; it did after his edit.

There are others I should thank. This book has been in gestation so long, and many friends have listened to me talk about it, and some colleagues have read early drafts and helped me find what was wrong and what little was right with the book. I hope those I don't name here—those who helped me recently when I needed encouragement to make it short and new and tight, and those at the beginning who barracked for me when this must have sounded like a strange undertaking—know that I thank them, too.

Over the last eight years hundreds of people, most of them strangers, some of them friends, some of them students, some of them fellow writers, have listened to me read from this book as it made itself up—in Brisbane, in Camden Haven, in Eugene, in Honolulu, in Iowa City, in Katoomba, in Melbourne, in Sydney, in Kew. In their sleep, sometimes, I'm sure. I want to thank them for listening and for helping me know that I had a book to be getting on with.

Daniel Slager at Milkweed committed to this book before anyone, and I will always be grateful for that. Patrick Thomas found in my manuscript the book I meant to write and helped me find it too. Alexandra Payne at the University of Queensland Press got the book from the start and kept on getting it; both nature writing and lyric nonfiction are new in Australia, and I'm thankful to Alex for taking the risk with such enthusiasm and sense. Judith Lukin-Amundsen found ways to refashion this mosaic of a book and to save me from myself. Judith, along with Alex and Patrick and Daniel, had a hand in the geomorphology of this book, and I'm glad they did. Though it's still me you have to blame. Thanks also to Madonna Duffy at UQP for her faith in the book, and to the sales team at Penguin for being inspired.

Thanks to Jake Mohan for the hard work that adapted the book, and who added a glossary, for American readers; to James Cihlar for managing the editorial process at Milkweed; and to Patrick Thomas, again, for some deft structural shifts. I'm also grateful to Betsy Donovan and Steve Foley for making my book look and feel the way I wanted it too. And to everyone at Milkweed Editions for the care and intelligence you've exerted on this book, and the fine work you do generally.

Finally and most of all, thanks to Maree, who lived through all of this with grace and generosity and love. I owe this book and so much else to you, my love.

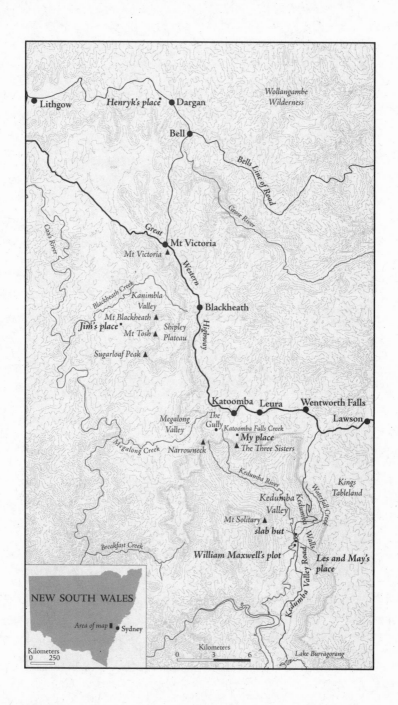

Lithgow

Henryk's place • Dargan

Wollangambe
Wilderness

Bell

Bells Line of Road

Grose River

Cox's River

Great

Mt Victoria

Mt Victoria ▲

Western

Blackheath Creek

Kanimbla
Valley

Mt Blackheath ▲

Jim's place ■

Mt Tosh ▲

Shipley
Plateau

Blackheath

Highway

Sugarloaf Peak ▲

Katoomba Leura Wentworth Falls

Megalong
Valley

The
Gully

Lawson

Katoomba Falls Creek

My place ■

Megalong Creek

Narrowneck ▲

The Three Sisters ▲

Kedumba River

Kings
Tableland

Kedumba
Valley

Waterfall Creek

Mt Solitary ▲

slab hut

Breakfast Creek

Kedumba Valley Road

Walls

William Maxwell's plot

Les and May's
place

NEW SOUTH WALES

Area of map ■ • Sydney

Kilometers
0   250

Kilometers
0   3   6

Lake Burragorang

249

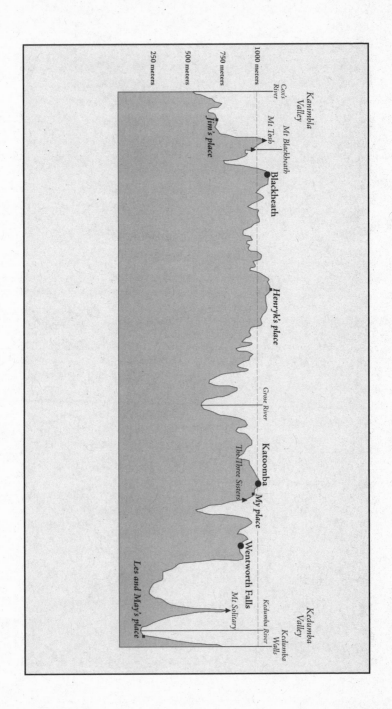

GLOSSARY

agist (v) To move cattle or horses for the purpose of grazing; in Australia, animals are often agisted from drought-affected regions to drought-free regions.

angophora (n) A genus of ten species of trees or large shrub in the family *Myrtaceae*, indigenous to eastern Australia. Angophora is closely related to Corymbia and Eucalyptus, and all three are often referred to as eucalypts.

banksia (n) A nectar- and cone-producing tree or woody shrub indigenous to Australia.

Bennett's wallaby (n) Common name for a type of *Macropus rufogriseus* or red-necked wallaby, a large marsupial indigenous to Australia.

Bentham's Gum (n) A type of eucalyptus tree.

billy (n) A metal pot used to boil water over a campfire.

blackfish (n) Common name for *Gadopsis marmoratus*, a freshwater fish indigenous to Australia.

bollard (n) Any of a series of short metal posts set at intervals to delimit an area, such as a roadway.

brigalow (n) Australian woodland, named after the common name for *Acacia harpophylla*, a tree indigenous to Australia.

brumby (n) A wild or unbroken horse.

bullock (n) Another term for a steer, a young bull, or an ox.

bushranger (n) In the early years of the British settlement of Australia, bushrangers were outlaws with the skills necessary to hide from authorities in the Australian bush. Compare to the outlaws of the Wild West in the United States.

bushwalking (n) Hiking, especially off-trail on rugged terrain.

burru (n) Gundungarra for *kangaroo*.

butcherbird (n) Common name for the genus *Cracticus*, a magpie-like songbird indigenous to Australia.

chook (n) A chicken.

cleanskins (n) Unbranded cattle.

crim (n) A criminal.

crook (adj) Unwell or injured: *Her tummy was crook*.

dray (n) A simple cart, often low to the ground and without side panels, pulled by a horse, ox, or other animal.

Driza-Bone (n) Trademark name for an Australian brand of long waterproof coat, a kind of oilskin or slicker.

esky (n) Australian term for a beverage cooler. Originally a trademarked brand name; now applied generically to all such containers. Short for *Eskimo*.

eucalypt; eucalyptus (n) A tree indigenous to Australia.

fibro (n) A building material made of compressed fibers cemented into rigid sheets. Popular in Australia and many other countries throughout the twentieth century, its use has been discontinued because it contains asbestos.

flying fox (n) A device used to travel along a suspended cord across a river or other expanse. Compare to a zip-line in American English.

friarbird (n) Common name for *Philemon meliphagidae*, a large Australian songbird.

frogmouth (n) Common name for the genus *Podargus*, a nocturnal bird indigenous to Australia.

geebung (n) Common name for the genus *Persoonia*, a shrub indigenous to Australia.

gelignite (n) A cheap, moldable explosive similar to dynamite.

goanna (n) Common name for the genus *Varanus*, a large monitor lizard indigenous to Australia. (Possibly derived from *iguana*.)

grey gum (n) A type of eucalyptus tree.

Gundungurra (n) A clan of aboriginal Australians in southeastern New South Wales, Australia. *Variation*: Gundong-gorra.

hessian (n) Burlap.

Holden (n) An Australian automaker, owned by General Motors since 1931.

humpy (n) A small temporary shelter built from bark and tree branches, traditionally used by aboriginal Australians.

ironbark (n) A type of eucalyptus tree.

ks (n) Vernacular term for *kilometers*.

kookaburra (n) A large terrestrial kingfisher bird indigenous to Australia.

kooradjie (n) Native Australian term for a healer. *Variations*: koradji, coraji.

kurrajong (n) Common name for *Sterculiaceae brachychiton*, a tree or shrub indigenous to Australia.

lairy (adj) Ostentatiously attractive; flashy.

laminex (n) A laminate for furniture and other surfaces; the name is a corporate trademark but is also used generically.

mallee gum (n) A type of eucalyptus tree.

mozzie (n) A mosquito.

mullock (n) Waste rock from which gold and other valuable minerals have been extracted.

Nattai (n) A landscape of massive sandstone escarpments in New South Wales.

paperbark (n) Common name for the genus *Melaleuca*, an evergreen tree or shrub indigenous to Australia.

ring-bark (v) To remove bark from a standing tree. Compare to *girdle* in American English.

RAAF (n) Royal Australian Air Force.

sclerophyll (n) A type of vegetation with hard leaves and short internodes (the distance between leaves along the stem), occurring in all parts of the world but most typical of Australia.

scribbly gum (n) Common name for *Eucalyptus haemastoma*, a type of eucalyptus tree.

sheoak (n) Common name for the genus *Allocasuarina*, a flowering tree indigenous to Australia.

silvertop ash (n) A type of eucalyptus tree.

snig (v) To drag a felled log by a chain or cable.

stockhorse (n) A hardy breed of horse bred especially for Australian conditions.

stone-curlew (n) Common name for the family *Burhinidae*, a bird indigenous to Australia.

stringybark (n) A type of eucalyptus tree.

sulky (n) A light, two-wheeled horse-drawn vehicle.

swag (n) A waterproof bedroll.

torch (n) A flashlight.

triple O (n) Phonetic name for Australia's emergency service's number of 000. Compare to 911 in the United States.

tute (n) Tutorial.

waratah (n) Common name for the genus *Telopea*, a large shrub or small tree indigenous to Australia.

watergum (n) Common name for *Tristaniopsis laurina*, a shade tree with yellow flowers, indigenous to Australia.

weatherboard demountable (n) Chiefly Australian term for a temporary, modular building designed to be disassembled and moved; compare to *mobile home* in American English. *Weatherboard* refers to the structure's siding made of timber (clapboard) or other thin material.

wold (n) An open, uncultivated piece of land.

ABOUT THE AUTHOR

Mark Tredinnick is a poet, essayist, and writing teacher; he lives in Burradoo, New South Wales—in the highlands southwest of Sydney in Australia's southeast. His writing has appeared in *Best Australian Essays*, *Orion*, *Isotope*, *Manoa*, and many other literary journals. His honors include the Newcastle Poetry Prize, the Gwen Harwood Poetry Prize, the Calibre Essay Prize, the Blake Poetry Prize, and the Wildcare Nature Writing Prize. Mark talks and teaches widely on writing, landscape, justice, and ecology. For over a decade he has run writing programs at the University of Sydney and at writers' centers in Australia and the United States.

MORE BOOKS FROM
MILKWEED EDITIONS

To order books or for more information, contact Milkweed at
(800) 520-6455 or visit our Web site (www.milkweed.org).

Shopping for Porcupine: A Life in Alaska
Seth Kantner

*The Future of Nature: Writing on a Human Ecology
from* Orion *Magazine*
Selected and Introduced by Barry Lopez

The Wet Collection
Joni Tevis

The Windows of Brimnes: An American in Iceland
Bill Holm

Hope, Human and Wild: True Stories of Living Lightly on the Earth
Bill McKibben

MILKWEED EDITIONS

Founded in 1979, Milkweed Editions is one of the largest independent, nonprofit literary publishers in the United States. Milkweed publishes with the intention of making a humane impact on society, in the belief that good writing can transform the human heart and spirit.

JOIN US

Milkweed depends on the generosity of foundations and individuals like you, in addition to the sales of its books. In an increasingly consolidated and bottom-line-driven publishing world, your support allows us to select and publish books on the basis of their literary quality and the depth of their message. Please visit our Web site (www.milkweed.org) or contact us at (800) 520-6455 to learn more about our donor program.

Milkweed Editions, a nonprofit publisher, gratefully acknowledges sustaining support from Anonymous; Emilie and Henry Buchwald; the Patrick and Aimee Butler Family Foundation; the Dougherty Family Foundation; the Ecolab Foundation; the General Mills Foundation; the Claire Giannini Fund; John and Joanne Gordon; William and Jeanne Grandy; the Jerome Foundation; Constance and Daniel Kunin; the Lerner Foundation; Sanders and Tasha Marvin; the McKnight Foundation; Mid-Continent Engineering; the Minnesota State Arts Board, through an appropriation by the Minnesota State Legislature, a grant from the Wells Fargo Foundation Minnesota, and a grant from the National Endowment for the Arts; Kelly Morrison and John Willoughby; the National Endowment for the Arts; the Navarre Corporation; Ann and Doug Ness; Ellen Sturgis; the Target Foundation; the James R. Thorpe Foundation; the Travelers Foundation; Moira and John Turner; Joanne and Phil Von Blon; Kathleen and Bill Wanner; and the W. M. Foundation.

THE M^cKNIGHT FOUNDATION

MINNESOTA
STATE ARTS BOARD

NATIONAL
ENDOWMENT
FOR THE ARTS
A great nation
deserves great art.

TARGET.

Interior design by Steve Foley
Typeset in Chaparral Pro
    by Steve Foley
Printed on acid-free, recycled (100% postconsumer waste), Rolland
    Enviro paper
by Friesens Corporation